Teaching Phonics & Word Study in the Intermediate Grades

❋ **A Complete Sourcebook** ❋

by Wiley Blevins

SCHOLASTIC
PROFESSIONAL BOOKS

New York ● **Toronto** ● **London** ● **Auckland** ● **Sydney**
Mexico City ● **New Delhi** ● **Hong Kong**

DEDICATION

I dedicate this book to the memory of Jeanne Chall.

She taught me. She guided me.

She inspired me.

Photo Credits:
Pages 7,15,24,187,253,255,262 and 276: Courtesy of author
Cover and all other photos courtesy of PhotoDisc

Illustration Credits:
Pages 248, 250, and 252: By Paige Billing-Frye
Pages 252 and 254: By Maxie Chambliss

Cover design by Joni Holst
Interior design by Grafica, Inc.

ISBN 0-439-16352-8

Table of Contents

Table of Contents

What Is Phonics?

"*At one magical instant in your early childhood, the page of a book—that string of confused, alien ciphers—shivered into meaning. Words spoke to you, gave up their secrets; at that moment, whole universes opened. You became, irrevocably, a reader.*"

—*Alberto Manguel*

It was almost midnight. The crowd outside the brightly lit building grew restless as the clock inched toward the eagerly awaited hour. Children clutched their parents' hands as the doors to the building slowly opened. As the crowd crammed into the building, onlookers stared in amazement. What awaited this breathless crowd wasn't a television star, a movie premiere, or the release of a new toy; rather, it was a book—the fourth in a series about a little boy named Harry Potter. These children (and adults) illustrate the power of books. For months they had been captivated by the promise of another tale about the adventures of a much-loved character. Indeed, they were so transported into this boy's magical world that they were prepared to tackle a 734-page novel with twists and turns unlike any they had previously read. Oh, the joys of reading!

All children deserve the promise that books hold. Whether they transport us to another world, make us laugh or cry, teach us something new, or introduce us to people we wouldn't otherwise meet, we are thankful for their gifts. In turn, all children deserve the gift of reading. And as educators, we bear the responsibility and honor of delivering that gift. As teachers of intermediate grade children, your students come to you with a wide range of reading skills and ability levels. Some have mastered most of the skills they'll need to decode and comprehend more complex text; others still struggle with the most basic and critical skills. Your task—and challenge—is to prepare each of these students for the demands of texts filled with new and long words and complex ideas.

Each year millions of teachers enter classrooms across our nation (and the world) facing this same challenge. They must make key decisions as they wrestle with how best to help their students improve their reading skills and develop a love of books. This guidebook is designed to help you, the intermediate grades teacher, better understand our unique and sometimes complex language and use that knowledge to improve and expand your students' reading skills. Its focus is on **advanced phonics**. Phonics involves the relationship between sounds and their spellings. Advanced phonics builds on the primary-grades skills (consonants, short vowels, silent *e*) and enables students to read multisyllabic words with often complex vowel and syllabication patterns. It also includes the study of structural analysis (prefixes, suffixes, roots) and fluency. As you explore advanced phonics, your students will gain insights into our fascinating language, get excited about words, and become fluent readers. You'll help them develop a passion for books and an understanding of how books can provide pleasure and information.

Teaching Phonics & Word Study in the Intermediate Grades • Scholastic Professional Books

Phonics: A Definition

According to a 1992 poll conducted by Peter D. Hart Research Associates, 62% of parents identified reading as one of the most important skills their children needed to learn. In 1994 the same polling firm conducted a survey for the American Federation of Teachers and the Chrysler Corporation and found that almost 70% of teachers identified reading as *the* most important skill for children to learn.

With such agreement on the importance of reading, what should be the primary goals of reading instruction? The following goals are often cited:

1. automatic word recognition (fluency)
2. comprehension of text
3. development of a love of literature and a desire to read

The first of these goals—automatic word recognition—is the primary focus of this book. To become skilled readers, students must be able to identify words quickly and accurately. And to do that, they must be proficient at decoding words. Decoding words involves converting the printed word into spoken language. A reader decodes a word by sounding it out, using structural analysis and syllabication techniques, or recognizing the word by sight. In order to sound out words, a reader must be able to associate a specific spelling with a specific sound. Phonics involves this relationship between sounds and their spellings.

Phonics is not a specific teaching method. In fact, there are many ways to teach phonics. However, what most types of phonics instruction have in common is that they focus on the teaching of sound-spelling relationships so that the reader can come up with an approximate pronunciation of a word and then check it against his or her oral vocabulary.

Approximately 84% of English words are phonetically regular. Therefore, teaching the most common sound-spelling relationships in English is extremely useful to readers. As Anderson et al. (1985) write, "English is an alphabetic language in which there are consistent, though not entirely predictable, relationships between letters and sounds. When children learn these relationships well, most of the words in their spoken language become accessible to them when they see them in print. When this happens, children are said to have 'broken the code.'"

One of the arguments against teaching phonics is that the approximately 16% of so-called **irregular** English words appear with the greatest frequency in text (about 80% of the time). As you will discover throughout this book, these words are not as irregular as they may seem. Although they must be taught as **sight words**, the reader has to pay attention to their spelling patterns in order to store them in his or her memory. Some detractors of teaching phonics also contend that reading develops in the same way as speaking—naturally. Foorman (1995) responds by saying "humans are biologically specialized to produce language and have done so for nearly one million years. Such is not the case with reading and writing. If it were, there would not be illiterate children in the world."

Clearly then, most children need instruction in learning to read. One of the critical early hurdles in reading instruction is helping children grasp the alphabetic principle. That is, in order to read, children must understand that this series of symbols we call the alphabet maps out the sounds of our language in roughly predictable ways. This alphabetic principle is a key insight into early reading. And it enables children to get off to a quick start in relating sounds to spellings and thereby decoding words.

Phonics in the Intermediate Grades: What and Why

Once children grasp the alphabetic principle and learn the most common sound-spellings they meet in primary grade texts, their next hurdle involves decoding multisyllabic words. Some older students find it extremely difficult to read these words. They can't recognize common spelling patterns or larger chunks of the words that may help in sounding them out. And many more of the words in the books they're now reading are new to them, are not in their speaking or listening vocabularies. Discovering the meanings of these unfamiliar words is critical to understanding the text. Learning advanced phonics skills helps. For example, one important aid in determining a word's meaning is understanding prefixes and roots, as there are significant differences between "relevant" and "*ir*relevant, "play" and "play*ful*."

Comprehension is certainly the most important part of reading. But how does the ability to decode words help a reader understand a text? The following flow chart illustrates that strong decoding ability is necessary for reading comprehension.

Phonics instruction helps the reader to map sounds onto spellings. This ability enables readers to decode words. **Decoding** words aids in the development of and improvement in word recognition. The more words one recognizes, the easier the reading task. Therefore, phonics instruction aids in the development of **word recognition** by providing children with an important and useful way to figure out unfamiliar words while reading.

When children begin to be able to recognize a large amount of words quickly and accurately, **reading fluency** improves. Reading fluency refers to the ease with which children can read a text. As more and more words become firmly stored in a child's memory (that is, the child recognizes more and more words on sight), he or she gains fluency and **automaticity** in word recognition. Having many opportunities to decode words in text is critical to learning words by sight. The more times a child encounters a word in text, the more likely he or she is to recognize it by sight and to avoid making a reading error (Gough, Juel, & Roper-Schneider, 1983).

Reading fluency improves **reading comprehension**. Since children are no longer struggling with decoding words, they can devote their full attention (mental energies) to making meaning from the text. As the vocabulary and concept demands increase in text, children need to be able to devote more of their attention to making meaning from text, and increasingly less attention to decoding. If children have to devote too much time to decoding words, their reading will be slow and labored. This will result in comprehension difficulties.

However, this is not the only skill a reader needs to make meaning from text. When they read, children need to be able to use three cueing systems. These systems represent signals in text that interact and overlap to help the reader understand what he or she is reading.

1. Graphophonic cues involve a reader's knowledge of sound-spelling relationships. Phonics instruction helps children to use these cues.

2. Syntactic cues involve a reader's knowledge of the grammar or structure of language. These cues do not help children sound out words. Rather, this knowledge helps the reader predict what type of word might appear in a certain place in a sentence. It might be a naming word (noun), an action word (verb), or a describing word (adjective). This cueing system also involves an understanding of word order and the use of function words, such as *the* and *an*. For example, read the following sentence and choose a word to fill in the blank.

We saw the _____ on the road.

All possible words to fill in the blank must be naming words. You determined this from your knowledge of English syntax.

Most children have an understanding of the basic syntactic structures of English when they enter school. However, oral language is different from "book language." Written material might pose difficulties for some children because their oral language patterns differ so much from the more formal language patterns of text. Reading many books aloud will help these children gain an understanding of the more formal syntactic structures used for writing. In particular, children may struggle with the vocabulary and structure of nonfiction texts. Reading numerous information books aloud and discussing their text structures will be beneficial to students.

3. Semantic cues involve a reader's knowledge of the world. This knowledge helps the reader to use cues in the text to discover the meaning of a word that fits into a specific place in a particular sentence. Readers use their semantic knowledge to determine if a text makes sense.

Teaching Phonics & Word Study in the Intermediate Grades • Scholastic Professional Books

Ten Important Research Findings About Phonics

Countless research studies have been conducted on phonics instruction. Much of this research has focused on the usefulness of phonics instruction and the best ways to teach children about sound-spelling relationships. Below is a list of ten of the top research findings regarding phonics.

#1: Phonics Instruction Can Help All Children Learn to Read

All children can benefit from instruction in the most common sound-spelling relationships and syllable patterns in English. This instruction helps children decode words that follow these predictable sound-spelling relationships and syllable-spelling patterns.

Phonics instruction is particularly beneficial for children at risk for learning difficulties. This might include children who come to school with limited exposure to books, have had few opportunities to develop their oral languages, are from low socio-economic families, have below-average intelligence, are learning English as a second language, or are suspected of having a learning disability. However, even children from language-rich backgrounds benefit from phonics instruction (Chall, 1967). As Chall states, "By learning phonics, students make faster progress in acquiring literary skills—reading and writing. By the age of six, most children already have about 6,000 words in their listening and speaking vocabularies. With phonics they learn to read and write these and more words at a faster rate than they would without phonics."

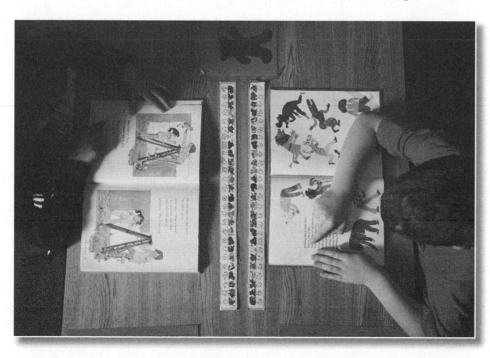

Phonics instruction is therefore an essential ingredient in reading instruction, as it teaches children how to read with accuracy, comprehension, fluency, and pleasure. The early ability to sound out words successfully is a strong predictor of future growth in decoding (Lundberg, 1984) and comprehension (Lesgold and Resnick, 1982). Weak decoding skills are characteristic of poor readers (Carnine, Carnine, and Gertsen, 1984; Lesgold and Curtis, 1981). Readers who are skilled at decoding usually comprehend text better than those who are poor decoders. Why this is so can be gleaned from the work of cognitive psychologists, who contend that we have a set amount of mental energy that we can devote to any task (Kahneman, 1973). Since decoding requires so much of this mental energy, little is left over for higher-level comprehension. As decoding skills improve and more and more words are recognized by sight, less mental energy is required to decode words and more mental energy can be devoted to making meaning from the text (Freedman and Calfee, 1984; LaBerge and Samuels, 1974).

In addition, successful early decoding ability is related to the number of words a reader encounters. That is, children who are good decoders read many more words than children who are poor decoders (Juel, 1991). This wide reading subsequently results in greater reading growth. Children not only learn more words, but they become more familiar with the common spelling patterns of English, which in turn helps them decode longer words.

Phonics instruction also helps get across the alphabetic principle (that the letters of the alphabet stand for sounds) by teaching the relationship between letters and the sounds they represent. Beginning readers learn better when their teachers emphasize these relationships (Chall, 1996).

#2: Explicit Phonics Instruction Is More Beneficial than Implicit Instruction

According to Chall (1996), "systematic and early instruction in phonics leads to better reading: better accuracy of word recognition, decoding, spelling, and oral and silent reading comprehension." The most effective type of instruction, especially for children at risk for reading difficulties, is **explicit (direct) instruction** (Adams, 1990; Chall, 1996; Honig, 1995; Evans and Carr, 1985; Stahl and Miller, 1989; Anderson et al., 1985). **Implicit instruction** relies on readers "discovering" clues about sound-spelling relationships. Good readers can do this; poor readers aren't likely to. Good readers can generalize their knowledge of sound-spelling relationships and syllable patterns to read new words in which these and other sound-spellings and patterns occur. Poor readers must rely on explicit instruction.

Teaching Phonics & Word Study in the Intermediate Grades • Scholastic Professional Books

Although explicit instruction has proved more effective than implicit instruction, the key element in its success is having many opportunities to read decodable words (words containing previously taught sound-spellings) (Stahl, Osborn, and Pearson, 1992; Juel and Roper-Schneider, 1985; Adams, 1990) and ample modeling of applying these skills to real reading. In fact, students who receive phonics instruction achieve best in both decoding and comprehension if the text they read contains high percentages of decodable words. In addition, by around second or third grade, children who've been taught by explicit phonics instruction generally surpass the reading abilities of their peers who've been taught by implicit phonics instruction (Chall, 1996).

Clearly, explicit phonics instruction and reviewing needs to occur for many students in the intermediate grades. Short daily lessons with decodable text reading practice can have a significant impact.

Phonics instruction can help students become active word detectives.

#3: Most Poor Readers Have Weak Phonics Skills and a Strategy Imbalance

Most poor readers have a strategy imbalance. They tend to over-rely on one reading strategy, such as the use of context clues, to the exclusion of other strategies that might be more appropriate (Sulzby, 1985). To become skilled, fluent readers, children need to have a repertoire of strategies to figure out unfamiliar words (Cunningham, 1990). These strategies include using a knowledge of sound-spelling relationships, using context clues, and using structural clues and syllabication. Younger and less skilled readers rely more on context than other, often more effective, strategies (Stanovich, 1980). This is partly due to their inability to use sound-spelling relationships to decode words. Stronger readers don't need to rely on context clues because they can quickly and accurately decode words by sounding them out.

Unfortunately, children who get off to a slow start in reading rarely catch up to their peers and seldom develop into strong readers (Stanovich, 1986; Juel, 1991). Those who experience difficulties decoding early on tend to read less and thereby grow less in terms of word recognition skills and vocabulary.

A longitudinal study conducted by Juel (1988) revealed an 88% probability that a child who is a poor reader at the end of first grade would still be a poor reader at the end of fourth grade. Stanovich (1986) refers to this as the "Matthew Effect": the "rich get richer" (children who are successful decoders early on read more and therefore improve in reading), and the "poor get poorer" (children who have difficulties decoding become increasingly distanced from the good decoders in terms of reading ability).

#4: Phonics Knowledge Has a Powerful Effect on Decoding Ability

Phonics knowledge affects decoding ability positively (Stanovich and West, 1989). Early attainment of decoding skill is important because this accurately predicts later skill in reading comprehension (Beck and Juel, 1995).

One way to help children achieve the ultimate goal of reading instruction, to make meaning of text, is to help them achieve automaticity in decoding words (Gaskins et al., 1988). Skilled readers recognize the majority of words they encounter in text quickly and accurately, independent of context (Cunningham, 1975-76; Stanovich, 1984). The use of graphophonic cues (knowledge of sound-spelling relationships) furthers word recognition abilities. In fact, a child's word recognition speed in first grade was found to be a strong predictor of reading comprehension ability in second grade (Lesgold and Resnick, 1982; Beck and Juel, 1995).

However, the inability to automatically recognize frequently encountered words affects reading in the following ways (Royer and Sinatra, 1994):

1. Since words can be stored in working memory for only about 10–15 seconds, slow decoding can result in some words "decaying" before the reader can process a meaningful chunk of text.

2. Devoting large amounts of mental energy to decoding words leaves less mental energy available for higher-level comprehension. This can result in comprehension breakdowns.

Teaching Phonics & Word Study in the Intermediate Grades • Scholastic Professional Books

#5: Good Decoders Rely Less on Context Clues than Poor Decoders

Good readers don't need to rely as much on context clues because their decoding skills are so strong (Gough and Juel, 1991). It's only when good readers can't use their knowledge of sound-spelling relationships to figure out an unfamiliar word that they rely on context clues. In contrast, poor readers, who often have weak decoding skills, over-rely on context clues to try to make meaning of text (Nicholson, 1992; Stanovich, 1986). Any reader, strong or weak, can use context clues only up to a certain point. It has been estimated that only one out of every four words (25%) can be predicted using context (Gough, Alford, and Holley-Wilcox, 1981). The words that are the easiest to predict are function words such as *the* and *an*. Content words—the words that carry the bulk of the meaning in a text—are the most difficult to predict. Researchers estimate that content words can be predicted only about 10% of the time (Gough, 1983). A reader needs to use his or her knowledge of phonics (sound-spelling relationships) to decode these words.

"The whole word method (meaning emphasis) may serve a student adequately up to about second grade. But failure to acquire and use efficient decoding skills will begin to take a toll on reading comprehension by grade 3."

—Jeanne Chall

#6: The Reading Process Relies on a Reader's Attention to Each Letter in a Word

Eye-movement studies have revealed that skilled readers attend to almost every word in a sentence and process the letters that compose each word (McConkie and Zola, 1987). Therefore, reading is a "letter-mediated" rather than a "whole-word-mediated" process (Just and Carpenter, 1987). Prior to these findings, it was assumed that readers did not process each letter in a word; rather they recognized the word based on shape, a few letters, and context.

Research has also revealed that poor readers do not fully analyze words; for example, some poor readers tend to rely on initial consonant cues only (Stanovich, 1992; Vellutino and Scanlon, 1987). Therefore, phonics instruction should help in focusing children's attention on all the letters or spellings that make up words and the sounds each represents by emphasizing full analysis of words. In addition, phonics instruction must teach children strategies to use this information to decode words. The reader has to pay attention to the spelling patterns in words in order to store the words in his or her memory. And by more fully analyzing the common spelling patterns of English, the reader becomes a better speller (Ehri, 1987).

Teaching Phonics & Word Study in the Intermediate Grades • Scholastic Professional Books

#7: Phonemic Awareness Is Necessary for Phonics Instruction to Be Effective

Before children can use a knowledge of sound-spelling relationships to decode words, they must understand that words are made up of sounds (Adams, 1990). Many children come to school thinking of words as whole units—*cat, dog, run*. Before they can learn to read, children must realize that these words can be broken into smaller units—and sounded out. **Phonemic awareness** is the understanding, or insight, that a word is made up of a series of discrete sounds. Without this insight, phonics instruction will not make sense to children. Some students with weak phonemic awareness skills are able to make it through the first few years of reading instruction by memorizing words. This strategy breaks down when the number of unique words in text increases in grades 3 and up. Therefore, if weak phonemic awareness skills are not detected and corrected, these students may enter the intermediate grades with a very serious reading deficit, intermediate-grade teachers will need to use one of the phonemic awareness programs listed on page 282 to help these students.

#8: Phonics Instruction Improves Spelling Ability

Reading and writing are interrelated and complementary processes (Pinnell, 1994). Whereas phonics is characterized by putting together sounds to form words that are printed, spelling involves breaking down spoken words into sounds in order to write them. To spell, or encode, a word a child must map a spelling onto each sound heard in the word.

Spelling development lags behind reading development. A word can generally be read before it can be spelled. The visual attention a child needs to recognize words is stored in his or her memory. This information—the knowledge of the spelling patterns, also known as **orthographic** knowledge—is used to spell. Spelling, however, requires greater visual recall than reading and places higher demands on memory.

Good spellers are generally good readers because spelling and reading share an underlying knowledge base. Poor readers, however, are rarely good spellers. Phonics is a particularly powerful tool in improving spelling because it emphasizes spelling patterns, which become familiar from reading. Studies show that half of all English words can be spelled with phonics rules that relate one letter to one sound. Thirty-seven % of words can be spelled with phonics rules that relate groups of letters to one sound. The other 13% must be learned by memorization. Good spellers have not memorized the dictionary; they apply the phonics rules they know and have a large store of sight words.

Writing, in turn, supports a child's reading development because it slows the process by focusing the child's attention on how print works. Poor spellers experience difficulties in both writing and reading. Poorly developed spelling ability also hinders vocabulary development (Adams, Treiman, and Pressley, 1996; Read, 1986).

#9: A Teacher's Knowledge of Phonics Affects His or Her Ability to Teach Phonics

A teacher's knowledge of phonics has a strong effect on his or her ability to teach phonics (Carroll, 1990; Moats, 1995). This understanding of the phonics of the English language enables the teacher to choose the best examples for instruction, provide focused instruction, and better understand and interpret students' reading and writing errors in relationship to their developing language skills. I highly recommend that all teachers take a basic course in phonics or linguistics to gain further insights into our language that can be used in the classroom in productive and purposeful ways.

#10: Knowledge of Common Syllable Patterns and Structural Analysis Improves the Ability to Read, Spell, and Learn the Meanings of Multisyllabic Words

For many children, reading long words is an arduous task. Explicit instruction in the six common spelling patterns, the most common syllable types (e.g., VCe, VCCV,), prefixes, suffixes, roots, and word origins helps students recognize larger word chunks, which makes decoding and figuring out meaning easier. For example, it may be efficient for a student to decode text containing simple CVC words such as *cat* and *ran* sound by sound; however, it is not efficient for him or her to decode text containing words such as *transportation* and *unhappy* sound by sound. Rather, it is more efficient for the child to recognize common word parts such as *trans, port, tion, un,* and *happy* and blend these larger chunks to sound out the word.

Teaching Phonics & Word Study in the Intermediate Grades • Scholastic Professional Books

Stages of Reading Development: Where Phonics Fits In

Before I begin discussing advanced phonics instruction in depth, I want to focus on the big picture. Knowing the stages of reading development can help put phonics in its proper perspective and enable you to make instructional decisions based on where each student fits in the continuum. I've chosen the stages of reading development proposed by Chall (1983) because they provide a clear and useful framework for how children learn to read. The time frames are general. (See next page.)

As Chall (1983) states, the value of this framework is that it "suggests that different aspects of reading be emphasized at different stages of reading development, and that success at the beginning is essential since it influences not only early reading achievement but also reading at subsequent stages of development." This framework highlights the need for reading programs to provide children with strong instruction in decoding words. It is also a warning that a prolonged stay in any one stage can result in serious reading problems.

As you read this book and assess the reading development of your students, keep in mind the Stages of Reading Development framework. Consider how you can use it to modify instruction. For example, the way you teach a fourth grade child stuck in Stage 2 is different from the way you teach a fourth grade child already in Stage 3.

Aside from providing balanced, strong reading instruction that meets the needs of all your children, the greatest gift you can give them is a love of reading. I am constantly reminded of Mrs. Fry, my fourth grade teacher. Throughout the school year, she read to us the entire *Little House* series by Laura Ingalls Wilder, as well as many other classics. The words seemed to melt off the page as she read. I can still remember the emotion in her voice. When the book was sad, her voice would crack, and we could feel the pain. When the book was happy, her voice sounded like it would burst from within her. She made me want to read everything she picked up. Indeed, many of us purchased our own *Little House* set of books or checked out of the library every book she "blessed" with these memorable readings. She brought books to life for hundreds of children during her career. It is that love of literature we can and must share with our students in order to lead them into a world of adventure, information, comfort, and wonderment.

The Six Stages of Reading Development

Stage 0: Birth to Age Six

Prereading The most notable change is the child's growing control over language. By the time a child enters grade 1 (at around age six), he or she has approximately 6,000 words in his or her listening and speaking vocabularies. During this stage, children also develop some knowledge of print, such as recognizing a few letters, words, and environmental print signs. Many children learn to write their names. It is common to see them "pretend" read a book that has been repeatedly read to them. At this stage, children bring more to the printed page than they take out.

Stage 1: Grades 1 Through 2

Initial Reading or Decoding During this time, children develop an understanding of the alphabetic principle and begin to use their knowledge of sound-spelling relationships to decode words.

Stage 2: Grades 2 Through 3

Confirmation, Fluency, and Ungluing from Print Children further develop and solidify their decoding skills. They also develop additional strategies to decode words and make meaning from text. As this stage ends, children have developed fluency; that is, they can recognize many words quickly and accurately by sight and are skilled at sounding out the words they don't recognize by sight. They are also skilled at using context clues.

Stage 3: Grades 4 Through 8

Learning the New During this stage, reading demands change. Children begin to use reading more as a way to obtain information and learn about the values, attitudes, and insights of others. Texts contain many words not already in a child's speaking and listening vocabularies. These texts, frequently drawn from a wide variety of genres, also extend beyond the background experiences of the children.

Stage 4: Throughout High School (Grades 9–12)

Multiple Viewpoints During this stage, readers encounter more complex language and vocabulary as they read texts in more advanced content areas. Thus the language and cognitive demands required increase. Students are also reading texts containing varying viewpoints and must analyze them critically.

Stage 5: Throughout College and Beyond

Construction and Reconstruction This stage is characterized by a "world view." Readers use the information in books and articles as needed; that is, they know which books (and articles) will provide the information they need and can locate that information without having to read the entire book. At this stage, reading is considered constructive; that is, readers take in a wide range of information and construct their own understanding for their individual uses based on their analysis and synthesis of the information. Not all readers progress to this stage.

From The Stages of Reading Development by Jeanne Chall ©1983, ©1996.

Learning About Sounds & Letters

"...*knowledge is power. The teacher with some knowledge of linguistics can be a far better kidwatcher, as well as be able to participate more learnedly in conversations and debates about teaching methodology.*"

—*Sandra Wilde*

Why is the most common vowel sound in English the colorless murmur we refer to as the schwa (/ə/) sound? Why do the vowels *e, i, o,* and *u* act as consonants in words such as *azalea, onion, one,* and *quick*; and the consonants *w* and *y* act as vowels in words such as *snow* and *fly*? Why don't the word pairs *five/give, low/how, paid/said,* and *break/speak* rhyme?

These and other questions might cause you to reconsider the teaching of reading and writing because of the seemingly irregular and unpredictable nature of the English language. However, 84% of English words do conform to regular spelling patterns. Of the remaining 16%, only 3% are highly unpredictable, such as *colonel* and *Ouija* (Bryson, 1990). Given the high degree of regularity of spelling, it's easy to see why teaching children the most common sound-spelling relationships in English and helping them to attend to common spelling patterns in words will help them with reading. It is important, therefore, for teachers to have a working knowledge of the many sounds in our language and the even greater number of spellings that can represent them.

Why Should I Know About Linguistics?

In 1995, Louisa Moats examined teacher preparation in the areas of reading and learning disabilities and surveyed teachers' background knowledge of language. Five of the fifteen questions she asked are listed here (answers provided).

---

1. How many speech sounds are in the following words?

ox (3)	**boil** (3)
king (3)	**thank** (4)
straight (5)	**shout** (3)
though (2)	**precious** (6)

2. Underline the consonant blends:
doubt, known, fir<u>st</u>, pu<u>mp</u>kin, <u>squ</u>awk, <u>scr</u>atch

3. What letters signal that a "g" is pronounced /j/? (*e, i, y*)

4. List all the ways you can think of to spell "long a"? (*a, ai, a-e, ey, ay, eigh*)

5. Account for the double "m" in *comment* or *commitment*: (The first *m* closes the syllable to make it short; *com* is a Latin morpheme—the smallest unit of meaning in language—as are *ment* and *mit*.)

22

The results of Moats' survey showed that the majority of teachers could benefit from additional training in linguistics. Only about half of the teachers surveyed could successfully answer most of the questions. Knowledge of phonics was particularly weak. Only about 10–20% of the teachers could identify consonant blends; almost none could consistently identify digraphs; less than half could identify the schwa sound in words; and only 30% knew the conditions in which the letters *ck* were used to stand for the /k/ sound. Moats contends that some of her survey results can be attributed to:

1. a lack of teacher training in phonics and linguistics.

2. the fact that most adult readers think of words in terms of spellings instead of sounds. Their knowledge of print may stand in the way of attending to individual sounds in words—a skill they no longer need to be conscious of because they have already acquired automaticity.

3. the fact that some adults have underdeveloped metalinguistic skills. That is, the skills they have acquired are sufficient for reading, but not sufficient for explicitly teaching reading and spelling.

During my years as a teacher, I've improved my ability to assess children's reading and writing skills because I've increased my understanding of the English language. The more I learn about English, the more regular its spelling seems. For example, at one time I thought of words such as *love* and *come* as being "irregular" since they didn't follow the typical *o-e* spelling for the long *o* sound. But when I realized how many words follow a similar spelling pattern (*shove, glove, above, some,* etc.), a regularity began to emerge. The *o-e* spelling pattern is not random; rather, it can represent either the /ō/ sound or the /u/ sound in words. Now, these are the two sounds I try out when confronted with this spelling pattern in an unfamiliar word. In addition, the more I learn about English and its spelling patterns, the more my students' reading and writing errors make sense. This knowledge has helped me to target specific difficulties students have had and to design appropriate instruction. If you have a basic knowledge of phonics and linguistics, you'll be able to help your students by (Moats, 1995):

- **interpreting and responding to student errors.** You can use student errors to modify instruction. For example, when a student substitutes *k* for *g* in a word, knowing that the sounds these two letters represent are formed in almost the same manner helps to explain the student's error. You can instruct students in the major difference between these two sounds (voicing).

- **choosing the best examples for teaching decoding and spelling.** You can help children distinguish auditorily confusing sounds such as /e/ and /i/, and use words for instruction that provide the clearest, simplest examples.

- **organizing and sequencing information for instruction.** You'll be able to separate the introduction of auditorily confusing sounds such as /e/ and /i/ and teach easier concepts before more complex ones (such as teaching consonants before consonant clusters).

- **using your knowledge of morphology to explain spellings.** Morphology is the study of units of meaning, or morphemes, such as root words (Latin, Greek). Use these to explain spelling patterns and guide children to figure out word meanings.

- **integrating the components of language instruction.** You'll be able to take better advantage of the "teachable moment" and more completely integrate the language arts.

Linguistics is the formal study of language and how it works. You don't have to be a linguist to be an effective teacher of reading and writing. However, a deeper understanding of our language can enhance any teacher's abilities. This chapter begins by defining a few basic terms associated with linguistics and another related area of study—**phonetics** (the study of speech sounds). It concludes by providing brief information on the sound-spellings covered in most intermediate-grade reading curriculums and word lists for instruction.

Teaching Phonics & Word Study in the Intermediate Grades • Scholastic Professional Books

The 44 Sounds of English

A phoneme is a speech sound. It's the smallest unit of sound that distinguishes one word from another. The word *phoneme* is derived from the Greek root *phon* (as in the word *telephone*), which refers to *voice* or *sound*. The following pairs of words differ by only one phoneme, the first—*cat/hat, men/pen.*

Since sounds cannot be written, we use letters to represent or stand for the sounds. A **grapheme** is the written representation (a letter or cluster of letters) of one sound. For example, the /b/ sound can be represented by the letter *b*; the /sh/ sound can be represented by the letters *sh*. The word *sat* has three phonemes (/s/ /a/ /t/) and three graphemes (s, a, t). The word *chop* also has three phonemes (/ch/ /o/ /p/) and three graphemes (ch, o, p).

Linguists disagree on the actual number of sounds in the English language. The number varies according to dialect, individual speech patterns, changes in stress, and other variables. However, for the sake of our study, we will deal with the 44 phonemes commonly covered in elementary school reading programs.

The 44 Sounds of English

CONSONANT SOUNDS

1. /b/ (bat)	10. /n/ (nest)	19. /ch/ (cheese)
2. /d/ (dog)	11. /p/ (pig)	20. /sh/ (shark)
3. /f/ (fan)	12. /r/ (rock)	21. /th/ (thumb)
4. /g/ (gate)	13. /s/ (sun)	22. /th̸/ (the)
5. /h/ (hat)	14. /t/ (top)	23. /hw/ (wheel)
6. /j/ (jump)	15. /v/ (vase)	24. /zh/ (treasure)
7. /k/ (kite)	16. /w/ (wagon)	25. /ng/ (ring)
8. /l/ (leaf)	17. /y/ (yo-yo)	
9. /m/ (mop)	18. /z/ (zebra)	

VOWEL SOUNDS

26. /a/ (cat)	33. /ī/ (bike)	40. /oi/ (boy)
27. /e/ (bed)	34. /ō/ (boat)	41. /ô/ (ball)
28. /i/ (fish)	35. /yo͞o/ (cube)	42. /û/ (bird)
29. /o/ (lock)	36. /ə/ (alarm)	43. /â/ (chair)
30. /u/ (duck)	37. /o͞o/ (moon)	44. /ä/ (car)
31. /ā/ (cake)	38. /o͝o/ (book)	
32. /ē/ (feet)	39. /ou/ (house)	

The 44 English phonemes are represented by the 26 letters of the alphabet individually and in combination. Therefore, a letter can sometimes represent more than one sound. For example, the letter *a* can stand for the sounds heard in words such as *at, ate, all, any, was,* and *father*. Likewise, a phoneme can sometimes be represented by more than one grapheme. For example, the /f/ sound can be represented by *f* (fan), *ph* (phone), or *gh* (laugh).

Adding to the complexity, some letters do not represent any sound in a word. For example, the letter *k* in the word *knot* is silent. In addition, some letters do not represent a unique or distinctive sound. The letter *c*, for instance, stands for either the /s/ sound (usually represented by the letter *s*), or the /k/ sound (usually represented by the letter *k*). The letters *q* and *x* also represent no distinctive sound.

To distinguish between a letter and a sound in writing, sounds are placed between **virgules**, or slashes. For example, to indicate the sound that the letter *s* stands for, we would write /s/. Other markings aid us in representing sounds in written form. These markings are called **diacritical marks**. The chart below shows some of the most common diacritical marks. The two most common are the macron and the breve. The **macron** (—) is used to represent long-vowel sounds, such as the /ā/ sound in *gate*. The **breve** (˘) is used to represent short-vowel sounds such as the /ă/ sound in *hat*. Short-vowel sounds can also be written using only the letter between virgules, such as /a/. The International Phonetic Alphabet has conventionalized the symbols for every sound of every language in the world. These differ somewhat from the symbols commonly found in dictionaries. For the sake of consistency, this book deals with only those markings and symbols commonly found in children's dictionaries and taught in elementary reading programs.

Diacritical Marks

Markings	Symbol	Example
macron	—	/ā/ as in cake
breve	˘	/ă/ as in cat
tilde	~	/ñ/ as in piñon
dieresis	¨	/ä/ as in car
circumflex	^	/ô/ as in ball

Teaching Phonics & Word Study in the Intermediate Grades • Scholastic Professional Books

Phonics instruction involves teaching the relationship between sounds and the spellings used to represent them. There are hundreds of spellings that can be used to represent the 44 English phonemes. Only the most common need to be taught explicitly. Throughout this book, when I refer to the most common sound-spelling relationships, I choose the term "sound-spelling" instead of the more common term "sound-symbol" because it is more accurate. Many sound-spelling relationships are represented by more than one symbol or letter. For example, the /ch/ sound is represented by the letters, or spelling, *ch*; the long /ē/ sound can be represented by the spellings *e, ea,* or *ee.* When teaching phonics, we want children to attend to these spelling patterns to develop their understanding of English **orthography**—the spelling system of our language.

The 44 English sounds can be divided into two major categories—consonants and vowels. A **consonant** sound is one in which the air flow is cut off either partially or completely when the sound is produced. In contrast, a **vowel** sound is one in which the air flow is unobstructed when the sound is made. The vowel sounds are the music, or movement, of our language.

Consonants

Of the 26 letters in the English alphabet, 21 are generally considered consonants. These are *b, c, d, f, g, h, j, k, l, m, n, p, q, r, s, t, v, w, x, y,* and *z.* The letters *w* and *y* sometimes act as vowels, as in the words *my, happy,* and *show.* Of the 44 English phonemes, 25 are consonant phonemes. (See the chart on page 25.) Eighteen of these phonemes are represented by a single letter, such as /b/ and /m/; seven are identified by a digraph, such as /sh/ and /ch/. A **digraph** is a letter cluster that stands for one sound. The letters *c, q,* and *x* do not have a unique phoneme assigned to them; the sounds that they stand for are more commonly represented by other letters or spellings.

Consonants can be further categorized according to (1) how they are produced, (2) where they are produced in the mouth, and (3) whether they are voiced. The five major categories of consonants based on their **manner of articulation** are:

1. plosives (stops): formed by closing or blocking off the air flow and then exploding a puff of air (examples: /b/, /p/, /d/, /t/, /g/, /k/). Place your hand in front of your mouth when producing these sounds. Do you feel a burst of air?

2. fricatives: formed by narrowing the air channel and then forcing air through it—this creates friction in the mouth (examples: /f/, /v/, /th/, /t͟h/, /z/, /s/, /zh/, /sh/). A subgroup of this category is the **affricative**, which is a sound produced by the sequence of a stop followed by a fricative (examples: /ch/, /j/).

3. nasals: formed when the mouth is closed, forcing the air through the nose (examples: /n/, /m/, /ng/). These sounds are also referred to as nasal stops.

4. liquids: formed by interrupting the airflow slightly, but no friction results (examples: /l/, /r/).

5. glides: sometimes called semivowels because they are formed in similar ways as vowels (examples: /w/, /y/, /h/).

In addition to how sounds are produced, where they are produced in the mouth distinguishes one sound from another. For example, the fricative /v/ is formed using the lips and teeth. Therefore, it is referred to as a **labiodental**. (labio = lips; dental = teeth). The fricative /z/ is formed using the front of the mouth. Therefore, it is referred to as an **alveolar**; the alveolar ridge is the name of the front of the mouth where the teeth arise. Similarly, the fricative /sh/ is formed using the roof of the mouth. Therefore, it is referred to as a **palatal**; the hard palate is the name of the roof of the mouth. Other labels you might encounter include **velar** (the velum, or soft palate, is the back of the mouth) and **bilabial** (both lips).

The chart that follows shows most of the consonant sounds according to where they are articulated. It also divides sounds according to those that are

Place of Articulation	Voiced	Unvoiced	Nasal
lips (bilabial)	/b/ (plosive)	/p/ (plosive)	/m/
front of mouth (alveolar)	/d/ (plosive) /z/ (fricative)	/t/ (plosive) /s/ (fricative)	/n/
back of mouth (velar)	/g/ (plosive)	/k/ (plosive)	/ng/
lips and teeth (labiodental)	/v/ (fricative)	/f/ (fricative)	
teeth (dental)	/t͟h/ (fricative)	/th/ (fricative)	
roof of mouth (palatal)	/zh/ (fricative) /j/ (affricative)	/sh/ (fricative) /ch/ (affricative)	

28

voiced and those that are **unvoiced**. When producing a voiced sound, the vocal cords vibrate. When producing an unvoiced sound, there's no vibration. To test this, place your hand on your throat. Then make the /b/ sound. You'll feel a vibration because this is a voiced sound. Now make the /p/ sound, the voiceless counterpart of the /b/ sound, and you won't feel vibration.

One aspect of consonant sounds that affects how we assess students' spelling is the issue of allophones. An **allophone** is a slightly different version of each phoneme. It generally results from the ease (or lack of ease) in articulating a sound in relation to its surrounding sounds. For example, pronounce the words *late* and *later*. The *t* in the word *later* sounds more like /d/. Pronounce the words *like* and *pill*. The *l* in *like* is pronounced with greater force and clarity than the *l* in *pill*. Therefore, when sounds are coarticulated, the surrounding sounds and the ease with which the mouth must move to form each sound affect the resulting sound. These slight sound variations don't bother us when we read, but children's invented spellings often reflect this.

Most of the consonant phonemes are highly reliable, or dependable. That is, when we see the most common letter or spelling for each consonant sound it generally stands for that sound. These regularities result in several generalizations that are helpful for the teacher of reading. The list on page 30 shows several of the most reliable consonant generalizations (Groff, 1977; Henderson, 1967; Mazurkiewicz, 1976). It's not necessary to teach these generalizations to students. It's better to point them out at appropriate moments to help students clarify and organize their understanding of English spelling patterns.

Consonants can appear by themselves or in combination with other consonants. Two consonants that appear together can be a cluster or a digraph. A **cluster** refers to two or more consonants that appear together in a word, each consonant retaining its own sound. For example, the cluster *sn* in *snail* represents the /sn/ sounds. The combination of sounds that the cluster stands for is called a **blend**. In contrast, sometimes when two consonants appear together in a word, they stand for one sound that is different from either sound of each individual consonant. This is called a **digraph**. The digraph *sh* stands for the /sh/ sound. This sound is not a combination of the /s/ and /h/ sounds, rather it is a new and unique sound. There are both consonant and vowel digraphs. An example of a vowel digraph is *oa,* which stands for the /ō/ sound.

Consonant Generalizations

1. Some letters represent no sound in words.

2. Some sounds are almost always represented by the same spelling, such as *th, v,* and *h.*

3. Some spellings appear to be purely arbitrary, such *igh* in *night* and *eau* in *beau.*

4. The English spelling system often uses doubled letters, especially in the middle of words. However, only one sound is produced unless the sounds cross morpheme boundaries, such as in *bookcase* or *unknown.*

5. Certain letters are almost never doubled: *j, k, q, w, x,* and *v.*

6. English spellings have been influenced by other languages, such as *qu* and *th* from Latin-French, *ou* and *ch* from French, and *ps* from Greek.

7. When the letter *c* comes before *e, i,* or *y* in a word, it usually represents the /s/ sound (examples: *cent, city, cycle*).

8. When double *c* comes before *e* or *i* in a word, it usually represents two sounds /ks/ (example: *success*).

9. When the letter *g* comes before *e, i,* or *y* in a word, it usually represents the /j/ sound.

10. When the letters *c* and *g* are followed by *e* at the end of words, they are usually pronounced /s/ and /j/, respectively (examples: *race, cage*).

11. When the letter *h* appears after *c* in a word, the letter pair can be pronounced /ch/, /k/, or /sh/. Try /ch/ first. Note that *ch* before another consonant is usually pronounced /k/ (example: *chlorine*).

12. The letters *sh* and *ph* almost always represent one sound—/sh/ and /f/, respectively.

13. The letters *gh* represent /g/ at the beginning of words and /f/ at the end of words. However, *gh* is often silent, as in *night.*

14. The digraph *th* has two pronunciations—/th/ and /t͡h/.

15. The digraph *wh* is pronounced /hw/. However, when it appears before the letter *o,* only the *h* is pronounced (example: *whole*).

16. The letters *se* indicate that the *s* may be pronounced /s/ or /z/. Try /z/ first, as in *these.*

17. When the letter *s* is followed by *y, i,* or *u* in the middle of words, it may be pronounced /zh/ or /sh/. Try /zh/ first (examples: *measure, fission*).

18. When the letter *i* follows *c, s, ss, sc,* or *t* in the last part of a word, it is usually silent and indicates that these graphemes represent /sh/ (example: *nation*).

19. When the letter *e* follows *v* and *z* at the end of words, it is silent and indicates that *v* and *z* rarely come at the end of words.

20. When the letter *e* follows *ng* at the end of words, it indicates that *ng* stands for /nj/ (example: *strange*).

21. When the letters *le* appear at the end of a word, the *l* is pronounced /ul/ (example: *table*).

22. When a word ends in *dure, ture, sure,* or *zure,* the first letter in each ending is pronounced /j/, /ch/, /sh/, /zh/, respectively (examples: *procedure, denture, ensure, azure*).

Teaching Phonics & Word Study in the Intermediate Grades • Scholastic Professional Books

Vowels

Nineteen of the 44 English phonemes are vowel phonemes. (See the chart on page 25.) The letters *a, e, i, o,* and *u* are classified as vowels. These five letters are used to represent many different sounds. Therefore, each vowel is used for a variety of purposes. The letter *o,* for instance, has at least ten distinct sounds assigned to it (*on, old, son, corn, room, look, word, lemon, out, oil*) and is used in more than 30 different ways (*oasis, old, road, though, shoulder, snow, on, gone, thought, soldier, one, son, enough, does, other, look, could, room, through, to, two, buoy, oil, boy, buoyant, out, how, drought, lemon, word, colonel, Ouija, board*).

In addition, the consonants *w* and *y* often act as vowels, as in the words *show, fly,* and *happy.* The letter *y* acts as a vowel when it appears at the end of a word or syllable. The letter *w* acts as a vowel when it is used in combination with another vowel, as in the words *few, how, slow, thaw,* and *threw.* As vowels, the letters *w* and *y* do not represent distinctive sounds.

The most important distinguishing characteristic of a vowel is its place of articulation. Depending on the approximate place in the mouth in which part of the tongue is raised, vowels can be produced in the front, central, or back part of the mouth. In addition, the degree to which the tongue is raised distinguishes sounds. The sounds can be produced with the tongue raised to a high, mid, or low degree. The following chart illustrates this.

Vowel Sounds			
	FRONT	**CENTRAL**	**BACK**
HIGH	/ē/		/ōō/
MID	/ī/ /e/	/ə/ (shwa) /ər/ (shwar)	/ō/ /ô/
LOW	/a/	/u/	/o/

Missing from this chart are the diphthongs. A **diphthong** is a sound in which the position of the mouth changes from one place to another as the sound is produced. The sounds /oi/ and /ou/ are commonly classified as diphthongs. In addition, two so-called long-vowel sounds—long *i* (/ī/) and long *u* (/yōō/)—are often classified as diphthongs. The long *u* sound is actually a combination of a consonant and vowel sound. To note the difference between a diphthong and other vowel sounds, say aloud the /ā/ sound as in *gate*. Notice how the mouth, tongue, and lips remain in the same position while the sound is produced. Now try the /oi/ sound as in *boy*. Note how the mouth, particularly the lips, changes position while the sound is being produced. This is characteristic of a diphthong. Interestingly, Southern dialects generally produce most of their vowels as diphthongs. This helps to explain the beautiful singsong, rhythmic nature of Southern speech.

In basal reading programs, vowels are generally classified into the following categories:

1. **long-vowel sounds:** The macron (—) is the diacritical mark used to represent long-vowel sounds. The word *macro* means *long* or *great*. Long-vowel sounds are also referred to as **glided sounds**. The long-vowel sounds covered in most basal reading programs include /ā/, /ē/, /i/, /ō/, and / yo͞o/, although long *i* and long *u* are generally classified as diphthongs by linguists. Common long-vowel spelling patterns include CVCe (*race*) and VCe (*age*). Long-vowel sounds are often represented by vowel digraphs such as *ai, ay, ee, ea, oa, ow, ey, igh,* and *ie*. The vowel sound in an **open syllable,** a syllable that ends in a vowel, is generally a long-vowel sound (*ti/ger, a/pron*).

2. **short-vowel sounds:** The breve (˘) is the diacritical mark used to represent short-vowel sounds. Often no mark is used. The short-vowel sounds include /a/, /e/, /i/, /o/, and /u/. Short-vowel sounds are also referred to as **unglided sounds**. The most common short-vowel spelling pattern is CVC (*cat*). Short-vowel sounds are usually represented by the single vowels *a, e, i, o,* and *u*. The vowel sound in a **closed syllable,** a syllable that ends in a consonant, is often a short-vowel sound (*bas/ket*).

3. **other vowel sounds:** The other vowel sounds include diphthongs (/oi/, /ou/), variant vowels (/o͞o/, /o͝o/, /ô /, /ä/), schwa (/ə /), and *r*-controlled vowels (/ôr/, /ûr/, /âr/). In addition to the letter *r*, the letters *l* and *w* also affect the vowel sound that precedes or follows.

Many vowel generalizations are unreliable. For example, the commonly taught generalization, "When two vowels go walking, the first does the talking" has been found to be only about 45% reliable. However, if you limit the generalization to the vowel digraphs *ai, ay, ee,* and *oa*, it becomes a highly useful generalization. The list that follows shows several of the most reliable vowel generalizations (Groff, 1977; Henderson, 1967; Mazurkiewicz, 1976). It's not necessary to teach these to students. Point them out at appropriate moments to help students clarify and organize their understanding of English spelling patterns.

Vowel Generalizations

1. A single vowel followed by one or two consonants usually stands for a short sound. However, it may be a long sound. Try the short sound first.

2. The letter *e* following a vowel and a consonant (other than *c, g, l, ng, s, th, v, z,* and *ur*) usually indicates that the vowel represents a long sound.

3. The letter *a* before *l* in a word, and in the spellings *au* and *aw*, usually represents the /ô/ sound.

4. When the vowel digraphs *ai, ay, ee,* and *oa* appear together in a word, the first vowel usually represents its long sound.

5. The letter *y* usually represents the long-*i* sound at the end of short words (example: *fly*), but the letters *y* and *ey* usually stand for the long-*e* sound in longer words (examples: *happy, monkey*).

6. Some vowel spellings are used in reading to distinguish word meanings (examples: *meat/meet*), but cause problems in spelling.

7. The final *e* (silent *e*, e-marker) accounts for many of the sound distinctions in words.

....

All the vowels, except *a*, can also act as consonants.

1. The letter *e* stands for the /y/ sound in the word *azalea*.

2. The letter *i* when it follows *c, s, ss, sc, t,* and *x* stands for the /sh/ sound (example: *nation*). The letter *i* can also stand for the /y/ sound as in *union, opinion, senior, brilliant, civilian, junior, onion, million, spaniel,* and *stallion*.

3. The letter *o* stands for the /w/ sound as in *one* and *once*.

4. The letter *u* when it follows *s* and *ss* stands for the /zh/ sound (example: *measure*). The letter *u* also stands for the /w/ sound as in *liquid, quiet, quick, queen, quill, quilt, suite, suave, language,* and *penguin*.

Notable sound-spellings from the list of "The 44 Sounds of English" (see page 25) that need special attention are the consonants *c, q,* and *x,* and the digraphs *gh* and *ph.* These consonants and digraphs do not represent distinctive sounds. Information on each of these includes the following:

The letter c

The letter *c* can stand for many sounds:

- It can stand for the /k/ sound as in *cat.* The letter *c* generally stands for the /k/ sound when it comes before the letter *a, o,* or *u* in a word (*cat, cot, cut*). This is sometimes referred to as the "hard" sound of *c.*

- It can stand for the /s/ sound as in *city.* The letter *c* generally stands for the /s/ sound when it comes before the letter *e, i,* or *y* in a word (*cent, cinder, cycle*). This is sometimes referred to as the "soft" sound of *c.*

- The word *cello* is an exception. In this word, the letter *c* stands for the /ch/ sound.

- The letter *c* usually stands for the /k/ sound when it is followed by a consonant as in *cliff* and *cry.* The consonant digraph *ck* also stands for the /k/ sound. Many consider the *c* silent in this digraph. The most notable exception to this is when the letter *c* is followed by the letter *h.* The letters *ch* can stand for the /k/ sound as in *chemistry* and *school* or the /ch/ sound as in *cheese.*

- When the letter *c* follows the letter *s* the two letters combined can stand for the /sk/ sounds as in *scold* and *scream*; or the *c* can be silent as in *science* and *scene.*

- When the letter *c* is doubled in a word, one of the *c*'s is usually silent. When they come before the letters *u* or *o,* the double *c*'s usually stand for the /k/ sound as in *occupy* and *tobacco.* When they come before the letters *e* or *i,* they usually stand for the /ks/ sounds as in *success, accident, access,* and *accept.* The *c* before *i* and *e* in these words stands for the /sh/ sound: *conscious, special, ocean, official, social, delicious, racial.* Note that the letter *i* is silent in these words.

Teaching Phonics & Word Study in the Intermediate Grades • Scholastic Professional Books

The letter q

- The letter *q* could be deleted from our alphabet and replaced with the letter *k*. The letter *q* almost always represents the /k/ sound and is usually followed by the letter *u*. In some words the letter *u* is silent (*antique, bouquet, croquet*). In most words the *u* stands for the /w/ sound (*quack, quail, quake, quart, quarter, queen, question, quick, quiet, quill, quilt, quirk, quit, quite, quiz, require, request, square,* and *squash*).

The letter x

- The letter *x* frequently stands for the /ks/ sounds as in *ax, box, fix, flax, fox, lox, mix, ox, sax, six, tax,* and *wax.*

- It also stands for the /gz/ sounds as in *exact, exit, exist, exam, auxiliary, exhaust,* and *exhibit.* We generally use /gz/ when the letter *x* appears between two vowels.

- The letter *x* can also stand for the /z/ sound as in *xylophone, anxiety, xylem,* and *Xerox.*

- There are words in which we use *x* as a letter (/eks/), as in *x-ray* and *x-ograph.*

- Other sounds that the letter *x* represents include the following: /ksh/ *anxious, anxiously*; /k/ *excite, exceed, excellent, except, excuse*; and /kzh/ *luxury.*

- The letter *x* is silent in the word *Sioux.*

The digraphs gh and ph

- The digraphs *gh* and *ph* can stand for the /f/ sound (*tough, phone*).

- The digraph *gh* can be silent as in *light*.

- The digraph *ph* almost always stands for the /f/ sound as in *phone* and *graph*. However, in the word *diphthong*, the *p* stands for the /p/ sound and the letter *h* is silent.

Teaching Phonics & Word Study in the Intermediate Grades • Scholastic Professional Books

How Phonics Is Taught

"Teach to mastery rather than just exposure."

—John Shefelbine

Many years ago, Flintstone lunch box in hand, I entered a small, rural classroom in a school building I had occasionally passed by and frequently wondered about. The large, brick building was old and run-down, but memories of the brightly illustrated books and seemingly fun activities my older sister brought home piqued my interest. On my first day of grade 1, my teacher, Mrs. Wershaw, distributed to each of us eager, neatly dressed six-year-olds a basal reader and introduced us to three characters we would grow to love—Dick, Jane, and Sally. In addition, she gave us a phonics workbook whose plaid cover had the same design as the girls' skirts at the Catholic school in a neighboring town. Mrs. Wershaw's combined approach to teaching us how to read (sight-word and phonics methods) was the key that unlocked the mysteries of print for me. And, even though some argue about the lack of engaging text in these early readers, I was enthralled by the ability to take those strange looking lines and squiggles on the page and turn them into something that made sense.

My strongest memory of the impact of these stories came one Friday afternoon. Mrs. Wershaw had a strict rule that we could not read ahead in our basals. So, on Friday when Sally fell headfirst into a clothes hamper, and I couldn't turn the page to discover the outcome, I had a weekend of tremendous anxiety. On Monday I raced into school to see if Sally was okay. She was! It was my first taste of suspense in books, and I was forever hooked.

You may be asking yourself, "Why is he telling me about early phonics instruction? I teach the intermediate grades!" Well, many of the instructional principles critical to early phonics instruction also apply to advanced phonics instruction. In addition, some of your students may be at a lower stage of reading development, and the instruction you give them will mirror that of the primary grades.

Two Ways to Teach Phonics

Generally speaking, phonics instruction falls into two camps, or approaches. The first is the *synthetic approach.* This method is also known as **direct** or **explicit phonics**. It follows a bottom-up model of learning to read. That is, children begin by learning to recognize letters, then blend words, and finally read connected text. Instruction roughly follows this sequence:

1. The letter names are taught.

2. The sound that each letter stands for is taught and reviewed. Some rules or generalizations might be discussed.

3. The principle of blending sounds to form words is taught.

4. Opportunities to blend unknown words in context are provided.

The following model illustrates the introduction of the /s/ sound using this approach:

Model: Write the letter *s* on the chalkboard. Explain to the children that the letter *s* stands for the /s/ sound, such as the first sound heard in the word *sat*. Write the letter *s* on the chalkboard as children chorally say the /s/ sound. Then write the word *sat* on the chalkboard, and have a volunteer circle the letter *s*. Slowly blend the word as you run your finger under each letter. Then ask the children for other words that begin with the /s/ sound. List these words on the chalkboard. Have volunteers circle the letter *s* in each word. Continue by providing children with simple words containing the /s/ sound to blend. Make sure these words can be decoded based on the sound-spelling relationships previously taught.

The second is the *analytic approach.* This method is also known as **indirect** or **implicit phonics**. It is sometimes referred to as the "discovery method." With this approach, children begin with words and are asked to deduce the sound-spelling relationship that is the focus of the lesson. Instruction roughly follows this sequence:

1. A list of words with a common phonic element is shown. For example, the words *sat, send,* and *sun* might be written on the chalkboard.

2. The children are asked to examine the words and discover what they have in common, focusing on finding a similar sound in each.

3. Once the common sound is discovered, the spelling that stands for the sound might be discussed.

4. The children are asked to verbalize a generalization about the sound and spelling, such as "the letter *s* stands for the /s/ sound."

The analytic approach gained popularity with teachers who believed that if children discovered these principles for themselves, they would better internalize them. However, one of the drawbacks of the analytic approach is that it relies on a child's ability to orally segment words. It isn't effective for children who can't break off the first sound in a given word, or who don't understand what is meant by the word *sound*. These children lack the **phonemic awareness** (the understanding that a word is made up of a series of discrete sounds) skills they need for the analytic approach to have meaning. And the method has proved least effective with students at risk for reading disorders.

Current research supports a combined approach to teaching phonics, with a heavy emphasis on synthetic (explicit) instruction (Anderson et al., 1985; Adams, 1990). Before I share my other recommendations for phonics instruction, it will be helpful for us to take a brief look at how children's decoding abilities develop. This will help to form the "big picture" within which instructional decisions can be made.

How Readers Develop

During the primary grades, most children are at a stage of reading development referred to as the Initial Reading, or Decoding, Stage (Chall, 1983). It is at this stage that children are taught sound-spelling relationships and how to blend sounds to form words. (For more information on reading development stages, see page 20.) Within each stage of reading development, children progress in roughly predictable ways. Several researchers, including Biemiller (1970) and Juel (1991), have looked at how children progress through the Initial Reading, or Decoding, Stage. Juel has outlined three stages, or levels of progression, within the Initial Reading Stage. She calls these stages the **Stages of Decoding**.

When you think about the stages of decoding, it's important to ask yourself, "What do children need instructionally to progress effectively through each stage?" Each stage has instructional implications, and an emphasis on any one without consideration of the others can result in problems. Well-designed instruction is the key to moving children through the three stages efficiently and effectively.

For example, one of the instructional problems I see frequently is that children can't connect the sound-spelling relationships they've been taught to the text they are given to practice decoding. That is, few words in these stories contain the sound-spelling relationship taught or are decodable based on the sound-spelling relationships learned. Therefore, having few opportunities to use their growing knowledge of sound-spelling relationships, the children are likely to undervalue the importance of the phonics they're learning. Why should they pay attention during phonics lessons when they rarely use what they learn? As a result, these children don't gain fluency, are forced to rely on meaning cues such as context and pictures, and lose out on important blending practice. Many researchers have found that most poor readers over-rely on meaning cues. They're likely stuck in an earlier stage of decoding, unable to progress because of flawed instruction (Stanovich, 1980).

The Stages of Decoding

1. **Selective-cue stage:** Readers learn about print and its purposes. Activities to help children gain this insight include labeling classroom objects, reading aloud Big Books, group-writing exercises such as shared and interactive writing, and reading patterned/predictable books. To read words, children rely on three possible cues: (1) **random cues**, which include almost any visual clue that will help the child to remember the word. It can be something as abstract as a thumbprint or smudge next to the word (Gough, 1991); (2) **environmental cues,** such as where the word is located on the page; and (3) **distinctive letters**, such as the *y* in *pony* or the two *ll's* in *yellow*.

2. **Spelling-sound stage:** Readers focus on graphophonic (phonics) cues to learn sound-spelling relationships and the importance of attending to each letter in a word. They learn how to blend words and make full use of their growing knowledge of sound-spelling relationships. Phonics instruction plays a crucial role at this stage.

3. **Automatic stage:** Readers use both contextual (meaning) and graphophonic (phonics) cues. It's at this point that readers develop fluency (accuracy and speed in decoding). Fluency is critical and comes with "over-learning"—constant review and repetition using sound-spelling knowledge to blend words in context. Automaticity, or fluency, is the result. This acquired automaticity enables readers to focus on the meaning of increasingly complex passages instead of the mechanics of reading. It is critical for students in grade 3 and above.

Teaching Phonics & Word Study in the Intermediate Grades • Scholastic Professional Books

Another frequently encountered problem is the trailing off of phonics instruction in grades 2 and beyond. In order to develop fluency and read multisyllabic words, children still need explicit instruction in more complex sound-spellings, syllabication patterns, and structural analysis, as well as information on word origins. They also need ample modeling and practice reading longer words. Research has found some very efficient ways to provide this instruction and practice. I'll expand on these techniques later in the book.

Characteristics of Strong Phonics Instruction

Active. Social. Reflective. These three words best express the phonics instruction to strive for in your classroom. Look to design a program that makes children aware of what they're doing, why they're doing it, and how they're progressing. This type of phonics instruction can be described as "metaphonics"—phonics combined with metacognition. As you develop an advanced phonics program, never lose sight of these goals: to provide children with (1) sufficient skills for breaking apart longer words to decode them and determine their meanings, and (2) ways to use these skills to read for pleasure and information. "The purpose of phonics instruction is *not* that children learn to sound out words. The purpose is that they learn to recognize words, quickly and automatically, so that they can turn their attention to comprehension of text" (Stahl, 1992).

You can use the checklist on page 43 to evaluate your phonics instruction. It's based on guidelines established by research and practice over the past several decades (Stahl, 1992; Chall, 1996; Vacca, 1995; Beck and McCaslin, 1978).

What About Scope and Sequence?

Sequence: One of the most difficult decisions to make when developing any phonics program is the order, or **sequence**, in which the sound-spelling relationships are taught. Educators have considerable debates about this issue. One of the key areas of dissent is how to teach vowel sounds. Some argue that long-vowel sounds should be taught first since these sounds are easier to auditorily discriminate than short-vowel sounds. In addition, the long vowels "say their names." One drawback to this approach is that there are many long-vowel spellings and introducing children to such complexities before they have gained key insights into how the "system" works might create serious

Evaluation Checklist

My Phonics Instruction...

❏ builds on a foundation of phonemic awareness and knowledge of how language works.

❏ is clear, direct, and explicit.

❏ contains instruction in blending and ample modeling of applying phonics skills.

❏ is integrated into a total reading program. Reading instruction must include these goals: decoding accuracy and fluency, increased word knowledge, experience with various linguistic structures, knowledge of the world, and experience in thinking about texts. Phonics is one important element.

❏ focuses on reading words and connected text, not learning rules.

❏ develops independent word recognition strategies, focusing attention on the internal structure of words, such as affixes, roots, and common spelling patterns.

❏ develops automatic word recognition skills (fluency) so that students can devote their attention to comprehension.

❏ contains repeated opportunities to apply learned sound-spelling relationships to reading and writing.

My Phonics Instruction Avoids...

Some phonics instructional strands fail because (Chall, 1996; Beck and McCaslin, 1978):

❏ instruction is hit-or-miss, instead of systematic.

❏ instruction is too abstract.

❏ children are not taught how to blend words.

❏ instruction is not connected to actual reading.

❏ there is not enough review and application.

❏ too many rules and sound-spelling relationships are taught.

❏ the pace of instruction is too fast.

❏ phonics is taught as the only way to figure out unfamiliar words.

❏ too much time is spent on tasks that have little relationship to reading. For example, children are asked to identify pictures of objects whose names contain a target sound, instead of looking at the letter and responding with its corresponding sound (Bateman, 1979).

problems. Others argue that short-vowel sounds and their one key spelling should be taught first because many simple CVC (consonant-vowel-consonant) words (such as *cat, sun, hit*) can be generated. Many of these "high utility" words appear in early reading materials, and it is thought that introducing them first makes it easier to teach the "system."

I offer the following recommendations regarding sequence:

- **Teach short-vowel sounds before long-vowel sounds.** Efficiency and ease of learning is critical. The simplicity of using short-vowel spellings and CVC words is beneficial to struggling readers.

- **Teach consonants and short vowels in combination so that words can be generated as early as possible.** Phonics is useless if it can't be applied, and what is not applied is not learned. By teaching short vowels and consonants in combination, you can create decodable connected text so children can apply their knowledge of learned sound-spelling relationships.

- **Make sure the majority of the consonants you teach early on are continuous consonants,** such as *f, l, m, n, r,* and *s*. This makes it easier to model blending because these consonant sounds can be sustained without distortion.

- **Use a sequence in which the most words can be generated.** For example, many words can be generated using the letter *t*; however, few can be generated using the letter *x*. Therefore, higher-frequency sound-spelling relationships should precede less-frequent ones.

- **Progress from simple to more complex sound-spellings.** For example, consonant sounds should be taught before digraphs (*sh, ch, th, wh, ph, gh, ng*) and blends (*br, cl, st*, etc.). Likewise, short vowel sound-spellings should be taught before long vowel sound-spellings, variant vowels, and diphthongs.

- **Once complex sound-spellings have been taught, focus on larger spelling patterns,** common syllable types and patterns, and useful word parts such as prefixes, suffixes, and roots.

Scope: Another major decision in teaching phonics is the **scope** of instruction: deciding which sound-spelling relationships are important enough to warrant instruction and which, because of their lower frequency in words, can be learned on an as-needed basis. The following chart shows the most

Teaching Phonics & Word Study in the Intermediate Grades • Scholastic Professional Books

frequent spellings of the 44 sounds covered in this book. These are the sounds and spellings covered in most basal reading programs. (See page 25 for information on the most important syllable patterns and types to teach.)

The percentages provided in parentheses are based on the number of each sound-spelling appeared in the 17,000 most frequently used words (Hanna et al., 1966). These included multisyllabic words.

The Most Frequent Spellings of the 44 Sounds of English

Sound	Common Spellings	Sound	Common Spellings
1. /b/	b (97%), bb	23. /hw/	wh (100%)
2. /d/	d (98%), dd, ed	24. /zh/	si (49%), s (33%), ss, z
3. /f/	f (78%), ff, ph, lf	25. /ng/	n (41%), ng (59%)
4. /g/	g (88%), gg, gh	26. /a/	a (96%)
5. /h/	h (98%), wh	27. /e/	e (91%), ea, e-e (15%)
6. /j/	g (66%), j (22%), dg	28. /i/	i (66%), y (23%)
7. /k/	c (73%), cc, k (13%), ck, lk, q	29. /o/	o (79%)
8. /l/	l (91%), ll	30. /u/	u (86%), o, ou
9. /m/	m (94%), mm	31. /ā/	a (45%), a-e (35%), ai, ay, ea
10. /n/	n (97%), nn, kn, gn	32. /ē/	e (70%), y, ea (10%), ee (10%), ie, e-e, ey, i, ei
11. /p/	p (96%), pp	33. /ī/	i-e (37%), i (37%), igh, y (14%), ie, y-e
12. /r/	r (97%), rr, wr	34. /ō/	o (73%), o-e (14%), ow, oa, oe
13. /s/	s (73%), c (17%), ss	35. /o͞o/	u (69%), u-e (22%), ew, ue
14. /t/	t (97%), tt, ed	36. /ə/	a (24%), e (13%), i (22%), o (27%), u
15. /v/	v (99.5%), f (of)	37. /o͞o/	oo (38%), u (21%), o, ou, u-e, ew, ue
16. /w/	w (92%)	38. /o͝o/	oo (31%), u (54%), ou, o (8%), ould
17. /y/	y (44%), i (55%)	39. /ou/	ou (56%), ow (29%)
18. /z/	z (23%), zz, s (64%)	40. /oi/	oi (62%), oy (32%)
19. /ch/	ch (55%), t (31%)	41. /ô/	o, a, au, aw, ough, augh
20. /sh/	sh (26%), ti (53%), ssi, s, si sci	42. /û/	er (40%), ir (13%), ur (26%)
21. /th/	th (100%)	43. /â/	a (29%), are (23%), air (21%)
22. /th/	th (100%)	44. /ä/	a (89%)

In addition to sound-spelling relationships, it's important to cover other aspects of phonics knowledge such as structural analysis and syllabication. Below is a recommended scope of skills for each grade (Chall, 1996; Blevins, 1998).

Kindergarten

- concepts of print
- alphabet recognition
- phonemic awareness
- blending
- sense of story
- building world knowledge

Grade 1

- phonemic awareness
- blending and word building
- short vowels (*a, e, i, o, u*—CVC pattern)
- consonants
- final *e* (*a_e, e_e, i_e, o_e, u_e*—CVCe pattern)
- long-vowel digraphs (*ai, ay, ea, ee, oa, ow*, etc.)
- consonant clusters (*br, cl, st*, etc.)
- digraphs (*sh, ch, th, wh*, etc.)
- some other vowels such as *oo, ou, ow, oi, oy*
- early structural analysis: verb endings (*-ing, -ed*), plurals, contractions, compound words
- connected text reading
- vocabulary development/world knowledge

Grades 2–3

- grade 1 skills review
- more complex vowel spellings
- more structural analysis (compound words, affixes, etc.)
- multisyllabic words
- syllabication strategies (common syllable spelling patterns)
- connected text reading
- vocabulary development/world knowledge

Grades 4–8

- more complex vowel spellings
- more structural analysis (compound words, affixes, etc.)
- multisyllabic words
- syllabication strategies (common syllable spelling patterns and types)
- word origins (Greek and Latin roots)
- connected text reading
- vocabulary development/world knowledge

Teaching Phonics & Word Study in the Intermediate Grades • Scholastic Professional Books

Beyond decisions about scope and sequence, I recommend that you make your instruction systematic. What do I mean by this? Systematic instruction follows a sequence that progresses from easy to more difficult. Systematic instruction includes constant review and repetition of sound-spelling relationships, application to reading and writing, and a focus on developing fluency through work with reading rate and decoding accuracy. Just because a program has a scope and sequence doesn't mean it's systematic. The instruction must be cumulative. The children's growing knowledge of sound-spellings must be reflected in the texts they're given to practice using these sound-spellings to decode words. In addition, the instruction must help children understand how words "work"—how to use knowledge of sound-spellings to blend the sounds in words. In essence, the system should not only be in the reading program, it should be in the children. They should be able to internalize how the "system" works through the type of instruction they are given.

Blending: Teaching Children How Words Work

Blending is a primary phonics strategy (Resnick & Beck, 1976). It is simply stringing together the sounds that each spelling stands for in a word in order to say the word. Some children seem to develop the ability to blend sounds in words naturally (Whaley and Kirby, 1980), whereas others need explicit teaching of this skill. It is critical to teach these children how to generalize sound-spelling relationships with new words (Golinkoff, 1978). Until a child can blend the sounds in words, phonics instruction will be of limited value. Research has revealed that students of teachers who spend more than average instructional time on modeling and reinforcing blending procedures achieve greater than average gains on first- and second-grade reading achievement tests (Rosenshine & Stevens, 1984; Haddock, 1976).

Two blending procedures have the greatest reading pay-off: **final blending** and **successive blending** (Resnick & Beck, 1976).

Final blending. With this strategy, the sound of each spelling is stated and stored. The whole word isn't blended until all the sounds in the word have been identified and pronounced. For example, for the word *sat*:

1. Point to the letter *s* and say /s/.

2. Point to the letter *a* and say /a/.

3. Slowly slide your finger under the letters *sa* and say /sa/ slowly.

4. Then, quickly slide your finger under the letters *sa* and say /sa/ quickly.

5. Next, point to the letter *t* and say /t/.

6. Slowly slide your finger under *sat* and say /sat/ slowly.

7. Circle the word with your finger and say, "The word is *sat*."

The main advantage of this procedure is that you can determine where a student is having difficulty as he or she attempts to blend an unfamiliar word. For example, if the student doesn't provide the correct sound for the spelling *s,* you know how to target further instruction. You also know if the student can't orally string together sounds. If a child correctly identifies /s/ for the letter *s* and /a/ for the letter *a*, but pronounces these two sounds in combination as "suh-aa," the student is not blending the sounds.

Successive blending. With this strategy, the sound that each spelling stands for is produced in sequence, without pauses. For example, for the word *sat*:

1. Point to the beginning of the word *sat*.

2. Run your finger under each letter as you extend the sound that each letter stands for. For example, you would say *ssssaaaat*. Do not pause between sounds. For example, don't say /s/ (pause) /a/ (pause) /t/. If the first sound is not a continuous consonant sound, quickly blend the first sound with the vowel sound that follows. For example, say *baaaat*.

3. Slowly compress the extended word. Therefore, go from *ssssaaaat* to *ssaat* to *sat*.

4. Circle the word with your finger and say, "The word is *sat*."

Teaching Phonics & Word Study in the Intermediate Grades • Scholastic Professional Books

Blending Multisyllabic Words: A Model

How do these techniques apply to multisyllabic words? When working with longer words, it's important for students to see larger word chunks and be able blend those chunks successively instead of sound by sound. For example, for the word *unhappy*:

1. Tell students that you first look for larger word parts within this long word.

2. Point to the prefix *un* and say its sounds—/un/. Then point to the word *happy*.

3. Slowly put together these two word parts—*un* and *happy*—to say the word *unhappy*.

4. Circle the word with your finger and say, "The word is *unhappy*."

5. Explain to students how the word parts also help you determine the meaning of the word. "I know that *un* often means 'not.' Therefore, *unhappy* must mean 'not happy.'"

If students don't readily recognize larger word parts, have them look for syllable chunks and use their knowledge of syllabication spelling patterns and sound-spellings to decode each chunk. More information on syllable spelling patterns can be found on page 170.

High-Frequency Words

High-frequency words play an important role in reading fluency. What are they, and how should they be taught? Of the approximately 600,000-plus words in English, a relatively small number appear frequently in print. Only 13 words (*a, and, for, he, is, in, it, of, that, the, to, was, you*) account for over 25% of the words in print (Johns, 1981), and 100 words account for approximately 50% (Fry, Fountoukidis, & Polk, 1985; Adams 1990; Carroll, Davies, and Richman, 1971). About 250 words make up 70–75% of all the words children use in their writing (Rinsland, 1945). Of these about 20% are function words such as *a, the,* and *and*.

Although high-frequency word lists disagree on the rank order of words, and many lists contain different words, there is general agreement on the majority of them. Many of the word lists are based on textbooks used in grades 1–8 (Harris and Jacobson, 1972). The Dolch Basic Sight Vocabulary (see page 52) contains 220 words (no nouns). Although this list was generated over 40 years ago, these words account for over 50% of the words found in textbooks today. In addition to this list, I've provided a list of the 150 most frequent words (in order of frequency) in printed school English according to the *American Heritage Word Frequency Book* (see page 51). These are the words most children should have mastered by grade 3. If they have not, concentrated review is in order.

Knowledge of high-frequency words is necessary for fluent reading. Although many of them carry little meaning, they affect the flow and coherence of text. Many of these words are considered "irregular" because they stray from the commonly taught sound-spelling relationships. Research shows that readers store these "irregular" words in their lexical memory in the same way they store so-called "regular" words (Gough and Walsh, 1991; Treiman and Baron, 1981; Lovett, 1987). That is, readers must pay attention to each letter and the pattern of letters in a word and associate them with the sounds that they represent (Ehri, 1992). Therefore, instruction should focus attention on each letter and/or letter pattern.

However, children don't learn "irregular" words as easily or quickly as "regular" ones. Early readers commonly confuse the high-frequency words *of, for,* and *from;* the reversible words *on/no* and *was/saw;* and words with *th* and *w* such as *there, them, their, then, what, were, where, this, these, went, will, that, this, when,* and *with* (Cunningham, 1995). Therefore, children need to be taught "irregular," high-frequency words with explicit instruction. I suggest the following sequence:

1. State aloud the word and use it in a sentence.

2. Write the sentence on the board. Underline the high-frequency word and read it aloud.

3. Discuss the word and mention any special features it contains.

4. Have the children spell aloud the word as you point to each letter.

5. Have the children write the word.

6. Have the children spell aloud the word again as they write it on a piece of paper.

7. Finally, write the word on a note card and display the card on the wall for future reference when reading or writing. Organize the words according to common spelling patterns. Periodically review the note card and any other high-frequency cards you've displayed.

Teaching Phonics & Word Study in the Intermediate Grades • Scholastic Professional Books

8. You can provide additional practice using individually given, timed speed drills and daily review. (See page 53 for a sample speed drill and page 54 for a speed drill template.) Select ten words you want to test students on, write them in random order on a sheet, and then have students read as many words as they can in one minute. Mark on a copy of the drill sheet the words they mispronounce. Have each student count the number of words he or she read correctly and mark this on a progress chart. Students find it highly motivating to track their own progress. Allow students additional opportunities to improve their speed drill times.

The Most Frequent Words

This chart contains the 150 most frequent words (in order of frequency) in printed school English according to the *American Heritage Word Frequency Book*.

the	can	been	three	had	made	right
of	an	long	word	not	over	look
and	your	little	must	will	did	think
a	which	very	because	each	down	such
to	their	after	does	about	only	here
in	said	words	part	how	way	take
is	if	called	even	up	find	why
you	do	just	place	out	use	things
that	into	where	well	them	may	help
it	has	most	as	then	water	put
he	more	know	with	she	go	years
for	her	get	his	many	good	different
was	two	through	they	some	new	away
on	like	back	at	so	write	again
are	him	much	be	these	our	off
but	see	before	this	would	used	went
what	time	also	from	other	me	old
all	could	around	I	its	man	number
were	no	another	have	who	too	
when	make	came	or	now	any	
we	than	come	by	people	day	
there	first	work	one	my	same	

Dolch Basic Sight Vocabulary 220

a	call	funny	just	only	small	use
about	came	gave	keep	open	so	very
after	can	get	kind	or	some	walk
again	carry	give	know	our	soon	want
all	clean	go	laugh	out	start	warm
always	cold	goes	let	over	stop	was
am	come	going	light	own	take	wash
an	could	good	like	pick	tell	we
and	cut	got	little	play	ten	well
any	did	green	live	please	thank	went
are	do	grow	long	pretty	that	were
around	does	had	look	pull	the	what
as	done	has	made	put	their	when
ask	don't	have	make	ran	them	where
at	down	he	many	read	then	which
ate	draw	help	may	red	there	white
away	drink	her	me	ride	these	who
be	eat	here	much	right	they	why
because	eight	him	must	round	think	will
been	every	his	my	run	this	wish
before	fall	hold	myself	said	those	with
best	far	hot	never	saw	three	work
better	fast	how	new	say	to	would
big	find	hurt	no	see	today	write
black	first	I	not	seven	together	yellow
blue	five	if	now	shall	too	yes
both	fly	in	of	she	try	you
bring	for	into	off	show	two	your
brown	found	is	old	sing	under	
but	four	it	on	sit	up	
buy	from	its	once	six	upon	
by	full	jump	one	sleep	us	

Sample High-Frequency Word Speed Drill

that	what	where	who	the	when	there	who	what	them
the	that	them	when	we	then	where	them	who	the
them	them	that	there	what	we	then	there	them	we
there	then	the	that	there	the	them	what	then	where
then	the	when	the	that	there	when	where	the	there
where	where	who	where	where	that	who	then	where	when
when	there	there	we	then	them	that	the	there	what
what	who	we	them	when	who	what	that	when	then
we	when	then	what	them	what	we	we	that	who
who	we	what	then	who	where	the	when	we	that

High-Frequency Word Speed Drill (blank form)

Teaching Phonics & Word Study in the Intermediate Grades • Scholastic Professional Books

SECTION FOUR

Creating Lessons for Success

"Patterns and morphological relationships are the keys to unlocking pronunciation, spelling, and meaning. All students should be issued these master keys."

—Patricia Cunningham

As I've visited classrooms across the country, I've seen a wide range of activities and instructional methods used to teach phonics. Many of these activities and methods have fallen under the umbrella of "explicit" phonics instruction. I have chosen those that are the most effective to help you develop guidelines for writing phonics lessons. Here are a few general dos and don'ts of phonics instruction (Groff, 1977; Blevins, 1998):

Phonics Lessons Do's

- **Use a logical sequence.** Explicitly teach the sound-spelling relationship, syllabication spelling pattern, or structural analysis skill. Progress to guided blending practice, then conclude with reading and writing opportunities.

- **Provide frequent, daily lessons.**

- **Keep the lessons relatively brief and fast-paced.**

- **Keep the lessons focused.** Cover only a small segment at a time.

- **Begin lessons with what students know.**

- **Create a classroom environment in which students become active word watchers** or word detectives—an environment in which there is a curiosity about words.

- **Provide a built-in review** of previously taught sound-spellings or spelling patterns in each lesson (through blending exercises, repeated readings, etc.).

- **Adjust pace or scope according to students' needs.** Don't set absolute deadlines for how much should be covered in a given time.

- **Regroup students according to their needs.**

- **Link phonics instruction to spelling** through dictation and free-writing activities.

- **Make learning public.** Create word walls, make letter charts, and share student writing.

- **Provide instruction that is reflective.** Gaskins et al. (1997), for example, uses the "Talk-To-Yourself Chart" with children to engage them in thinking about words. Here is a completed chart for the word *high*.

Teaching Phonics & Word Study in the Intermediate Grades • Scholastic Professional Books

1. The word is _high._

2. Stretch the word. I hear ___2___ sounds.

3. I see ___4___ letters because _igh_ stands for one sound.

4. The spelling pattern is _igh._

5. This is what I know about the vowel: _It is the long i sound—/ī/._

6. Another word on the Word Wall with the same vowel sound is _light._

Phonics Lessons Don'ts

Here are fice things to avoid in phics instruciton.

- **Avoid having students continually wait for turns.** Instead, use choral response techniques or every-pupil response cards.

- **Avoid instruction in which students are not directly told** what they are being asked to understand and how they should respond.

- **Avoid immediately correcting students' errors.** Provide feedback only after allowing students an opportunity to self-monitor and self-correct.

- **Avoid inadequately addressing exceptions to the generalizations being learned.**

- **Avoid using incorrect language or terminology:**

  1. Instead of saying, "You can hear the _f_ sound," say, "You can hear the /f/ sound." _f_ is a letter, not a sound.

  2. Rather than saying, "What sounds do you _see_ at the end of _mint_?" say, "What sounds do you hear at the end of the word _mint?_" You see letters; you hear sounds.

  3. Instead of saying, "The letter _t_ makes the /t/ sound," say, "The letter _t_ stands for or represents the /t/ sound." Letters are inanimate objects, they do not make sounds.

  4. Instead of saying, "The blend _st_ stands for the /st/ sound," say, "The letters (cluster) _st_ stand for the /st/ sounds." Cluster refers to a group of letters blend refers to a group of sounds.

  5. Instead of saying, "The following letters are diphthongs," say, "The following vowel pair (digraph) stands for the /oi/ sound." A diphthong is a sound, a vowel pair, or digraph, is a group of letters.

Sample Lessons and Word Lists

The following sample lessons are set up as templates for you to use when writing your phonics lessons. The lessons are brief and follow a simple 5-step procedure:

▸ **Step 1—Review and Warm-Up:** repeated reading and warm-up

▸ **Step 2—Introduce New Skill:** explicit instruction of sound-spelling relationship, spelling pattern, or word analysis skill

▸ **Step 3—Guided Practice:** blending and word-building exercises

▸ **Step 4—Apply to Text:** reading connected text

▸ **Step 5—Apply to Writing:** dictation and writing

Some components of the lessons, such as the warm-up exercises and reading of connected text, will be determined by the materials you have available.

Classroom Spotlight

Ways to Use Word Lists

You can use the words in the word lists throughout this section during phonics and spelling instruction in the following ways:

- to create word lists for blending practice

- to create connected text for reading practice

- to create word lists for word sorts

- to create word lists to be sent home for reading practice

- to create word lists to add to a word wall

- to create word lists for dictation (spelling)

- to create activity pages

Consonant Digraphs

Guidelines:

- Consonant digraphs are two consonants that appear together in a word and stand for one sound. The consonant digraphs include *sh, ch, th, wh, ph, gh,* and *ng.*

- Teach the consonant digraphs after the children have learned the single consonants. Help your students become aware of these unique letter pairs by challenging them to be on the lookout for the digraphs in words.

Teaching Phonics & Word Study in the Intermediate Grades • Scholastic Professional Books

Consonant Digraphs

Phonic Principle: The cluster *sh* stands for the /sh/ sound.

Step 1: Review and Warm-Up. Begin by displaying index cards with the sound-spellings or spelling patterns previously taught. Flip through the cards rapidly as students chorally say the sound(s) each represents. Then have students reread a story or passage containing previously taught sound-spelling relationships.

Step 2: Introduce New Skill. Explain to students that when we encounter the letters *s* and *h* together in words, they often stand for a new sound. Point out that the letters *sh* stand for the /sh/ sound, as in the words *ship* and *dish*. Write the words *ship* and *dish* on the chalkboard as you display a picture of each. Make sure the pictures are labeled. Then blend each word aloud as you run your finger under each letter. Have a volunteer underline the letters *sh*. Point to the letters *sh* and ask students to state the sound that the letters stand for. Continue by having students generate a list of words containing the /sh/ sound in the initial and final position. List these words on the chalkboard in separate columns.

Step 3: Guided Practice. Write the following words and sentences on the chalkboard. Note that all the words are decodable based on the sound-spelling relationships previously taught. (This should always be the case.) The first line focuses on words with the /sh/ sound in the initial position. A contrast is provided to focus students' attention on the importance of each letter in a word. The second line focuses on words with the /sh/ sound in the final position. The third line contains multisyllabic words with /sh/. The sentences contain some high-frequency words previously taught.

- sack, shack, hop, shop

- dish, fish, mash, rush

- wishing, shoestring, shuffle, shadow

- The shopkeeper shut the door at nine.

- I should've bought those red dishes for Shirley.

Now distribute the following spelling-card set to each child: *ash, ish, ush, m, f, w, r, st, sp, ll, ing, ed*. Have children build as many words as possible. Ask them to write the words on a sheet of paper. Circulate around the room and model blending when necessary.

Step 4: Apply to Text. Provide students with connected reading practice.

Step 5: Apply to Writing. Dictate the following words and sentence. Have the children write the words and sentence on a sheet of paper. For students having difficulty segmenting the sounds or syllables in each word, extend the word (you might wish to clap on each sound or syllable to provide another clue). Next, write the words and sentence on the chalkboard. Have children self-correct their papers. Don't grade this dictation practice. It's designed to help children segment words and associate sounds with spellings.

- shot, shopkeeper, shared

- She was shopping for shoes.

Consonant-Digraph Words for Instruction

/ch/ as in cheese

Initial Position

chain	chart	cheep	chew	chin	chow
chair	chase	cheerful	chick	chip	chuckle
chalk	chat	cheese	chicken	chipmunk	chug
change	cheap	cheeseburger	child	chirp	chum
chap	cheat	cherry	children	chocolate	chunk
chapter	check	chess	chilly	choose	churn
charge	check-up	chest	chime	chop	
charm	checker	chestnut	chimney	chose	

Final Position

beach	hunch	quench	trench	itch	stitch
bench	inch	ranch	batch	latch	stretch
branch	lunch	reach	catch	match	switch
bunch	much	rich	clutch	notch	watch
church	munch	sandwich	crutch	patch	witch
clinch	peach	search	ditch	pitch	
couch	perch	such	fetch	scratch	
crunch	pinch	teach	hitch	sketch	
each	punch	touch	hutch	snatch	

More Multisyllabic /ch/ Words

chairman	checkbook	chosen	hatchet	reattach
challenge	cheesecake	approach	hopscotch	research
chamber	cherish	attach	launching	richness
champion	chickadee	beseech	leeches	speechless
charcoal	childhood	bleachers	lunchroom	spinach
chariot	chimpanzee	catcher	merchandise	stagecoach
charitable	chisel	cockroach	parchment	
charter	chopstick	duchess	patchwork	
chatter	chortle	enchantment	preacher	

Note: The /ch/ sound is frequently represented by the digraph *ch* as in *cheese* or *lunch*. The digraph *ch* is not reliably constant. It can also stand for the /k/ sound in words of Greek origin such as *chemical, character, chorus, orchestra, stomach,* and *school* (the word *ache* is of Anglo-Saxon origin); or the /sh/ sound in words of French origin as in *Chicago, chiffon,* and *machine.*

/sh/ as in shark

Initial Position

shack	shampoo	she	sherbet	shock	shorts	show
shade	shape	shear	shield	shoe	shot	shower
shadow	share	shed	shift	shoelace	should	shuck
shake	shark	sheep	shin	shoot	shoulder	shut
shall	sharp	sheet	shine	shop	shout	shy
shallow	shave	shelf	ship	shore	shove	
shame	shawl	shell	shirt	short	shovel	

Final Position

ash	cash	dash	fresh	leash	push	splash
blush	clash	dish	gash	mash	rash	trash
brush	crash	fish	gush	mesh	rush	wash
bush	crush	flash	lash	mush	smash	wish

Other /sh/ Spellings

action	attention	fraction	patient	station	vacation
addition	delicious	nation	social	suspicion	vicious

More Multisyllabic /sh/ Words

shabby	shimmer	shortstop	boyish	furnish	rubbish
shaggy	shingle	shrubbery	bushel	garish	selfish
shaken	shipment	shuffle	dishrag	harshly	snapshot
shameful	shipwreck	shuttle	dishwasher	marshal	starfish
shamrock	shoestring	shyness	eggshell	mushroom	tarnish
sharpen	shopkeeper	accomplish	establish	polish	vanish
sheepish	shoreline	anguish	fashion	publish	washboard
shellfish	shortage	banish	fishnet	punish	washcloth
shepherd	shortcut	barbershop	foolish	radish	whiplash
sheriff	shorthand	bloodshot	freshman	rosebush	workshop

Note: The /sh/ sound is frequently represented by the digraph *sh* as in *shark* and *fish*. The digraph *sh* is a very reliable spelling for this sound. Whenever we see the letters *sh* together in a word they stand for the /sh/ sound unless they appear in separate syllables, such as in *mishap* or *dis-honor*. The /sh/ sound can be represented by many other spellings such as *s* (*sure*, *sugar*), *ti* (*nation*), *ch* (*machine*), and *ci* (*special*). The *ch* spelling for the /sh/ sound occurs mostly in words of French origin such as *chalet, chamois, chef, machine, parachute, sachet, cliché, chic, Chevrolet, Michigan,* and *Chicago.*

/zh/ as in treasure

Medial Position

Asia	casual	exposure	measure	rouge	television	vision
azure	decision	garage	occasion	sabotage	treasure	
bon jour	equation	luxurious	pleasure	seizure	usual	

Note: The /zh/ sound is never represented by the letters *zh*. This letter combination doesn't appear in English words. The /zh/ sound is, instead, represented by a wide range of spellings including the following: *si* (*vision, occasion*), *s* (*pleasure, measure*), *g* (*rouge, garage*), *z* (*azure*), *zi* (*brazier*), *ssi* (*scission*), *ti* (*equation*), *x* (*luxurious*).

/th/ as in thumb (voiceless)

Initial Position

thank	thermos	think	thistle	through
Thanksgiving	thick	third	thorn	throw
thaw	thief	thirst	thought	thumb
theater	thimble	thirsty	thousand	thump
theme	thin	thirteen	three	thunder
thermometer	thing	thirty	thread	

Final Position

bath	both	fifth	math	oath	south	with
Beth	broth	fourth	moth	path	teeth	worth
birth	cloth	growth	mouth	Ruth	thief	wreath
booth	death	length	north	sixth	tooth	

More Multisyllabic /th/ Words

thankful	thresh	author	henceforth	pathway
therapist	throbbing	birthplace	hither	plaything
thicken	throughout	blacksmith	method	ruthless
thirtieth	thumbnail	eighteenth	methodical	sympathy
thirteenth	thunderbolt	eleventh	mother	tablecloth
thorough	thunderous	faithful	otherwise	tollbooth
thoughtful	afterthought	father	overthrow	washcloth
thoughtless	another	fifteenth	parentheses	wither
thousandth	anthem	gather	pathetic	within

Note: This /th/ sound is most frequently spelled by the digraph *th* as in *thin* or *bath*. The digraph *th* represents two sounds—the voiceless /th/ sound as in *thin* and the voiced /th/ sound as in *the*. The letters *th* are fairly reliable for these two sounds. However, sometimes the letters *th* stand for the /t/ sound as in *Thomas* and *thyme*, and sometimes they are silent as in *isthmus*. When the letters *th* appear together in a word, but are in separate syllables (example: *boathouse*) the *t* stands for /t/ and the *h* stands for /h/.

Teaching Phonics & Word Study in the Intermediate Grades • Scholastic Professional Books

/th/ as in the (voiced)

Initial Position

than	the	them	there	they	those	thus
that	their	then	these	this	though	

Medial/Final Position

bathe	gather	smooth	together	whether

More Multisyllabic /th/ Words

themselves	thereby	therefore	therein

Note: This /th/ sound is most frequently spelled by the digraph *th* as in *the* or *that*. Most of the words containing the /th/ sound are of higher-frequency in English than those containing the /th/ sound. The digraph *th* represents two sounds—the voiceless /th/ sound as in *thin* and the voiced /th/ sound as in *the*. The letters *th* are fairly reliable for these two sounds. However, sometimes the letters *th* stand for the /t/ sound as in *Thomas* and *thyme*, and sometimes they are silent as in *isthmus*. When the letters *th* appear together in a word, but are in separate syllables (example: *boathouse*), the *t* stands for /t/ and the *h* for /h/.

/hw/ as in wheel

Initial Position

whack	wheelbarrow	whey	whinny	whistle
whale	wheelchair	which	whip	white
wham	when	whiff	whir	whittled
what	whenever	while	whirl	whiz
whatever	where	whim	whisk	whoops
wheat	wherever	whimper	whisker	whopper
wheel	whew	whine	whisper	why

More Multisyllabic /hw/ Words

whereabouts	whichever	whippoorwill	whirlwind	whitewash

Note: The /hw/ sound is rapidly disappearing from the English language. Many dialects do not distinguish the /hw/ sound in *whether* from the /w/ sound in *weather*. Listen carefully as you say aloud these words. Do you pronounce the beginning sound differently? When making the /hw/ sound, /h/ (just a puff of air) is vocalized before /w/. The jaws are apart to produce /h/, then close as the lips come closer together to produce /w/. You should be able to feel a slight vibration of the lips. The /hw/ sound is represented by the digraph *wh*. This spelling appears only at the beginning of a word or syllable. The digraph *wh* can also represent /h/ as in *who, whom, whose,* and *whole*.

/ng/ as in ring

Medial/Final Position

angry	hang	rang	strangler	young	junk	sink
bang	hung	ring	strong	bank	link	sunk
clang	hunger	rung	strength	brink	mink	tank
clung	king	sang	thing	drink	pink	thank
finger	linger	sing	wing	drunk	rank	wink
gang	long	song	wrangler	honk	sank	
gong	longer	sprung	wringer	ink	shrunk	

More Multisyllabic /ng/ Words

accusingly	cunning	greeting	occurring	sweet-smelling
adjoining	daring	hangar	overdoing	tantalizing
admiringly	drawing	helpings	pleasing	trimmings
amazing	dwelling	increasing	pudding	unceasing
anything	earning	knowingly	rasping	uninteresting
banging	earring	lightning	recording	unknowing
being	evaluating	linger	seemingly	warning
belong	exhilarating	longing	springboard	
clippings	finger	making	springtime	
convincingly	glancing	meaning	sterling	
crossing	good-looking	misleading	surprisingly	

Note: The /ng/ sound is frequently represented by the letters *ng* as in *ring.* This sound never occurs at the beginning of a word or syllable and always follows a vowel sound. The letters *ng* are only moderately reliable for this sound. At the end of words, the letters *ng* always stand for the /ng/ sound. However, within words the two letters *n* and *g* can cause confusion. For example, the letter *n* alone may stand for the /ng/ sound and the *g* for /g/ as in *finger*; or the letter *n* may stand for the /n/ sound and the *g* for the /g/ sound as in *ungrateful, ongoing,* or *engulf.* The letters *ng* can also stand for the /n/ and /j/ sounds as in *angel, change, plunge,* and *ranger.* The letter *n* alone can represent the /ng/ sound when followed by *k* as in *pink, rank, think,* and *sink.* In the words *linger* and *mango* you also hear the /g/ sound after /ng/

Teaching Phonics & Word Study in the Intermediate Grades • Scholastic Professional Books

Consonant Clusters

Guidelines:

- Consonant clusters are two consonants that appear together in a word, with each retaining its sound when blended. The sounds that each cluster stands for is called a blend. Therefore, the term cluster refers to the written form and the term blend refers to the spoken form.

- The clusters are highly reliable; that is, when we see these letter combinations in words, they almost always stand for the blended sounds of each consonant. The one major exception is *sc*, which can stand for the /sk/ sounds as in *scare* or the *c* can be silent as in *science*. In addition, the consonant cluster *ck* stands for one sound, the /k/ sound.

- There are three major categories of consonant clusters: *r*-blends (*br, cr, dr, fr, gr, pr, tr*), *s*-blends (*sc, sk, sl, sm, sn, sp, st, sw*), and *l*-blends (*bl, cl, fl, gl, pl, sl*). In addition, a few other consonant clusters can be formed such as *tw* and *qu*. There are also three-letter consonant clusters such as *str, spr, spl, scr, squ, thr, chr, phr,* and *shr*. The clusters *thr, phr,* and *shr* are comprised of a digraph and a consonant. The cluster *ngth* as in *strength* is made up of two digraphs—*ng* and *th*.

- Teach the consonant clusters after children have learned the single consonant sound-spellings.

- Teach beginning clusters before ending clusters.

Consonant Clusters

Phonic Principle: *s*-blends

Step 1: Review and Warm-Up. Begin by displaying index cards with the sound-spellings or spelling patterns previously taught. Flip through the cards rapidly as students chorally say the sound(s) each represents. Then have students reread a story or passage containing previously taught sound-spelling relationships.

Step 2: Introduce New Skill. Write the words *snake, stone,* and *spot* on the chalkboard. Underline the letters *sn, st,* and *sp* in each word. Explain that these letters stand for the /sn/, /st/, and /sp/ sounds, respectively. Point out that often when *s* and another consonant appears together in a word, the sounds that both letters stand for are blended together. Blend each word aloud as you run your finger under each letter. Have a volunteer underline the letters *sn, st,* and *sp.* Point to each of these clusters and ask students to state the sounds the letters stand for. Continue by having students generate a list of words containing these sounds. List the words on the chalkboard.

Step 3: Guided Practice. Write the following words and sentences on the chalkboard. Note that all the words are decodable based on the sound-spelling relationships previously taught. The first line contains contrasts to focus children's attention on the importance of each letter in a word. The sentences contain some high-frequency words previously taught.

- sell, spell, sack, stack

- sneak, speak, stop, spot

- snapshot, snowflake, spaceship, stampede

- The rainstorm caused water to flood the streets.

- The spider slipped out of its snug web.

Now distribute the following spelling-card set to each child: *a, o, e, s, t, n, ll, m, p, s, sh.* Have students build as many words as possible. Ask them to write the words on a sheet of paper. Circulate around the room and model blending when necessary.

Step 4: Apply to Text. Provide students with connected reading practice.

Step 5: Apply to Writing. Dictate the following words and the sentence. Have the children write the words and sentence on a sheet of paper. For students having difficulty segmenting the sounds in each word, extend the word or segment syllable by syllable. Then, write the words and sentence on the chalkboard. Have the children self-correct their papers. Don't grade this dictation practice. It's designed to help children segment words and associate sounds with spellings.

- snack, stoplight, sparkle

- The snowfall was spectacular!

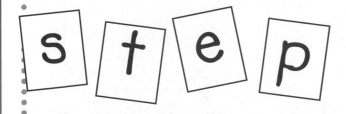

Teaching Phonics & Word Study in the Intermediate Grades • Scholastic Professional Books

Consonant-Cluster Words for Instruction

r-blends

br

brace	bray	brisk	brush	broadcast
Brad	bread	broad	bracelet	bronco
braid	break	broil	bracket	brontosaurus
brain	breath	broke	brambles	broomstick
braise	breathe	bronze	brandish	brother
brake	breeze	brood	bravery	brotherhood
bran	brew	brook	breakdown	
branch	brick	broom	breakfast	
brand	bride	broth	breathless	
brass	bridge	brought	briefcase	
brat	bright	brown	brighten	
brave	brim	browse	brilliant	
brawl	bring	bruise	brittle	

cr

crab	cried	crunch	crazy	critical
crack	croak	crust	creation	criticize
craft	crook	cry	creativity	crocodile
crane	crop	cracker	creature	crossroad
crash	cross	crackle	cricket	crossword
crawl	crow	cradle	criminal	cruelty
creek	crowd	cranberry	crinkle	crumble
creep	crown	crawfish	cripple	crusade
crib	crumb	crayon	crisscross	crystallized

dr

drab	dread	drive	dragonfly	driftwood
draft	dream	droop	dramatic	driveway
drag	dress	drop	draperies	drizzle
drain	drew	drove	drastic	droplets
drake	drift	drug	drawback	drugstore
drank	drill	drum	dreadful	drummer
drape	drink	dry	dreamlike	
draw	drip	dragon	dribble	

fr

frail	freeze	fringe	fruit	frantic	freshmen	frustration
frame	freight	frizz	fry	freckles	Friday	frying
France	fresh	frog	fraction	freeway	friendliness	
frank	friend	from	fragile	freezer	frighten	
freak	fright	front	fragment	frenzy	frostbite	
free	frill	frost	framework	frequency	frozen	

gr

grab	grate	grill	grow	graduation	gratitude	groceries
grace	grave	grim	growl	grammar	gravity	grotesque
grade	gravy	grime	grown	grandchild	greasy	grounder
graft	gray	grin	grub	grandeur	greatness	gruesome
grain	graze	grind	grudge	grandfather	greenery	
gram	grease	grip	gruff	grandmother	greenhouse	
grand	great	grit	grump	grandstand	greetings	
grant	greed	groan	graceful	granite	griddle	
grape	green	groom	gracias	grapefruit	grievance	
graph	greet	grouch	gracious	grasshopper	grimace	
grasp	grew	ground	gradual	grassland	gritty	
grass	grid	group	graduate	grateful	grizzly	

pr

praise	proof	prediction	presumably	probably	pronounce
prance	prop	prefer	pretty	problem	propeller
pray	proud	prejudice	pretzel	procedure	prophet
press	prove	preliminary	prevention	proclamation	prosperous
price	prowl	preoccupied	priceless	produce	protect
pride	prune	preparation	prickly	product	protective
priest	pry	prepare	primarily	profession	protein
prince	practical	prescription	primitive	professor	protest
print	practice	present	princess	profit	provide
prison	prayer	president	principal	program	province
prize	precaution	pressure	priority	project	provoke
probe	precious	presto	prisoner	promise	
prod	predict	prestigious	privilege	pronoun	

tr

trace	tree	trout	traffic	transport	tribune	trouser
track	trek	truck	tragedy	transportation	tribute	truckload
trade	tribe	true	trailer	trapeze	triceratops	truly
trail	trick	trunk	traitor	travel	trickery	trumpet
train	trim	trust	trample	traveler	trillion	truthful
tramp	trip	truth	tranquil	treacherous	trimmings	tryout
trap	troll	try	transfer	treasurer	triumphant	
trash	tromp	tractor	transformation	treatment	trivial	
tray	troop	trademark	transition	tremble	trophy	
tread	trot	tradition	translator	tremendous	tropical	
treat	trough	traditional	transplant	trespasser	trouble	

l-blends

bl

blab	bleat	blip	blow	blackout	blizzard
black	bleed	blob	blue	bladder	bloodhound
blade	bleep	block	bluff	blanket	blossom
blame	blend	blonde	blunt	bleachers	blubber
blank	bless	blood	blush	blessings	blueberry
blast	blew	bloom	blackberry	blindfold	bluebird
blaze	blind	blot	blackbird	blissful	blueprint
bleach	blink	blouse	blackboard	blister	blunder

cl

clack	class	cling	cloth	clamber	cleanup	closet
clad	claw	clink	clothes	clamor	clergyman	clothesline
claim	clay	clip	cloud	clarify	cleverness	clothing
clam	clean	cloak	clove	clarinet	client	clubhouse
clamp	clear	clock	clown	classic	climate	clumsy
clan	cleat	clod	club	classical	climber	cluster
clang	clerk	clog	cluck	classmate	clinical	
clap	click	clomp	clue	classroom	clipboard	
clash	cliff	close	clump	clatter	clockwise	
clasp	climb	closet	clutch	cleanliness	closeness	

fl

flag	fleck	flip	flu	flagpole	fledgling	fluorescent
flake	fleet	float	fluff	flagship	flexible	fluster
flame	flesh	flock	fluid	flashback	flicker	flutter
flap	flew	flood	fluke	flashbulb	flimsy	flyer
flare	flex	floor	flunk	flashlight	flipper	
flash	flick	flop	flush	flatland	floppy	
flat	flight	floss	flute	flatten	flounder	
flaw	fling	flour	fly	flatter	flourish	
flea	flint	flow	flabbergasted	flavor	flower	

gl

glad	gleam	gloat	gloss	glacial	gleeful	glorious
glance	glee	glob	glove	glacier	glimmer	glossary
glare	glide	globe	glow	gladness	glisten	glossy
glass	glitch	gloom	glue	glamorous	glitter	

pl

place	plate	plod	placid	plastic	pleasure	plunder
plaid	play	plot	plaintive	plateau	plentiful	
plain	plead	plow	planet	platform	plenty	
plan	please	plug	plankton	player	pliers	
plane	pleat	plum	planner	playground	plumage	
plank	pledge	plump	plantation	plaza	plumber	
plant	plink	placement	plaster	pleasant	plummet	

sl

slab	sleep	slight	slow	slaughter	slippery
slack	sleet	slim	slug	sleazy	slither
slam	sleeve	slime	slump	sleepless	slobber
slant	slept	sling	slush	sleepy	sloppy
slap	slice	slip	sly	slender	slouchy
slate	slick	slit	slacker	slightly	slowly
sled	slid	slope	slander	slingshot	slugger
sleek	slide	slot	slapstick	slipper	

Teaching Phonics & Word Study in the Intermediate Grades • Scholastic Professional Books

s-blends

sc

scab	scare	score	scandal	scoundrel
scald	scarf	scour	scarecrow	sculpture
scale	scat	scout	scarlet	scurry
scalp	scold	scuff	scatter	scuttle
scamp	scoop	scallion	scooter	
scan	scoot	scallop	scoreboard	
scar	scope	scaly	scornful	
scarce	scorch	scamper	scorpion	

sk

skate	skip	skateboard	skillet	skyline
sketch	skirt	skedaddle	skillful	skyrocket
ski	skit	skeleton	skimmer	
skid	skull	skeptical	skinny	
skill	skunk	sketchy	skipper	
skin	sky	skidproof	skirmish	

sm

smack	smear	smog	smallpox	smolder
small	smell	smoke	smelling	smoothest
smart	smile	smooth	smitten	smother
smash	smock	smudge	smoky	smuggle

sn

snack	snarl	snob	snakebite	snowball
snag	snatch	snoop	snappy	snowdrift
snail	sneak	snore	snapshot	snowfall
snake	sneeze	snout	sneaker	snowman
snap	sniff	snow	sniffle	snowmobile
snare	snip	snug	snorkel	snuggle

sp

space	spell	sponge	spaghetti	spectacular	spiral
span	spend	spoon	spaniel	spectator	spirit
spare	spent	sport	sparkle	speculate	spiritual
spark	spike	spot	sparrow	speculation	spontaneous
spat	spill	spout	spasm	speechless	spoonful
speak	spin	spur	spatter	spellbound	spotless
spear	spine	spy	special	spellings	spotlight
speck	spire	spacecraft	specialize	spider	
speech	spoil	spaceship	specific	spinach	
speed	spoke	spacious	specimen	spindle	

st

stack	state	stink	stagger	station	stirrup
staff	stay	stir	staircase	stationery	stocking
stage	steak	stitch	stallion	statue	stomach
stain	steal	stock	stamina	steadfast	stomachache
stair	steam	stone	stammer	steadily	stopwatch
stake	steel	stool	stampede	steady	storage
stale	steep	stoop	standard	steamboat	storekeeper
stalk	steer	stop	standstill	steeple	storybook
stall	stem	store	stanza	stegosaurus	stovepipe
stamp	step	storm	staple	stepfather	stubborn
stand	stew	story	stapler	stepmother	student
star	stick	stove	starfish	stereo	sturdy
starch	stiff	style	starlight	sticky	stutter
stare	still	stable	starter	stiffness	
start	stilt	stadium	starvation	stimulate	
starve	sting	stagecoach	statement	stingy	

sw

swam	swatch	sweet	swim	swoop	sweatshirt
swamp	swarm	swell	swine	swagger	sweeper
swan	sway	swept	swing	swallow	sweeten
swap	sweat	swerve	swish	swampland	swiftness
swat	sweep	swift	switch	sweater	swollen

Teaching Phonics & Word Study in the Intermediate Grades • Scholastic Professional Books

Three Letter Consonant Clusters

scr

scram	scrawl	screw	scrabble	screwdriver
scrap	scream	script	scramble	scribble
scrape	screech	scroll	scrapbook	scrimmage
scratch	screen	scrub	scraper	scrutiny

squ

square	squeak	squid	squirm	squirt
squash	squeal	squint	squirrel	squish
squat	squeeze			

str

straight	streak	strike	struck	streetcar
strain	stream	string	strum	stretcher
strand	street	strip	straddle	stricken
strange	strength	stripe	straighten	stronger
strap	stretch	stroke	strainer	structure
straw	strict	stroll	stranger	struggle
stray	stride	slrong	strawberry	

spr

sprain	spray	spring	spruce	sprinkle
sprang	spread	sprint	springboard	sprinkler
sprawl	sprig	sprout	springtime	sprinter

spl

splash	splint	split	splashdown	splendid	splinter

thr

thrash	throat	through	threadbare	throttle
thread	throb	thrush	threshold	throughout
thrill	throne	thrashing		

Other Consonant Clusters

tw

tweed	twelve	twig	twine	twist	twentieth	twilight
tweet	twice	twin	twirl	tweezers	twenty	twinkle

qu

quack	quality	quarter	quench	quick	quilt	quiz
quail	quarrel	quartz	quest	quiet	quirk	quote
quake	quart	queen	question	quill	quit	

Ending Consonant Clusters

ct

act	fact	distract	exact	impact	overreact
pact	duct	enact	extract	interact	subtract

ft

cleft	graft	rift	swift	makeshift	witchcraft
craft	left	shaft	thrift	snowdrift	
draft	lift	shift	tuft	spacecraft	
drift	loft	sift	aircraft	spendthrift	
gift	raft	soft	airlift	uplift	

ld

bald	gold	scold	behold	stepchild	withheld
bold	held	shield	billfold	stronghold	withhold
build	hold	sold	blindfold	threshold	
child	mild	told	brainchild	unfold	
cold	mold	weld	foothold	untold	
field	old	wild	household	upheld	
fold	scald	beheld	retold	windshield	

lp

help	gulp	scalp	yelp

74

Teaching Phonics & Word Study in the Intermediate Grades • Scholastic Professional Books

lt

belt	fault	kilt	salt	deadbolt	somersault
bolt	felt	knelt	tilt	default	
built	guilt	melt	welt	exalt	
colt	halt	pelt	asphalt	heartfelt	
dealt	jolt	quilt	assault	revolt	

mp

blimp	clamp	shrimp	hump	pump	tramp
bump	clump	skimp	jump	stamp	tromp
camp	cramp	slump	lamp	stomp	trump
champ	crimp	damp	limp	stump	trumpet
chimp	ramp	dump	lump	swamp	
chomp	romp	grump	plump	thump	

nd

and	find	lend	trend	command	rebound
band	found	mend	wand	compound	recommend
bend	friend	mind	wind	correspond	remind
bind	grand	mound	wound	demand	reprimand
bland	grind	pound	abound	extend	respond
blend	ground	round	apprehend	firsthand	surround
blind	hand	sand	armband	greyhound	suspend
blonde	hind	send	around	mastermind	understand
bond	hound	sound	attend	offend	unkind
bound	husband	spend	bandstand	offhand	unwind
brand	intend	stand	beforehand	pretend	
end	kind	strand	behind	profound	
extend	land	tend	beyond	quicksand	

nk

bank	drink	junk	plunk	stink	wink
blank	dunk	link	rank	stunk	chipmunk
blink	frank	mink	rink	sunk	kerplunk
bunk	honk	wink	sank	tank	outrank
chunk	hunk	pink	sink	think	rethink
drank	ink	plank	skunk	trunk	

nt

absent	invent	scent	ballpoint	evident	peppermint
ant	lent	sent	blueprint	experiment	pinpoint
bent	lint	spent	cement	fingerprint	prevent
bunt	meant	splint	checkpoint	frequent	represent
cent	mint	tent	compliment	implant	torment
dent	paint	tint	consent	invent	transplant
faint	pint	want	content	lament	underwent
front	plant	went	disenchant	manhunt	viewpoint
grant	print	account	eggplant	misrepresent	
hint	rent	amount	enchant	newsprint	
hunt	runt	appoint	event	paramount	

pt

apt	slept	accept	except	intercept	rainswept
kept	wept	concept	inept	overslept	windswept

rd

bird	herd	afford	boulevard	landlord	record
board	lard	backyard	discard	leotard	safeguard
cord	sword	barnyard	discord	lifeguard	scorecard
guard	toward	blackbird	disregard	lovebird	shipyard
hard	word	bodyguard	hummingbird	mockingbird	smorgasbord
heard	yard	bombard	jailbird	postcard	songbird

rk

ark	fork	mark	work	birthmark	landmark	trademark
bark	hark	park	aardvark	bookmark	pitchfork	
clerk	jerk	perk	ballpark	disembark	postmark	
dark	lark	stork	berserk	earmark	remark	

sk

ask	desk	disk	dusk	mask	risk	task	asterisk

sp

clasp	crisp	gasp	rasp	wasp

Teaching Phonics & Word Study in the Intermediate Grades • Scholastic Professional Books

st

best	fast	most	twist	combust	goalpost	resist
blast	fest	must	west	conquest	headfirst	robust
boast	fist	nest	wrist	consist	innermost	sawdust
bust	ghost	past	adjust	contrast	insist	signpost
cast	gust	pest	aghast	defrost	invest	stardust
chest	jest	post	almost	detest	manifest	steadfast
coast	just	quest	arrest	disgust	mistrust	suggest
contest	last	rest	assist	distrust	newscast	telecast
cost	least	roast	bedpost	downcast	outlast	unjust
crust	list	rust	bombast	enlist	overcast	utmost
dentist	lost	test	broadcast	enthusiast	persist	
dust	mast	toast	checklist	exist	protest	
east	mist	trust	coexist	forecast	request	

Double Consonants

ss

bass	class	fussy	guess	lesson	messy	passage
bless	dress	glass	hiss	mass	miss	press
brass	dresser	gloss	kiss	mess	moss	session
chess	fuss	grass	less	message	pass	toss

ll

ball	collect	fell	hello	mill	silly	stall	village
bell	dell	fill	hill	pill	skill	still	wall
belly	dill	follow	holler	pillow	skull	swell	well
bill	doll	football	hollow	roll	small	tall	will
bull	dollar	frill	hull	shallow	smaller	taller	willow
call	drill	gill	ill	sell	smell	tell	yell
cell	dull	grill	jell	session	smelly	till	yellow
cellar	dwell	gull	kill	shell	spell	toll	
chill	fall	hall	mall	sill	spill	valley	

tt

attic	bitter	cottage	flutter	kitten	rattle
batter	bottle	critter	glitter	letter	sitter
battle	butter	fatter	gutter	little	smitten
better	cattle	fitter	hotter	matter	tattered
bitten	chatter	flatter	kettle	mitten	

ff

bluff	cliff	fluff	puff	staff
buff	coffee	gruff	scuff	stiff
buffet	cuff	huff	sniff	stuff

bb

blubber	cubby	hobble	rabbit	wobble
bubble	dabble	lobby	rubble	
chubby	gobble	pebble	stubble	

dd

bidding	hidden	meddle	puddle	saddle
bladder	huddle	muddle	redder	sudden
fiddle	ladder	muddy	riddle	waddle
haddock	madder	paddle	rudder	

pp

apple	grapple	happy	preppy	sipping	supper
dapple	happen	pepper	puppy	stopper	zipper

zz

buzz	dazzle	fizz	guzzle	nuzzle	sizzle
buzzer	dizzy	fuzz	jazz	puzzle	

gg

baggy	digger	goggle	mugger	soggy
bigger	egg	jiggle	rugged	suggest
biggest	foggy	juggle	saggy	wiggle
buggy	giggle	logger	slugger	

Teaching Phonics & Word Study in the Intermediate Grades • Scholastic Professional Books

Silent Letters

Guidelines:

Most of the letters in our alphabet are silent in words at one time or another. Frequently consonants are silent because the pronunciation of a particular word has changed over time, but the spelling has remained constant. Silent consonants also occur in words borrowed from other languages. Our inner speech seems to ignore silent letters when we read.

The following list, based on Hanna's 17,000 most frequent words (Burmeister, 1971), shows the 15 most frequent silent letters and their corresponding sounds.

1. tch /ch/ (hatch)
2. dg /j/ (lodge)
3. wr /r/ (write)
4. kn /n/ (know)
5. gn /n/ (gnaw, sign)
6. mb /m/ (lamb)
7. ps /s/ (psychology)
8. lk /k/ (talk)
9. lm /m/ (calm)
10. rh /r/ (rhino)
11. dj /j/ (adjust)
12. wh /h/ (who)
13. bt /t/ (debt)
14. gh /g/ (ghost)
15. mn /m/ (hymn)

The chart below shows the conditions under which each letter is silent and provides some sample words for instruction.

LETTER(S)	CONDITION	SAMPLE WORDS
b	• silent before *t* and after *m* unless this letter and the *b* are in separate syllables (example: *timber*)	debt, doubt, subtle, lamb, climb, comb, crumb, dumb, thumb, plumb, tomb, numb
c	• silent in the cluster *ck*	back, pick, sack, lick
	• silent occasionally after *s*	science, scene, scenery, scenic, scent, scientific, scientist, scissors, sciatic, scintillate
	• silent in a few other words	Connecticut, indict
ch	• rarely silent	yacht
d	• rarely silent (sometimes a result of lazy pronunciation)	handkerchief, Wednesday, grandmother

LETTER(S)	CONDITION	SAMPLE WORDS
g	• silent when it comes before *n* or *m*	gnat, gnaw, gnarl, gnu, gnarled, gnash, gneiss, gnocchi, gnome, Gnostic, sign, design, assign, resign, phlegm
h	• silent when it follows *r* or *k*	rhyme, rhapsody, rhatany, rhea, rhebok, rheumatic, rhesus, rhetoric, rheumatic, rhexis, rhinestone, rhino, rhinoceros, rhizome, Rhode Island, rhodium, rhombus, rhubarb, rhythmic, rhythm, rhyton, khaki, khaddar, khamsin, khan, Khartoum, Khmer
	• sometimes silent when it follows *x*	exhaust
	• often silent between a consonant and the unstressed vowel	shepherd
	• silent after vowels at the end of a word	oh, hurrah
	• sometimes silent at the beginning of a word	honor, honesty, honorary, hors d'oeuvre, hour, heir, heiress, heirloom
k	• silent before *n* at the beginning of a word or syllable	know, knife, knew, knapsack, knack, knee, kneel, knob, knit, knight, knock, knot, knowledge, knave, knead, knickers, knotty, knoll, known, knuckle
l	• silent usually before *f, k, m,* or *v*	calf, talk, calm, salve
	• silent in the *-ould* spelling pattern	would, could, should
m	• rarely silent	mnemonic
n	• silent after *m* (this is considered to be morphophonemic because the *m* is maintained in all derivatives of the word and pronounced in many other forms of the word such as *hymnal*)	autumn, hymn

Teaching Phonics & Word Study in the Intermediate Grades • Scholastic Professional Books

LETTER(S)	CONDITION	SAMPLE WORDS
p	● silent before *n, s,* or *t*	pneumonia, psychology, ptomaine, pneumatic, psalm, psaltery, pseudo, pseudonym, psoriasis, psyche, psychotic, psyche, psychic, psyllium, ptarmigan, pterodactyl, Ptolemy, ptosis
s	● silent sometimes when it follows *i*	island, debris, aisle
	● silent in the word *Arkansas*	
t	● silent in words with *-sten* and *-stle*	fasten, listen, castle, whistle, bristle, bustle, gristle, hustle, rustle, thistle
	● silent in words borrowed from French that end in *-et, -ot,* or *-ut*	bouquet, ballet, depot, debut
th	● rarely silent	asthma, isthmus
u	● silent sometimes when it follows *g* or *q*	guard, opaque
w	● silent before *r* at the beginning of a word or syllable	wrong, write, wrap, wrapper, wrath, wreath, wreck, wreckage, wren, wrench, wrestle, wrestler, wriggle, wring, wrinkle, wrist, wristwatch, write, writer, writhe, writings, wrote, wrought, wring, wry
	● silent in a few other words	two, answer, sword
	● silent in words beginning with *who-*	who, whose, whole
x	● rarely silent	Sioux
z	● rarely silent	rendezvous

Silent Letters

Phonic Principle: silent letter spelling *wr*

Step 1: Review and Warm-Up. Begin by displaying index cards with the sound-spellings or spelling patterns previously taught. Flip through the cards rapidly as students chorally say the sound(s) each represents. Then have students reread a story or passage containing previously taught sound-spelling relationships.

Step 2: Introduce New Skill. Explain to students that sometimes a letter stands for no sound in a word; it is silent. Point out that when the letters *wr* appear together at the beginning of a word such as *write,* the letter *w* is silent. Put the word *write* on the chalkboard, then blend the word aloud as you run your finger under each letter. Have a volunteer underline the letters *wr*. Point to the letters *wr* and ask students to state the sound that the letters stand for. Continue by having students suggest words that begin with *wr*. Encourage them to become "word explorers" and search through classroom books for these words. List these words on the chalkboard.

Step 3: Guided Practice. Write the following words and sentences on the chalkboard. Note that all the words are decodable based on the sound-spelling relationships previously taught. The sentences contain some high-frequency words previously taught.

- **rap, wrap, wing, wring**

- **wreckage, wrongdoing, wristwatch, wrinkled**

- **I have written two books.**

- **The worm wriggled out of the soil.**

Now distribute the following letter-card set to each child: *wr, a, e, i, s, t, p, ck*. Have students build as many words as possible. Ask them to write the words on a sheet of paper. Circulate around the room and model blending when necessary.

Step 4: Apply to Text. Provide students with connected reading practice.

Step 5: Apply to Writing. Dictate the following words and the sentence. Have students write them on a sheet of paper. For students having difficulty segmenting the sounds in each word, extend the word or segment it syllable by syllable. Have students write one syllable at a time. Then, write the words and sentence on the chalkboard and have students self-correct their papers. Don't grade this dictation practice. It's designed to help children segment words and associate sounds with spellings.

- **write, wrinkle, wrecking**

- **Are those your writings?**

Long Vowels

Guidelines:

● Begin instruction with simple, one-syllable words. Start with CVCe (consonant-vowel-consonant-*e*) words, since this pattern is an extremely useful and unencumbered long-vowel pattern. Word lists are provided on pages 86–88. The silent *e* (also known as final *e* or the *e*-marker) acts as a diacritical mark, alerting the reader that the preceding vowel probably stands for a long vowel sound. There are four basic, one-syllable patterns in the English language, including the CVCe pattern (Eldredge, 1996).

1. The **closed syllable** pattern is the most common. There's one vowel in the syllable and the syllable ends with a consonant. Most of the words using this pattern contain short-vowel sounds. There are 13 variations: CVC (*cup*), CVCC (*hand*), CCVCC (*fresh*), CCVC (*trip*), CVCCC (*match*), CVCCe (*judge*), CCVCCC (crutch), CCVCCe (*grudge*), CCCVCC (*script*), VCC (*add*), VC (*in*), CCCVC (*scrap*), VCCC (*inch*)

2. The **vowel team (vowel digraph) pattern** is the second most common. There are 12 variations: CVVC (*heat*), CCVVC (*treat*), CVVCC (*reach*), CVV (*pay*), CCVV (*play*), CVVCe (*leave*), CCVVCC (*bleach*), CCVVCe (*freeze*), CCCVVC (*sprain*), VVC (*oat*), VVCC (*each*), CCCVV (*three*)

3. The **vowel-consonant–silent *e* pattern** is the third most common. There are 4 variations: CVCe (*race*), CCVCe (*shave*), CCCVCe (*strike*), VCe (*ate*)

4. The **open syllable** pattern is the fourth most common. There is only one vowel letter in the syllable and the syllable ends with the vowel's sound. There are two variations: CCV (*she*), CV (*we*)

● Use contrasts in instruction (*rat/rate, hat/hate*) so that students can see how one letter can make all the difference in a word's vowel sound. Following is a list of contrasts for CVC and CVCe words. Contrasts can also be made for words with vowel digraphs (*pan/pain, cot/coat, red/read*).

A Note About Silent *e*

The silent *e* is important in English spelling (Moats, 1995). For example, the silent *e* helps to keep some words from looking like plurals (*please*, not *pleas*; and *moose*, not *moos*). Since the letter *v* doesn't appear at the end of words, the silent *e* in words such as *dove, love, shove,* and *above* gives them orthographic regularity. Although this silent *e* doesn't indicate that the preceding *o* stands for the long *o* sound, it does indicate that the preceding *o* is **not** a short *o* sound. In essence, the silent *e* helps to create a spelling pattern that is consistent and far from random. The final *e* also indicates when the letter *g* or *c* stands for its "soft" sound (*page, race*).

Short-Vowel/Long-Vowel Contrasts

bit / bite	grad / grade	past / paste	slid / slide
can / cane	hat / hate	pin / pine	slim / slime
cap / cape	hid / hide	plan / plane	slop / slope
cod / code	hop / hope	rag / rage	spin / spine
cub / cube	kit / kite	rat / rate	strip / stripe
cut / cute	mad / made	rid / ride	tap / tape
dim / dime	man / mane	rip / ripe	twin / twine
fad / fade	mat / mate	rob / robe	us / use
fat / fate	not / note	rod / rode	van / vane
fin / fine	pal / pale	scrap / scrape	wag / wage
glob / globe	pan / pane	shin / shine	

● In addition to silent *e,* many vowel spellings are formed by vowel digraphs, also known as vowel pairs or vowel teams. These include *ea, ee, oa, ai, ay,* and others. The following chart shows the predictability of various vowel digraphs, many of which are long-vowel digraphs (Burmeister, 1968).

Vowel digraph	Predictability	Vowel digraph	Predictability
ai	/ā/ (pain) 74%, air (chair) 15%	ou	/ə/ (trouble) 41%, /ou/ (house) 35%
ay	/ā/ (say) 96%	au	/ô/ (haul) 94%
ea	/ē/ (seat) 51%, /e/ (head) 26%	aw	/ô/ (hawk) 100%
ee	/ē/ (feet) 86%, eer (steer) 12%	oo	/o͞o/ (food) 59%, /o͝o/ (foot) 36%
ey	/ē/ (key) 58%, /ā/ (convey) 20%, /ī/ (geyser) 12%	ei	/ā/ (reign) 40%, /ē/ (deceit) 26%, /i/ (foreign) 13%, /ī/ (seismic) 11%
oa	/ō/ (boat) 94%	ie	/ē/ (chief) 51%, /ī/ (lie) 17%, /ə/ (patient) 15%
ow	/ō/ (snow) 50%, /ou/ (how) 48%	ew	/yo͞o/ (few) 95%
oi	/oi/ (soil) 98%	ui	/o͞o/ (fruit) 53%, /i/ (build) 47%
oy	/oi/ (boy) 98%		

Teaching Phonics & Word Study in the Intermediate Grades • Scholastic Professional Books

Long Vowels

Phonic Principle: The letters *ea* and *ee* stand for the /ē/ sound.

Step 1: Review and Warm-Up. Begin by displaying index cards with the sound-spellings or spelling patterns previously taught. Flip through the cards rapidly as students chorally say the sound(s) each represents. Then have students reread a story or passage containing previously taught sound-spelling relationships.

Step 2: Introduce New Skill. Explain to students that the letters *ee* and *ea* can stand for the /ē/ sound as in *feet* and *seat*. Write the words *feet* and *seat* on the chalkboard. Then blend the words aloud as you run your finger under each letter. Have a volunteer underline the letters *ee* or *ea*. Point to the letters and ask students to state the sound that the letters stand for. Continue by having students generate a list of words containing the /ē/ sound. List these words on the chalkboard. Have volunteers circle the letters *ee* or *ea* in all the words containing these spellings for the /ē/ sound.

Step 3: Guided Practice. Write the following words and sentences on the chalkboard. Note that all the words are decodable based on the sound-spelling relationships previously taught. The first line focuses on short-vowel/long-vowel contrasts. The sentences contain some high-frequency words previously taught.

- bet, beat, fed, feed

- leaflet, needed, beanbag, deepen

- My teammate is the best!

- Keeping the seeds in the bag is important.

Distribute the following spelling-card set to each student: *eat, eed, eep, eak, eam, b, t, cr, p, bl, s, tr, sp, f, n, br*. Have the students build as many words as possible. Ask them to write the words on a sheet of paper. Circulate around the room and model blending when necessary.

Step 4: Apply to Text. Provide students with connected reading practice.

Step 5: Apply to Writing. Dictate the following words and sentence. Have the students write the words and sentence on a sheet of paper. For students having difficulty segmenting the sounds in each word, extend the word or segment it syllable by syllable. Have the students write one syllable at a time. Write the words and the sentence on the chalkboard, then have the students self-correct their papers. Don't grade this dictation. It's designed to help children segment words and associate sounds with spellings.

- reading, feed, heater

- We are eating green beans and peas.

One-Syllable CVCe Words for Instruction

a_e (long a)

ace	cave	gave	late	quake	shape	trace
age	chase	gaze	made	race	shave	trade
bake	crane	glaze	make	rage	skate	vane
base	crate	grace	male	rake	slate	vase
blade	date	grade	mane	rate	snake	wade
blame	daze	grape	mate	rave	space	wage
blaze	drape	grate	name	safe	spade	wake
brace	face	grave	pace	sake	stage	waste
brake	fade	haste	page	sale	stake	wave
brave	fake	hate	pale	same	stale	whale
cage	fame	haze	pane	save	state	
cake	flake	jade	paste	scale	take	
came	flame	lace	pave	scrape	tale	
cane	frame	lake	place	shade	tame	
cape	game	lame	plane	shake	tape	
case	gate	lane	plate	shame	taste	

EXCEPTIONS: advantage, are, average, breakage, cabbage, climate, courage, delicate, furnace, have, manage, message, palace, passage, private, purchase, senate, separate, surface, village

i_e (long i)

bike	file	like	pine	slice	swine	wife
bite	fine	lime	pipe	slide	tide	wipe
bride	five	line	price	slime	tile	wise
chime	glide	live	pride	smile	time	write
crime	hide	mice	rice	spice	twice	
dice	hike	mile	ride	spike	twine	
dime	hive	mine	ripe	spine	vine	
dine	kite	nice	rise	stride	while	
dive	lice	nine	shine	strike	white	
drive	life	pile	side	stripe	wide	

EXCEPTIONS: active, aggressive, automobile, determine, engine, examine, expressive, favorite, figurine, give, justice, live, machine, magazine, massive, native, notice, office, opposite, police, practice, promise, representative, routine, service

Teaching Phonics & Word Study in the Intermediate Grades • Scholastic Professional Books

o_e (long o)

bone	code	hole	lone	pole	slope	stove	whole
broke	cone	home	mole	robe	smoke	stroke	woke
choke	dome	hope	nose	rode	spoke	those	zone
chose	drove	hose	note	rope	stole	tone	
close	globe	joke	poke	rose	stone	vote	

EXCEPTIONS: above, become, come, done, glove, gone, improve, lose, love, lovely, move, movement, none, purpose, remove, shove, some, something, welcome, whose

u_e (long u)

cube	cute	fuse	mule	use

EXCEPTIONS: assure, conclude, include, measure, pleasure, rule, sure, treasure, crude, duke, dune, flute, June, prune, rude, rule, tube, tune

Multisyllabic CVCe Words for Instruction

aflame	contemplate	explode	microscope	senile	telephone
alpine	crusade	fireplace	microwave	separate	tightrope
animate	cupcake	gateway	mistake	shapeless	tradewind
anyplace	daytime	handmade	nickname	shipmate	upgrade
appetite	demonstrate	handshake	nightingale	shoelace	upscale
arcade	dictate	headline	nineteen	sideways	wasteland
awake	disgrace	hesitate	offstage	snowflake	whaleboat
backbone	dislike	homemade	outrage	staircase	wildlife
bathrobe	drainpipe	humane	overcame	statement	
bedtime	eliminate	illustrate	overtake	stockpile	
birthplace	enclose	inhale	pancake	subscribe	
blockade	engage	inside	parade	suitcase	
bookcase	episode	intimidate	persuade	summertime	
calculate	escape	keepsake	pipeline	sunrise	
candidate	estate	landscape	porcupine	sunshine	
capsize	estimate	lateness	profane	sunstroke	
celebrate	evaluate	lemonade	provide	tailgate	
cheesecake	exchange	lifeboat	rattlesnake	tailpipe	
classmate	excite	maypole	reptile	teammate	
coincide	exhale	mealtime	sacrifice	teenage	

Long-Vowel Words for Instruction

/ā/ as in cake

bake	grade	shape	chain	raid	hay
blade	grape	skate	claim	rain	jay
brace	grapes	space	drain	rail	lay
brake	lake	stage	fail	raise	may
brave	late	take	faint	sail	maybe
cage	made	tale	faith	snail	pay
cake	make	tape	frail	Spain	play
came	male	trace	grain	stain	player
case	maze	trade	jail	strain	pray
cave	name	vase	laid	tail	ray
chase	page	wade	maid	trail	say
date	place	wake	mail	train	spray
face	plate	wave	main	vain	stay
fade	race	whale	nail	waist	stray
flake	rake	aid	paid	wait	sway
flame	sale	aim	pail	bay	today
game	same	bait	pain	clay	tray
gate	save	braid	paint	day	way
gave	shade	Braille	plain	gay	
grace	shake	brain	praise	gray	

More Multisyllabic /ā/ Words

abstain	explain	overpaid	subway
afraid	faraway	paintbrush	throwaway
away	hallway	paycheck	unchain
birthday	holiday	payday	unpaid
complain	mailbox	pigtail	waistband
contain	mainland	railway	waitress
crayon	maintain	raindrop	yesterday
decay	mermaid	refrain	
entertain	midday	runway	

Teaching Phonics & Word Study in the Intermediate Grades • Scholastic Professional Books

/ē/ as in feet

be	bean	dirty	shield	wheel	lobby
me	beat	dizzy	shriek	lean	lucky
we	bleach	dusty	siege	leap	many
bee	bleak	duty	thief	leash	mommy
beech	cheap	easy	yield	least	muddy
beef	cheat	eighty	peel	meal	navy
beep	clean	family	peep	mean	ninety
beet	cream	forty	queen	meat	only
cheek	deal	fifty	reef	neat	party
cheep	dear	funny	screech	pea	penny
cheese	dream	fuzzy	screen	peach	plenty
creep	each	gravy	see	peak	pony
deed	east	happy	seed	plead	pretty
deep	eat	jelly	seek	pleat	puppy
deer	feast	kitty	seem	reach	quickly
fee	flea	lady	seen	read	sandy
feed	gleam	lately	seep	real	seventy
feel	heal	babies	sheep	scream	shiny
feet	heap	belief	sheet	sea	silly
flee	heat	believe	sleep	seal	sixty
free	jeans	berries	sleet	seam	sleepy
greed	lead	brief	speech	seat	slowly
green	leaf	brownie	speed	sneak	smoothly
greet	leak	Charlie	steel	speak	sticky
heed	any	chief	steep	steal	story
jeep	baby	cities	street	steam	strawberry
keep	beauty	cookies	sweep	stream	sunny
knee	bunny	field	sweet	tea	thirsty
meet	candy	fierce	teen	teach	thirty
need	carry	grief	teeth	team	tiny
peek	chilly	niece	three	treat	tricky
beach	city	parties	tree	weak	ugly
bead	county	pennies	weed	wheat	windy
beak	daddy	pierce	week	yeast	
beam	daisy	relief	weep	zeal	

More Multisyllabic /ē/ Words

absentee	cartwheel	esteem	mainstream	proofread	succeed
agreed	decease	freedom	mislead	reason	sunbeam
antifreeze	decrease	freeway	nosebleed	seashell	teapot
asleep	defeat	guarantee	outreach	seasick	treetop
beneath	degree	heartbeat	overeat	seaweed	upbeat
between	disagree	impeach	peanut	sixteen	
bloodstream	eighteen	indeed	pedigree	sleepless	
bumblebee	employee	indiscreet	proceed	steamship	

/ī/ as in bike

bike	hike	pike	spike	by	blind	died	high
bite	hive	pine	splice	cry	child	dries	knight
bride	ice	pipe	stride	dry	climb	flies	light
chime	kite	price	strive	fly	find	fries	might
chive	life	rice	tide	fry	grind	lie	night
dime	like	ride	time	my	hind	pie	right
dine	line	ripe	tire	pry	kind	skies	sigh
dive	lime	rise	twice	shy	mild	spies	sight
drive	live	shine	twine	sky	mind	tie	slight
fine	mice	side	whine	sly	rind	tries	thigh
fire	mile	size	white	spy	wild	bright	tight
five	mine	slice	wide	try	wind	fight	
grime	nice	slide	wife	why	cries	flight	
hide	nine	spice	wise	bind	die	fright	

More Multisyllabic /ī/ Words

airtight	exemplify	gratify	midnight	overnight	simplify
amplify	falsify	headlight	modify	oversight	stoplight
brightness	flashlight	highlight	moonlight	playwright	starlight
bullfight	foresight	highway	multiply	reply	sunlight
daylight	frighten	imply	nightfall	satisfy	tonight
delight	gaslight	insight	occupy	sightless	upright

90

Teaching Phonics & Word Study in the Intermediate Grades • Scholastic Professional Books

/ō/ as in boat

ago	broke	pole	croak	bow	doe
bold	choke	pose	float	bowl	foe
bolt	chose	robe	foam	crow	goes
cold	close	rode	goal	flow	hoe
colt	clothes	rope	goat	flown	Joe
fold	clove	rose	groan	glow	toe
go	code	slope	Joan	grow	woe
gold	cone	smoke	load	grown	
hold	cope	spoke	loaf	know	
jolt	cove	stone	loan	known	
mold	dome	stove	moan	low	
no	dose	stroke	moat	mellow	
old	doze	those	oak	mow	
poll	drove	throne	oats	row	
pro	froze	tone	roach	show	
roll	globe	vote	road	shown	
scold	grove	whole	roam	slow	
scroll	hole	woke	roast	snow	
so	home	wrote	soak	sparrow	
sold	hope	yoke	soap	stow	
stroll	hose	zone	throat	swallow	
told	joke	boat	toad	throw	
toll	lone	cloak	toast	thrown	
troll	nose	coach	whoa	tow	
volt	note	coal	below	willow	
alone	phone	coast	blow	window	
bone	poke	coat	blown	yellow	

More Multisyllabic /ō/ Words

boatload	follow	rainbow	sailboat	snowman
coatrack	oatmeal	roadbed	seacoast	trainload
elbow	pillow	roadway	shadow	
fellow	railroad	rowboat	snowdrift	

/yōō/ as in cube

cube	puke	January	unit	mew	fuel
cute	use	menu	united	pew	hue
fume	bugle	museum	university	preview	rescue
fuse	community	music	unusual	review	value
huge	future	pupil	usual	view	beautiful
mule	human	regular	Utah	argue	beauty
muse	humid	uniform	few	continue	
mute	humor	union	hew	cue	

Other Vowel Sounds

Guidelines:

Some vowel digraphs stand for sounds that are not commonly classified as long or short vowels. These include the following, which I've classified according to the way they are grouped in most basal reading programs:

Variant Vowels

/ōō/ (food), /ōō/ (foot), /ô/ (ball, cause, claw, for)

Note that the *o* in *for* can also be classified as an *r*-controlled vowel (see next page). The vowel digraph *oo* has a long and a short sound assigned to it. The long sound is more frequent in words than the short sound. Therefore, when students encounter this vowel digraph in a word, they should try the long sound first. The only way for students to know which sound is correct is to try both sounds and see which forms a word that is in their speaking or listening vocabularies (assuming they have heard the word before).

Diphthongs

/oi/ (boil, boy), /ou/ (house, cow)

Diphthongs are vowel sounds formed by a gliding action in the mouth. That is, unlike other vowel sounds, the tongue and lip positions often change as the sound is formed. For example, say and extend the /a/ sound. Notice the position of the lips and tongue. Do they change while forming the sound? No.

Teaching Phonics & Word Study in the Intermediate Grades • Scholastic Professional Books

Now say the /oi/ sound. Notice how the lips are thrust forward and close together as the sound begins, but quickly retract and open slightly as the sound is concluded. This gliding action is characteristic of diphthongs. Many linguists also consider the long-*i* and long-*u* sounds diphthongs. As mentioned earlier, people speaking in a Southern dialect form many vowel sounds in this manner, which accounts for much of the liveliness, beauty, and sing-song nature of Southern speech.

r-Controlled Vowels

/âr/ (ch<u>air</u>), /ûr/(f<u>er</u>n, b<u>ir</u>d, h<u>ur</u>t), /är/ (p<u>ar</u>k, fath<u>er</u>)

The letter *r* affects the sound of the vowel that precedes it in many ways. The following suggested sequence for teaching *r*-controlled vowels is based on frequency and predictability of spellings (Groff, 1977; Blevins, 1997):

1. /ûr/ (ir, er, ur) **2.** /ôr/ (or, or-e, oar)

3. /âr/ (ar) **4.** /≠r/ (ar-e, air, eir, ear)

In addition to the letter *r*, the letters *l* and *w* have effects on the vowels that precede or follow them (i.e., <u>wa</u>ter, f<u>all</u>, t<u>alk</u>). Instead of trying to explain to students the intricacies of how the vowel sound is affected by these consonants, the sounds are best taught as spelling patterns such as *ar, er, ir, or, ur, air, ear, are, all, alk,* and *wa.*

Schwa

/ ə / (<u>a</u>lone, happ<u>e</u>n, d<u>i</u>rect, gall<u>o</u>p, circ<u>u</u>s)

Some linguists don't consider the schwa a separate sound; rather they think of it as an allophone—a variant of a particular sound caused by a reduction in stress on that sound in a word. The schwa is also known as a murmur or neutral sound. Up to 22 different spellings of the schwa sound have been identified (Hanna et al., 1966). It is difficult to teach rules for identifying this sound in words. Some educators suggest telling students to try the short sound of a questionable vowel when decoding multisyllabic words (Chall and Popp, 1996); others have suggested telling students to say "uh" for every vowel sound in a word they are unsure of. They believe that this approximation will be close enough for the student to identify the word if it is in the student's speaking or listening vocabulary.

Other Vowel Sounds

Phonic Principle: The letters *oi* and *oy* stand for the /oi/ sound.

Step 1: Review and Warm-Up. Begin by displaying index cards with the sound-spellings or spelling patterns previously taught. Flip through the cards rapidly as students chorally say the sound(s) each represents. Then have students reread a story or passage containing previously taught sound-spelling relationships.

Step 2: Introduce New Skill. Explain to the students that the letters *oi* and *oy* stand for the /oi/ sound as in *boil* and *boy*. Write the words *boil* and *boy* on the chalkboard. Then blend the words aloud as you run your finger under each letter. Have a volunteer underline the letters *oi* or *oy*. Point to the letters and ask students to state the sound that the letters stand for. Continue by having students generate a list of words containing the /oi/ sound. List these words on the chalkboard.

Step 3: Guided Practice. Write the following words and sentences on the chalkboard. Note that all the words are decodable based on the sound-spelling relationships previously taught. Contrasts are given in the first line. The sentences contain some high-frequency words previously taught.

- box, boy, pint, point

- coin, joyful, toys, noisily

- The boy is enjoying the game.

- I found five coins.

Then distribute the following spelling-card set to each student: *oi, oy, b, l, c, n, j*. Have children build as many words as possible. Ask them to write the words on a sheet of paper. Circulate around the room and model blending when necessary.

Step 4: Apply to Text. Provide students with connected reading practice.

Step 5: Apply to Writing. Dictate the following words and sentence. Have the students write the words and sentence on a sheet of paper. Then write the words and sentence on the chalkboard. Have the students self-correct their papers. Don't grade this dictation. It's designed to help students segment words and associate sounds with spellings.

- **boyish, pointing, coiled**

- **We gave her the royal treatment.**

Words for Instruction for Other Vowel Sounds

schwa — /ə/ as in alarm

about	afraid	alarm	anew	ashamed	awake
above	again	alas	annoy	ashore	aware
account	ago	alone	another	aside	away
adult	agree	along	apart	asleep	awhile
afloat	ahead	America	appear	avoid	awoke
afoot	ajar	among	applause	await	

Note: The /ə/ sound is referred to as the schwa sound or murmur sound. It is graphically represented by an upside-down e. Some linguists don't consider it a sound, rather a phonetic variant or allophone. The ə / sound can be spelled with any vowel: a (alone), e (happen), i (direct), o (gallop), u (circus). Several multisyllabic words beginning with a as their first unaccented syllable contain this sound. Above is a list of these words. The schwa sounds appears in most multisyllabic words and is the most common sound in English.

r-controlled vowel — /â/ as in chair

air	pair	dare	mare	spare	swear
chair	stair	fare	pare	square	wear
fair	bare	flare	rare	stare	
flair	blare	glare	scare	bear	
hair	care	hare	share	pear	

Multisyllabic /â/ Words

affair	compare	midair	repair	welfare
airfare	debonair	millionaire	silverware	wheelchair
aware	declare	nightmare	solitaire	
beware	despair	prepare	underwear	
billionaire	impair	questionnaire	warfare	

Note: The /â/ sound is an r-controlled vowel sound. The diacritical mark above the a is known as a circumflex.

Teaching Phonics & Word Study in the Intermediate Grades • Scholastic Professional Books

r-controlled sound — /û/ as in bird

blur	purr	circle	squirm	fern	person
burn	purse	circus	squirt	germ	river
burst	spur	dirt	stir	her	serve
church	surf	dirty	swirl	herd	sister
churn	Thursday	fir	third	jerk	stern
curb	turkey	firm	thirst	letter	swerve
curl	turn	first	twirl	merge	term
curse	turtle	flirt	whirl	mother	under
curve	urge	girl	after	nerve	verb
fur	bird	quirk	better	other	verge
hurt	birth	shirt	certain	over	verse
nurse	birthday	sir	clerk	perch	water
purple	chirp	skirt	ever	perk	winter

More Multisyllabic /û/ Words

adverb	converge	heartburn	observe	rebirth	sunburn
blackbird	disturb	intern	overturn	reserve	superb
concern	diverge	midterm	preserve	return	unhurt
conservative	headfirst	nightshirt	proverb	suburb	

Note: The /û/ sound is an *r*-controlled vowel sound. The diacritical mark above the *u* is known as a circumflex.

r-controlled sound — /ä/ as in car

arch	barn	dart	jar	part	star
Arctic	car	far	lard	party	start
ark	card	farm	large	scar	starch
arm	cart	garden	march	scarf	tar
art	charge	guard	mark	shark	tart
artist	charm	hard	marsh	sharp	yard
bar	chart	harm	mart	smart	yarn
bark	dark	harp	park	spark	

Teaching Phonics & Word Study in the Intermediate Grades • Scholastic Professional Books

More Multisyllabic /ä/ Words

aardvark	bazaar	cigar	guitar	leotard	recharge
ajar	bodyguard	depart	impart	lifeguard	seminar
alarm	bombard	discard	jaguar	outsmart	superstar
backyard	bookmark	disembark	junkyard	postcard	trademark
ballpark	caviar	enlarge	landmark	postmark	upstart

Note: The /ä/ sound is often an *r*-controlled vowel sound. The diacritical mark above the *a* is known as a dieresis.

variant or *r*-controlled sound /ô/ as in ball

bore	north	sworn	small	Paul	law
born	or	thorn	stall	pause	lawn
chore	porch	torch	tall	sauce	lawyer
chord	pore	tore	wall	sausage	paw
cord	pork	torn	audience	taught	pawn
core	port	wore	August	vault	raw
cork	scorch	worn	author	awful	saw
corn	score	halt	autumn	bawl	shawl
door	scorn	malt	because	brawl	slaw
dorm	shore	salt	caught	caw	sprawl
for	short	chalk	cause	claw	squawk
force	snore	stalk	clause	crawl	straw
fork	sore	talk	daughter	dawn	strawberry
form	sort	walk	dinosaur	draw	thaw
fort	sport	all	fault	drawn	yawn
forth	store	ball	fraud	fawn	
horn	stork	call	haul	flaw	
horse	storm	fall	haunt	gnaw	
more	sword	hall	launch	hawk	
morning	swore	mall	laundry	jaw	

More Multisyllabic /ô/ Words

assault	default	exalt	jigsaw	snowball
baseball	distraught	football	pitfall	withdraw
boardwalk	enthrall	install	seesaw	

Note: The /ô/ sound is referred to as the broad *o* sound. The diacritical mark above the *o* is known as a circumflex.

diphthong — /oi/ as in boy

avoid	coin	moist	poison	voice	decoy	joyful	soy
boil	foil	moisture	rejoice	annoy	destroy	loyal	toy
broil	hoist	noise	soil	boy	employ	ploy	voyage
choice	join	oil	spoil	cowboy	enjoy	Roy	
coil	joint	point	toil	coy	joy	royal	

More Multisyllabic /oi/ Words

ahoy	checkpoint	overjoy	recoil	tenderloin	viewpoint
appoint	corduroy	pinpoint	rejoin	turmoil	
ballpoint	disappoint	purloin	sirloin	turquoise	

diphthong — /ou/ as in house

about	found	ouch	sound	chow	growl	towel
bounce	grouch	out	sour	clown	how	tower
bound	ground	pouch	south	cow	howl	town
cloud	hound	pound	spout	crowd	now	vow
couch	house	pout	sprout	crown	owl	wow
count	loud	proud	trout	down	plow	
crouch	mound	round	allow	drown	powder	
doubt	mouse	scout	bow	fowl	power	
flour	mouth	shout	brow	frown	prowl	
foul	noun	snout	brown	gown	sow	

More Multisyllabic /ou/ Words

abound	blowout	downtown	hometown	slowdown
account	breakdown	dropout	lighthouse	spellbound
aloud	campground	dugout	lookout	sundown
amount	campout	earthbound	loudmouth	surround
announce	compound	eyebrow	mispronounce	thundercloud
around	countdown	fallout	newfound	touchdown
astound	devour	firehouse	paramount	warehouse
background	devout	foreground	pronounce	without
ballgown	discount	hangout	runabout	workout
blackout	doghouse	holdout	runaround	

Teaching Phonics & Word Study in the Intermediate Grades • Scholastic Professional Books

variant — /o͞o/ as in spoon

bloom	groom	pool	snoop	blue	grew	rude
boo	hoop	proof	soon	clue	knew	rule
boom	hoot	roof	spook	due	new	tube
boot	igloo	room	spool	glue	news	tune
broom	loom	root	spoon	sue	screw	duty
coo	loop	school	stool	true	shrew	July
cool	loose	scoop	too	blew	stew	junior
coop	loot	scoot	tool	brew	threw	numeral
doom	moo	shampoo	toot	chew	crude	solution
food	mood	shoo	tooth	crew	flute	truth
fool	moon	shoot	troop	dew	June	tuna
gloom	moose	sloop	zoo	drew	prune	
goose	noon ooze	smooth	zoom	flew	reduce	

More Multisyllabic /o͞o/ Words

afternoon	cartoon	courtroom	mushroom	seafood
aloof	cashew	curfew	outgrew	switcheroo
anew	childproof	fireproof	overdo	taboo
baboon	classroom	harpoon	platoon	tattoo
balloon	cockatoo	interview	raccoon	troubleshoot
bathroom	cocoon	kangaroo	renew	typhoon
caboose	corkscrew	macaroon	review	withdrew

Note: The /o͞o/ sound is referred to as the long sound of *oo*.

Two *oo*'s

The letters *oo* can stand for two sounds about the same percentage of time. Therefore, I often advise students to try both sounds when confronted with an unfamiliar word that contains this spelling. If the word is in their speaking or listening vocabularies, then the approximation resulting from trying one of the sounds will help the students figure out the word. On the Word Wall, I write the /o͞o/ words on moon shapes and the /o͝o/ words on book shapes as visual reminders of the sound the letters *oo* stand for in each word listed.

variant — /o͝o/ as in book

afoot	crook	hood	notebook	stood	wool
book	foot	hoof	rook	took	
brook	football	hook	rookie	wood	
cook	good	look	shook	wooden	
cookie	good-bye	nook	soot	woof	

More Multisyllabic /o͝o/ Words

brotherhood	driftwood	mistook	redwood	understood
checkbook	fatherhood	motherhood	scrapbook	unhook
childhood	likelihood	notebook	sisterhood	underfoot
deadwood	livelihood	outlook	textbook	

Note: The /o͝o/ sound is referred to as the short sound of *oo*.

Teaching Phonics & Word Study in the Intermediate Grades • Scholastic Professional Books

What Are Phonograms?

A **phonogram** is a letter or series of letters that stands for a sound, syllable, or series of sounds without reference to meaning. For example, the phonogram -*ay* contains two letters and stands for the long *a* sound. It can be found in words such as *say, may*, and *replay*. The phonogram -*ack* contains three letters, stands for two sounds (/a/ /k/), and can be found in words such as *pack, black*, and *attack*. Phonograms are often referred to as **word families**. The words *face, space,* and *replace* belong to the same word family because they all contain the ending -*ace*. The ending -*ace* is a phonogram. During the past two decades, increased attention has been paid to phonograms and their use in reading instruction. In the classrooms I visit, I see more and more word walls containing word lists organized primarily around phonograms.

A linguistic term sometimes substituted for phonogram is **rime**. Rime is generally used in combination with the term **onset**. Onset and rime refer to the two parts of a syllable. In a syllable, a rime is the vowel and everything after it. For example, in the one syllable word *sat*, the rime is -*at*. The onset is the consonant, consonant blend, or digraph that comes before the rime in a syllable. In the words *sat, brat*, and *chat*, the onsets are *s, br,* and *ch*, respectively. A two-syllable word, such as *pancake*, has two onsets and two rimes. What are the onsets in the word *pancake*? (*p, c*) What are the rimes? (-*an, -ake*) Some words such as *at, out,* and *up* contain no onset.

Phonograms Provide a Reading Boost

Phonograms have been used in reading and spelling instruction dating as far back as the *New England Primer* and *Webster's Blue Back Spelling Books* of the 1600s, 1700s, and 1800s. Phonograms have been used during spelling instruction because word patterns are the most effective vehicle for teaching spelling. The most common phonograms appear in many of the words students will encounter in elementary stories. Teaching students that words contain recognizable chunks, and teaching them to search for these word parts or patterns is an important step in developing reading fluency. As students encounter more and more multisyllabic words, they gain an understanding that words may contain recognizable parts (phonograms, suffixes, prefixes, smaller words). This insight is critical to decoding words quickly and efficiently.

Another value of phonograms is that they are reliable and generalizable. Of the 286 phonograms that appeared in the primary-level texts reviewed in one classic study, 272 (95%) were pronounced the same in every word in which they were found (Durrell, 1963). In addition, these 272 reliable phonograms can be found in 1,437 of the words common to the speaking vocabularies of primary-age children (Murphy, 1957).

Many educators have noted the utility of phonograms in early reading instruction, as is illustrated by the abundance of word walls containing word lists organized by phonograms. In fact, a relatively small number of phonograms can be used to generate a large number of words. According to Wylie and Durrell (1970), nearly 500 primary-grade words can be derived from only 37 phonograms:

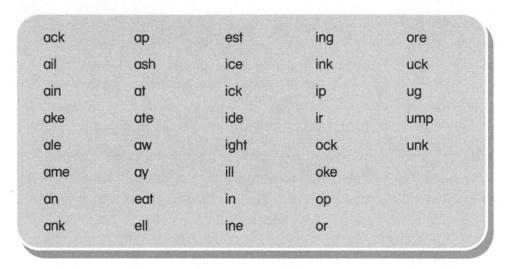

ack	ap	est	ing	ore
ail	ash	ice	ink	uck
ain	at	ick	ip	ug
ake	ate	ide	ir	ump
ale	aw	ight	ock	unk
ame	ay	ill	oke	
an	eat	in	op	
ank	ell	ine	or	

Wylie and Durrell also made some important instructional findings about phonograms:

- **Long-vowel phonograms** (*-eat, -oat*) were learned as easily as short-vowel phonograms (*-ed, -op*).

- **Long-vowel phonograms with final *e*** (*-ake, -ide, -ope*) were as easily learned as other long-vowel phonograms.

- **Phonograms containing variant vowels** (*-ood, -ook*), *r*-controlled vowels (*-ear, -are*), and diphthongs (*-out, -oint*) were almost as easy to learn as long- and short-vowel phonograms.

- **Phonograms ending in a single consonant** (*-at, -ot*) were easier to learn than phonograms ending in consonant blends (*-ast, -imp*).

Teaching with Phonograms

One instructional method that uses phonograms is decoding by analogy (Cunningham, 1975–76; Wagstaff, 1994; Fox, 1996). When decoding by analogy, students look for recognizable chunks within a word to help them figure it out. Cunningham (1995) contends that our brain works as a "pattern

Teaching Phonics & Word Study in the Intermediate Grades • Scholastic Professional Books

detector." As we develop as readers and our knowledge of English orthography increases, we detect more and more of these spelling patterns. Teaching students to decode by analogy helps make them aware of the patterns in our written language. At left is how one teacher might model the use of analogies to decode the word *sticking*.

Using phonograms in phonics instruction also helps some students internalize more complex phonics concepts, such as *r*-controlled vowels (Wagstaff, 1994). To explain to students how the *r* in the word *far* affects the sound that the *a* stands for is difficult. However, teaching students the phonogram *-ar* and providing them practice reading words such as *bar, car, far, jar,* and *star* is simpler and arguably more efficient.

> **Model** When I look at this word, I see three parts that remind me of other words I know. First I see the letters *st*, as in the word *stop*. These two letters stand for the /st/ sound. I also see the word part *-ick* as in the word *pick*. Then I see the common vowel ending *-ing*. If I blend together these three word parts, I get the word *sticking*.

Phonogram Cautions

Although phonograms can provide a boost to early reading instruction, I offer a strong word of caution. Never make phonograms the sole focus of early reading instruction; they provide the developing reader only limited independence in word analysis. Beginning readers who rely primarily on phonograms to decode by analogy are less skilled at word identification than beginning readers who analyze words fully (Bruck & Treiman, 1992). Fully analyzing words focuses students' attention on all of the word's sound-spelling relationships.

As you can see, analyzing words in their entirety is essential. Much of what students learn about English orthography (the spelling patterns of English) comes from constantly analyzing words and being exposed to lots and lots of print. Eventually, multiple exposures to words enable the reader to recognize words by sight and recognize common spelling patterns in unfamiliar words—an important goal in developing reading fluency. The best explanation of how this happens can be gleaned from the work of Ehri (1995). She provides us with a clear model of the four phases students go through in making every word a sight word:

1. **Pre-alphabetic phase (logographic):** Children recognize symbols, such as the "golden arches" of McDonald's, and attach a word or meaning to them. Or, they might recognize a special feature of a word. For example, a child might remember the word *yellow* because it contains two "sticks" in the middle.

2. **Partial alphabetic phase:** Children are beginning to learn sound-spelling relationships, yet are using only some phonic cues to figure out words. For instance, a child may guess the word *kitten* based on his use of picture clues and his knowledge of the sounds associated with the letters *k* and *n*. However, this same child probably wouldn't be able to distinguish the word *kitten* from the word *kitchen* because he can't fully analyze the word.

3. **Full alphabetic phase:** Children are using their knowledge of sound-spelling relationships and analyzing words in their entirety. Much practice decoding and multiple exposures to print help children begin to develop an awareness of spelling patterns.

4. **Consolidated alphabetic phase (orthographic):** The awareness of spelling patterns is stronger, and children are beginning to use this knowledge to decode words they don't know quickly and accurately. Now, when a child sees the word *stack*, instead of analyzing the word sound by sound, she almost instantly recognizes the familiar *st* combination from words such as *step* and *stop*, and the word part *-ack*. The efficiency with which this child decodes words is greater than in the previous phase. This child has had many opportunities to fully analyze words, decode many words, and attend to word parts within words.

As children repeatedly encounter words, many are learned as sight words. This is the ultimate goal of fast, efficient decoding. Some children require as few as 4–5 exposures to new words to learn them by sight. For struggling readers, that number jumps to 50–100 (Honig, 1996). Learning words by sight requires analyzing many words in their entirety and wide reading. Beginning readers who are taught to look only for phonograms, or other word chunks, are being treated as skilled readers instead of the developing readers they are. In addition, no reading program can teach the vast number of phonograms children will encounter in words. Therefore, although using phonograms to decode by analogy is helpful, it is not sufficient. Children must be able to use a variety of decoding strategies, including decoding by analogy, blending, recognizing sight words, and using context clues, to figure out the complete range of words in the English language.

How to Use Phonogram Lists

You can use the phonogram lists on pages 105–161 to develop word lists for phonics and spelling instruction. The lists contain one-syllable and multisyllabic words and are organized by vowel sound. Within each list, the words and phrases are listed in alphabetical order beginning with single consonant words, then proceeding to multisyllabic words.

Teaching Phonics & Word Study in the Intermediate Grades • Scholastic Professional Books

Long-a Phonograms

-ace

brace	place	deface	misplace	unlace
face	race	disgrace	replace	workplace
grace	space	embrace	retrace	
lace	trace	everyplace	shoelace	
mace	anyplace	fireplace	staircase	
pace	birthplace	horse race	suitcase	

-ade

blade	trade	charade	lampshade	ready-made
fade	wade	crusade	lemonade	renegade
glade	accolade	custom-made	marmalade	serenade
grade	arcade	decade	masquerade	shoulder blade
jade	barricade	escapade	parade	tirade
made	blockade	grenade	persuade	unmade
shade	cavalcade	homemade	promenade	upgrade
spade	centigrade	invade	razor blade	

-age

age	stage	enrage	offstage	space age
cage	wage	front page	old age	teenage
page	backstage	ice age	outrage	upstage
rage	bird cage	middle age	rampage	
sage	engage	minimum wage	rib cage	

-aid

aide	paid	bridesmaid	mermaid	unafraid
braid	raid	first aid	nursemaid	underpaid
laid	afraid	foreign aid	overpaid	unpaid
maid	band-aid	hearing aid	repaid	visual aid

Teaching Phonics & Word Study in the Intermediate Grades • Scholastic Professional Books

-ail

ail	mail	trail	derail	pigtail
bail	nail	wail	detail	prevail
Braille	pail	Abigail	dovetail	retail
fail	quail	airmail	fan mail	shirttail
frail	rail	blackmail	fingernail	thumbnail
Gail	sail	cocktail	hangnail	toenail
hail	snail	cottontail	monorail	
jail	tail	curtail	nature trail	

-ain

brain	slain	ascertain	explain	retain
chain	Spain	birdbrain	freight train	scatterbrain
drain	sprain	bloodstain	maintain	sustain
grain	stain	complain	migraine	tearstain
main	strain	contain	obtain	terrain
Maine	train	disdain	refrain	Ukraine
pain	vain	domain	regain	unchain
plain	abstain	Elaine	remain	
rain	acid rain	entertain	restrain	

-aint

faint	paint	quaint	saint	taint

-aise

raise	praise	mayonnaise

-ait

bait	gait	strait	trait	wait	await

-ake

bake	lake	stake	earthquake	namesake
brake	make	take	fruitcake	overtake
cake	quake	wake	handshake	pancake
drake	rake	awake	intake	rattlesnake
fake	sake	cheesecake	keepsake	remake
flake	shake	clambake	milkshake	shortcake
Jake	snake	cupcake	mistake	snowflake

Teaching Phonics & Word Study in the Intermediate Grades • Scholastic Professional Books

-ale

bale	sale	whale	impale	fairy tale
Dale	scale	exhale	inhale	garage sale
gale	stale	female	telltale	nightingale
male	tale	for sale	upscale	tattletale
pale				

-ame

blame	flame	name	aflame	inflame
came	frame	same	ball game	nickname
dame	game	shame	became	overcame
fame	lame	tame	defame	surname

-ane

cane	pane	airplane	hurricane	weathervane
crane	plane	candy cane	inhumane	windowpane
Jane	sane	cellophane	insane	
lane	vane	Great Dane	mundane	
mane	wane	humane	profane	

-ange

change	strange	exchange	long-range	rearrange
grange	arrange	interchange	prearrange	shortchange
range	downrange			

-ape

cape	nape	tape	escape	red tape
drape	scrape	agape	fire escape	reshape
gape	shape	egg-shape	landscape	shipshape
grape				

-ase

base	vase	briefcase	home base	suitcase
case	bookcase	erase	staircase	data base
chase				

Teaching Phonics & Word Study in the Intermediate Grades • Scholastic Professional Books

-aste

baste	haste	paste	taste	waste

-ate

ate	assassinate	detonate	fumigate	irrigate
crate	associate	devastate	generate	isolate
date	birthrate	deviate	graduate	legislate
fate	blind date	discriminate	gravitate	liberate
gate	calculate	dislocate	gyrate	liquidate
grate	candidate	dominate	hallucinate	locate
hate	captivate	donate	helpmate	lubricate
Kate	carbohydrate	duplicate	hesitate	mandate
late	celebrate	educate	hibernate	manipulate
mate	cellmate	elaborate	humiliate	medicate
plate	cheapskate	elate	hyphenate	meditate
rate	checkmate	elevate	ice skate	migrate
skate	circulate	eliminate	illuminate	motivate
slate	classmate	emancipate	illustrate	mutilate
state	communicate	emigrate	imitate	narrate
abbreviate	complicate	equate	immigrate	nauseate
accelerate	concentrate	escalate	impersonate	navigate
accommodate	confiscate	estate	indicate	nominate
accumulate	congratulate	estimate	infiltrate	officiate
activate	contaminate	evacuate	inflate	operate
advocate	contemplate	evaluate	ingrate	ornate
aggravate	cooperate	evaporate	initiate	out-of-date
agitate	coordinate	exaggerate	inmate	overate
alienate	create	exasperate	inoculate	overrate
alleviate	cultivate	excavate	insinuate	overstate
allocate	debate	exhilarate	instigate	participate
amputate	decorate	exterminate	integrate	penetrate
animate	dedicate	fascinate	interrogate	percolate
annihilate	deflate	first-rate	intimidate	playmate
anticipate	delegate	fluctuate	intoxicate	populate
appreciate	deliberate	formulate	investigate	primate
asphyxiate	demonstrate	frustrate	invigorate	procrastinate

Teaching Phonics & Word Study in the Intermediate Grades • Scholastic Professional Books

pulsate	relate	separate	tailgate	vaccinate
punctuate	retaliate	situate	terminate	validate
radiate	reverberate	speculate	tolerate	vibrate
real estate	roller skate	stagnate	translate	vindicate
rebate	rotate	stalemate	underrate	violate
recuperate	second-rate	stimulate	update	
regulate	sedate	strangulate	up-to-date	
reiterate	segregate	suffocate	vacate	

-ave

brave	grave	shave	brainwave	misbehave
cave	knave	slave	engrave	shockwave
crave	pave	wave	forgave	tidal wave
Dave	rave	aftershave	heat wave	
gave	save	behave	microwave	

-ay

bay	pray	decay	milky way	stowaway
clay	ray	delay	Norway	subway
day	say	display	okay	Sunday
fray	slay	essay	one-way	throwaway
gay	spray	everyday	railway	today
gray	stay	faraway	relay	tooth decay
hay	stray	halfway	repay	underway
jay	sway	hallway	role-play	weekday
lay	tray	headway	runaway	x-ray
may	way	highway	runway	yesterday
nay	away	holiday	someway	
pay	birthday	hooray	stairway	
play	blue jay	ice tray	stingray	

-aze

blaze	faze	graze	raze	stargaze
craze	gaze	haze	ablaze	trailblaze
daze	glaze	maze	amaze	

-eak

break	beefsteak	daybreak	housebreak	newsbreak
steak	coffee break	heartbreak	jailbreak	outbreak

-eigh

neigh	weigh	sleigh		

-ey

hey	prey	whey	obey	survey
grey	they	disobey		

Long-e Phonograms

-e

be	he	me	she	we

-ea

flea	plea	tea	deep-sea	sweet pea
pea	sea			

-each

beach	breach	peach	reach	impeach
bleach	leach	preach	teach	outreach

-ead

bead	lead	read	mislead	speed-read
knead	plead	lip-read	proofread	

-eak

beak	freak	sneak	streak	misspeak
bleak	leak	speak	tweak	pip-squeak
creak	peak	squeak	weak	Chesapeake

110

Teaching Phonics & Word Study in the Intermediate Grades • Scholastic Professional Books

-eal

deal	seal	zeal	fair deal	ordeal
heal	squeal	appeal	for real	piecemeal
meal	steal	big deal	ideal	reveal
peal	teal	conceal	misdeal	unreal
real	veal	congeal	oatmeal	

-eam

beam	scream	bloodstream	drill team	pipe dream
cream	seam	daydream	ice cream	sour cream
dream	steam	double-team	mainstream	sunbeam
gleam	stream	downstream	moonbeam	whipped cream
ream	team			

-ean

bean	glean	mean	dry clean	jelly bean
clean	Jean	wean	green bean	
dean	lean			

-eap

cheap	heap	leap	reap	junkheap

-ear

clear	near	tear	crystal-clear	pierced ear
dear	rear	year	disappear	reappear
fear	shear	all clear	far and near	Shakespeare
gear	smear	appear	leap year	unclear
hear	spear			

-ease

cease	lease	decrease	press release	world peace
crease	peace	elbow grease	release	
grease	decease	increase	time-release	

-east

beast	least	Far East	Middle East	Near East
feast	yeast			

-eat

beat	heat	seat	deadbeat	overeat
bleat	meat	treat	defeat	repeat
cheat	neat	wheat	heartbeat	retreat
cleat	peat	backseat	mistreat	upbeat
feat	pleat	browbeat	off-beat	

-eath

heath	wreath	beneath	bequeath	underneath
sheath				

-eave

cleave	leave	sheave	weave	sick leave
heave				

-ee

bee	tee	degree	oversee	sugar-free
fee	three	disagree	pedigree	tax-free
flee	tree	emcee	peewee	tee-hee
free	wee	employee	queen bee	teepee
glee	absentee	fiddle-de-dee	referee	Tennessee
knee	agree	guarantee	refugee	worry-free
Lee	bumblebee	home-free	shopping spree	
see	caffeine-free	jamboree	sightsee	
spree	carefree	nominee	spelling bee	

-eech

beech	leech	speech	free speech	figure of speech
breech	screech			

-eed

bleed	greed	tweed	full speed	refereed
breed	heed	weed	guaranteed	seaweed
creed	need	agreed	indeed	succeed
deed	reed	disagreed	nosebleed	tumbleweed
feed	seed	exceed	overfeed	up to speed
freed	speed	force-feed	proceed	

Teaching Phonics & Word Study in the Intermediate Grades • Scholastic Professional Books

-eek

cheek	leek	reek	week	cheek-to-cheek
creek	meek	seek	midweek	hide-and-seek
Greek	peek	sleek		

-eel

feel	peel	wheel	Ferris wheel	high heel
heel	reel	cartwheel	genteel	newsreel
kneel	steel			

-eem

| deem | seem | teem | esteem | redeem | self-esteem |

-een

green	teen	evergreen	Kathleen	sixteen
keen	between	fifteen	movie screen	smokescreen
queen	canteen	fourteen	preteen	sunscreen
screen	colleen	go-between	prom queen	thirteen
seen	eighteen	Halloween	seventeen	unseen

-eep

beep	jeep	sheep	weep	oversleep
cheep	keep	sleep	asleep	skin-deep
creep	peep	steep	beauty sleep	
deep	seep	sweep	knee-deep	

-eer

deer	sneer	root beer	engineer	pioneer
jeer	steer	auctioneer	musketeer	racketeer
peer	career	buccaneer	mutineer	volunteer
queer	reindeer			

-eet

beet	meet	street	bittersweet	indiscreet
feet	sheet	sweet	cold feet	parakeet
fleet	skeet	tweet	discreet	Wall Street
greet	sleet			

-eeze

breeze	sneeze	tweeze	antifreeze	freezer
freeze	squeeze	wheeze	deep freeze	sea breeze

-iece

niece	apiece	centerpiece	hairpiece	timepiece
piece				

-ief

brief	thief	debrief	fire chief	handkerchief
chief	belief	disbelief	good grief	relief
grief				

-ield

field	shield	yield	mine field	windshield

Long-i Phonograms

-ibe

bribe	tribe	diatribe	inscribe	subscribe
scribe	describe	imbibe	prescribe	transcribe

-ice

dice	price	thrice	device	sacrifice
lice	rice	twice	entice	self-sacrifice
mice	slice	vice	sale price	
nice	splice	advice	suffice	

-ide

bride	snide	confide	misguide	worldwide
glide	stride	decide	outside	coincide
hide	tide	divide	provide	insecticide
pride	wide	fireside	reside	
ride	bedside	inside	riptide	
side	chloride	joyride	roadside	
slide	collide	landslide	subside	

Teaching Phonics & Word Study in the Intermediate Grades • Scholastic Professional Books

-ie

die	tie	bow tie	mud pie	apple pie
lie	vie	hog-tie	necktie	underlie
pie	black tie	magpie	tongue-tie	

-ied

cried	clarified	glorified	notified	replied
died	deep-fried	horrified	occupied	satisfied
dried	defied	identified	pacified	supplied
fried	denied	implied	personified	terrified
lied	dignified	justified	petrified	tongue-tied
spied	disqualified	magnified	preoccupied	unsatisfied
tried	dissatisfied	modified	qualified	untied
applied	exemplified	multiplied	relied	verified

-ier

brier	crier	drier	flier

-ies

cries	butterflies	French fries	mystifies	replies
dies	certifies	glorifies	neckties	satisfies
dries	clarifies	horrifies	notifies	signifies
flies	defies	identifies	occupies	simplifies
lies	demystifies	implies	outcries	solidifies
pies	denies	justifies	pacifies	specifies
skies	disqualifies	lullabies	personifies	stupefies
spies	dissatisfies	magnifies	pigsties	supplies
ties	dragonflies	modifies	preoccupies	terrifies
tries	drip-dries	mortifies	qualifies	unifies
applies	exemplifies	mud pies	ratifies	unties
beautifies	family ties	multiplies	relies	verifies

-ife

fife	rife	wife	jackknife	nightlife
knife	strife	housewife	larger-than-life	wildlife
life				

-igh

high	nigh	sigh	thigh

-ight

blight	slight	firelight	limelight	searchlight
bright	tight	fistfight	midnight	skintight
fight	airtight	flashlight	moonlight	stage fright
flight	all right	foresight	night-light	starlight
fright	all-night	forthright	not quite	stoplight
knight	birthright	good night	out-of-sight	sunlight
light	bullfight	green light	outright	tonight
might	civil right	headlight	overnight	twilight
night	copyright	highlight	oversight	upright
plight	daylight	hindsight	playwright	uptight
right	delight	insight	prizefight	
sight	eyesight			

-ike

bike	Mike	alike	hunger strike	motorbike
dike	pike	childlike	ladylike	unlike
hike	spike	dislike	lifelike	warlike
like	strike	hitchhike	look-alike	

-ild

child	wild	brainchild	hogwild	stepchild
mild				

-ile

file	vile	exile	reconcile	woodpile
mile	while	infantile	reptile	worthwhile
Nile	awhile	juvenile	senile	
pile	bibliophile	meanwhile	single file	
smile	crocodile	nail file	stockpile	
tile	domicile	profile	turnstile	

Teaching Phonics & Word Study in the Intermediate Grades • Scholastic Professional Books

-ime

chime	slime	lifetime	part-time	springtime
crime	time	maritime	pastime	sublime
dime	anytime	meantime	peacetime	summertime
grime	bedtime	nighttime	prime time	wartime
lime	bigtime	old-time	showtime	
mime	daytime	overtime	small-time	
prime	dinnertime	pantomime	sometime	

-ind

bind	kind	change of mind	never mind	unkind
blind	mind	colorblind	one-track mind	unwind
find	rind	humankind	peace of mind	
grind	wind	lemon rind	remind	
hind	behind	mastermind	snow-blind	

-ine

dine	alpine	deadline	hot line	refine
fine	assign	decline	incline	shoeshine
line	baseline	define	intertwine	sideline
mine	beeline	divine	iodine	skyline
nine	borderline	entwine	lifeline	storyline
pine	canine	feline	neckline	streamline
shine	checkout line	goal line	outline	sunshine
shrine	clothesline	gold mine	outshine	underline
spine	cloud nine	grapevine	picket line	undermine
swine	coal mine	guideline	pipeline	valentine
vine	coastline	hairline	porcupine	
whine	combine	headline	punch line	
airline	confine	hemline	recline	

-ipe

gripe	snipe	wipe	peace pipe	tailpipe
pipe	stripe	bagpipe	pinstripe	unripe
ripe	swipe	overripe	sideswipe	windpipe

-ire

fire	aspire	crossfire	inspire	satire
hire	attire	desire	live wire	spitfire
spire	backfire	entire	on fire	surefire
tire	barbed wire	expire	overtire	transpire
wire	bonfire	flat tire	perspire	umpire
acquire	campfire	haywire	require	vampire
admire	cease-fire	hot-wire	retire	
afire	conspire	inquire	sapphire	

-ise

guise	chastise	disguise	likewise	televise
rise	clockwise	enterprise	otherwise	unwise
wise	comprise	exercise	revise	
advertise	compromise	franchise	sunrise	
advise	despise	high-rise	supervise	
arise	devise	improvise	surprise	

-ite

bite	white	frostbite	overbite	Snow White
kite	write	ignite	parasite	socialite
mite	appetite	impolite	polite	termite
quite	black-and-white	incite	recite	unite
rite	dynamite	invite	reunite	
site	excite	meteorite	satellite	
sprite	finite	not quite	snakebite	

-ive

chive	live	beehive	high dive	survive
dive	strive	connive	high five	take five
drive	thrive	contrive	nine-to-five	test drive
five	alive	crash-drive	nosedive	
hive	archive	deep-sea dive	revive	
jive	arrive	deprive	skydive	

-uy

buy	guy	wise guy

Teaching Phonics & Word Study in the Intermediate Grades • Scholastic Professional Books

-y

by	blow-dry	exemplify	multiply	rely
cry	butterfly	falsify	mummify	reply
dry	camera-shy	firefly	mystify	satisfy
fly	certify	fortify	nearby	signify
fry	clarify	glorify	notify	simplify
my	classify	gratify	nullify	small fry
ply	comply	horrify	occupy	solidify
pry	crucify	horsefly	outcry	specify
shy	deep-fry	hush-a-by	pacify	standby
sky	defy	identify	passerby	stupefy
sly	demystify	imply	personify	supply
spy	deny	intensify	petrify	terrify
try	dignify	July	pigsty	testify
why	disqualify	justify	preoccupy	tsetse fly
ally	dissatisfy	lullaby	purify	unify
amplify	dragonfly	magnify	qualify	verify
apply	drip-dry	modify	ratify	war cry
beautify	electrify	mortify	rectify	

-ye

bye	lye	bye-bye	good-bye	private eye
dye	rye	eye to eye	Popeye	shut-eye
eye	bull's eye			

Long-o Phonograms

-o

go	dynamo	Mexico	pueblo	stop and go
no	get-up-and-go	Navajo	radio	studio
pro	golf pro	New Mexico	ratio	to and fro
so	gung-ho	no-go	ready, set, go	Tokyo
ago	heave-ho	no-no	rodeo	touch and go
Alamo	hello	piccolo	Romeo	video
buffalo	Idaho	Pinocchio	so-so	yes and no
calico	info	pistachio	status quo	yo-yo
do-si-do	long ago	portfolio	stereo	

-oach

broach	poach	approach	reproach	stagecoach
coach	roach	cockroach		

-oad

load	carload	hit the road	railroad	unload
road	crossroad	overload	truckload	workload
toad	freeload			

-oak

cloak	croak	oak	soak	poison oak

-oal

coal	foal	goal	charcoal

-oam

foam	loam	roam

-oan

groan	Joan	loan	moan

-oast

boast	roast	toast	pot roast	coast-to-coast
coast				

-oat

bloat	goat	cutthroat	raincoat	steamboat
boat	moat	dreamboat	rock the boat	sugarcoat
coat	oat	lifeboat	rowboat	turncoat
float	throat	overcoat	scapegoat	
gloat	afloat	petticoat	sore throat	

-obe

globe	probe	bathrobe	earlobe	wardrobe
lobe	robe	disrobe	space probe	

Teaching Phonics & Word Study in the Intermediate Grades • Scholastic Professional Books

-ode

code	rode	area code	episode	Morse code
lode	strode	decode	erode	penal code
mode	à la mode	dress code	explode	zip code
node	abode	electrode	implode	

-oe

doe	hoe	toe	mistletoe	tic-tac-toe
foe	Joe	woe	Sloppy Joe	tippy-toe

-oke

broke	smoke	yoke	cowpoke	provoke
choke	spoke	artichoke	dead broke	slowpoke
coke	stoke	awoke	go for broke	sunstroke
joke	stroke	cloud of smoke	heatstroke	
poke	woke			

-old

bold	old	billfold	household	stronghold
cold	scold	blindfold	ice-cold	threshold
fold	sold	choke hold	out cold	toehold
gold	told	common cold	pot of gold	unfold
hold	age-old	enfold	retold	untold
mold	behold	foothold	stranglehold	withhold

-ole

dole	whole	Creole	loophole	porthole
hole	buttonhole	cubbyhole	manhole	pothole
mole	cajole	fishing pole	north pole	tadpole
pole	camisole	flagpole	parole	totem pole
role	casserole	foxhole	peephole	
stole	console	keyhole	pigeonhole	

-oll

droll	roll	toll	egg roll	rock and roll
knoll	scroll	troll	enroll	steamroll
poll	stroll	drum roll	payroll	unroll

-olt

bolt	jolt	volt	lightning bolt	revolt
colt	molt	deadbolt		

-ome

chrome	home	Rome	metronome	palindrome
dome	Nome	foster home	mobile home	syndrome
gnome				

-one

bone	zone	dethrone	monotone	telephone
clone	accident-prone	dial tone	outshone	time zone
cone	alone	end zone	ozone	tombstone
drone	backbone	funny bone	pay phone	twilight zone
hone	baritone	grindstone	pinecone	war zone
lone	birthstone	headphone	postpone	wishbone
phone	buffer zone	headstone	rhinestone	xylophone
prone	car phone	hormone	saxophone	Yellowstone
shone	cobblestone	jawbone	sno-cone	
stone	condone	microphone	stepping-stone	
tone	cyclone	milestone	T-bone	

-ope

cope	nope	slope	horoscope	stethoscope
dope	pope	antelope	jump rope	telescope
hope	rope	elope	microscope	tightrope
mope	scope	envelope	periscope	towrope

-ose

chose	prose	enclose	open and close	pug nose
close	rose	expose	oppose	runny nose
hose	those	fire hose	overexpose	suppose
nose	decompose	impose	panty hose	
pose	dispose	nose-to-nose	propose	

Teaching Phonics & Word Study in the Intermediate Grades • Scholastic Professional Books

-ost

ghost	post	goalpost	innermost	topmost
host	almost	guidepost	outpost	trading post
most	bedpost	hitching post	signpost	utmost

-ote

note	vote	antidote	keynote	promote
quote	wrote	devote	misquote	remote
rote	anecdote	footnote	outvote	

-ove

| clove | drove | stove | wove | by Jove |
| cove | grove | trove | alcove | |

-ow

blow	low	stow	game show	right-to-know
bow	mow	tow	high and low	scarecrow
crow	row	aglow	low blow	sideshow
flow	show	below	no show	skid row
glow	slow	blow by blow	outgrow	talent show
grow	snow	ebb and flow	overflow	talk show
know	sow	fashion show	rainbow	undertow

-own

blown	known	sown	full-blown	well-known
flown	mown	thrown	full-grown	windblown
grown	shown	disown	homegrown	

Short-a Phonograms

-ab

blab	drab	jab	slab	rehab
cab	flab	lab	stab	sand crab
crab	gab	nab	tab	taxicab
dab	grab	scab	backstab	

-ack

back	rack	backpack	heart attack	piggyback
black	sack	backtrack	hijack	quarterback
clack	shack	blackjack	icepack	racetrack
crack	slack	camelback	jumping jack	railroad track
hack	smack	crackerjack	knapsack	ransack
Jack	snack	drawback	laugh track	setback
knack	stack	feedback	lumberjack	sidetrack
lack	tack	flapjack	off-track	soundtrack
Mack	track	flashback	one-track	thumbtack
pack	whack	fullback	panic attack	unpack
quack	attack	haystack	paperback	wisecrack

-act

fact	artifact	enact	interact	riot act
pact	attract	exact	matter of fact	subtract
tact	compact	extract	overact	transact
tract	contract	impact	overreact	
abstract	distract	in fact	react	

-ad

bad	fad	pad	granddad	shoulder pad
Brad	glad	sad	ink pad	Sinbad
Chad	had	tad	ironclad	too bad
clad	lad	doodad	launching pad	Trinidad
dad	mad	egad	nomad	undergrad

-aft

craft	graft	waft	life raft	spacecraft
daft	raft	aircraft	mine shaft	witchcraft
draft	shaft			

-ag

bag	flag	nag	snag	beanbag
brag	gag	rag	stag	dishrag
crag	jag	sag	tag	dog tag
drag	lag	shag	wag	doggie bag

Teaching Phonics & Word Study in the Intermediate Grades • Scholastic Professional Books

grab bag	mailbag	saddlebag	tea bag	windbag
jet lag	name tag	sandbag	trash bag	zigzag
litterbag	price tag	sleeping bag	washrag	
lollygag	ragtag			

-am

am	Pam	swam	flimflam	telegram
clam	ram	tam	grand slam	traffic jam
cram	Sam	yam	in a jam	Uncle Sam
dam	scam	Abraham	madame	
gram	scram	anagram	milligram	
ham	sham	diagram	outswam	
jam	slam	exam	program	

-amp

camp	cramp	ramp	tramp	summer camp
champ	damp	scamp	vamp	writer's cramp
clamp	lamp	stamp	postage stamp	

-an

ban	plan	cancan	hangman	overran
bran	ran	caravan	Japan	Pakistan
can	scan	catamaran	lawman	sandman
clan	span	caveman	life span	sedan
Dan	tan	deadpan	madman	spic-and-span
fan	than	dishpan	moving van	suntan
flan	van	dustpan	oat bran	time span
man	attention span	frying pan	orangutan	trashcan
pan	began	handyman	outran	

-ance

chance	prance	circumstance	finance	romance
dance	stance	enhance	folk dance	song and dance
France	trance	entrance	freelance	square dance
glance	advance	fat chance	last chance	tap dance
lance	break dance	fighting chance	rain dance	

Teaching Phonics & Word Study in the Intermediate Grades • Scholastic Professional Books

-anch

blanch	branch	ranch

-and

band	armband	crash-land	handstand	quicksand
bland	baby grand	demand	headband	reprimand
brand	backhand	disband	helping hand	rubber band
gland	bandstand	dreamland	homeland	secondhand
hand	beforehand	expand	kickstand	shorthand
land	close-at-hand	fantasy land	longhand	Thailand
sand	command	firsthand	misunderstand	understand
stand	contraband	grandstand	name-brand	wasteland
strand	cowhand	hand-in-hand	offhand	

-ang

bang	gang	rang	sprang	chain gang
clang	hang	sang	twang	mustang
fang	pang	slang	boomerang	overhang

-ank

bank	frank	sank	blankety-blank	military rank
blank	Hank	shrank	blood bank	outrank
clank	lank	spank	data bank	point-blank
crank	plank	tank	draw a blank	savings bank
dank	prank	thank	fish tank	think tank
drank	rank	yank	gangplank	

-ant

ant	pant	slant	enchant	power plant
can't	plant	disenchant	gallivant	supplant
chant	rant	eggplant	implant	transplant
grant	scant			

Teaching Phonics & Word Study in the Intermediate Grades • Scholastic Professional Books

-ap

cap	sap	backslap	gift wrap	overlap
chap	scrap	baseball cap	gingersnap	recap
clap	slap	bottle cap	handicap	road map
flap	snap	burlap	hubcap	thinking cap
gap	strap	catnap	kidnap	tourist trap
lap	tap	dunce cap	kneecap	unwrap
map	trap	firetrap	madcap	wiretap
nap	wrap	gender gap	mishap	
rap	yap	generation gap	mousetrap	

-ash

bash	gash	slash	balderdash	succotash
brash	hash	smash	corned beef hash	whiplash
cash	lash	stash	diaper rash	
clash	mash	thrash	eyelash	
dash	rash	trash	mishmash	
flash	sash	backlash	news flash	

-ask

ask	cask	flask	mask	task

-asm

chasm	plasm	spasm	enthusiasm	sarcasm

-asp

clasp	gasp	grasp	hasp	rasp

-ast

blast	vast	contrast	gymnast	outlast
cast	aghast	downcast	half-mast	overcast
fast	all-star cast	enthusiast	iconoclast	sandblast
last	at last	flabbergast	miscast	steadfast
mast	bombast	forecast	newscast	telecast
past	broadcast	full blast	outcast	typecast

-at

at	mat	vat	cowboy hat	muskrat
bat	pat	acrobat	democrat	nonfat
brat	rat	alley cat	dingbat	pack rat
cat	sat	aristocrat	diplomat	place mat
chat	scat	baby fat	doormat	thermostat
fat	slat	bureaucrat	format	tomcat
flat	spat	chitchat	habitat	welcome mat
gnat	splat	combat	hardhat	wildcat
hat	that	copy cat	laundromat	wombat

-atch

batch	match	thatch	cabbage patch	mismatch
catch	patch	arm patch	detach	mix and match
hatch	scratch	attach	dispatch	reattach
latch	snatch	boxing match	knee patch	unlatch

-ath

bath	path	aftermath	bubble-bath	steam bath
math	wrath	birdbath	psychopath	warpath

-ax

ax	lax	tax	climax	relax
fax	max	wax	earwax	
flax	sax	candle wax	income tax	

Short-e Phonograms

-ead

bread	thread	drop dead	homestead	redhead
dead	tread	egghead	instead	sleepyhead
dread	ahead	figurehead	knucklehead	spearhead
head	arrowhead	forehead	letterhead	straight ahead
lead	bald head	French bread	misread	widespread
read	behead	gingerbread	overhead	
spread	blockhead	hardhead	proofread	

Teaching Phonics & Word Study in the Intermediate Grades • Scholastic Professional Books

-ealth

health	stealth	wealth

-eath

death	bad breath	out of breath	scared to death	starve to death
breath	kiss of death			

-eck

check	neck	bottleneck	pain in the neck	rubberneck
deck	peck	double-check	paycheck	shipwreck
fleck	speck	hit the deck	raincheck	spot-check
heck	wreck	neck and neck	roughneck	turtleneck

-ed

bed	red	bobsled	inbred	underfed
bled	shed	bottle-fed	infrared	unwed
bred	shred	bunkbed	moped	waterbed
fed	sled	city-bred	newlywed	well-bred
fled	sped	coed	overfed	well-fed
Fred	Ted	deathbed	sickbed	
led	wed	early to bed	spoon-fed	
Ned	biped	ill-bred	thoroughbred	

-edge

dredge	hedge	pledge	wedge	on edge
edge	ledge	sledge		

-eft

cleft	left	theft

-eg

beg	leg	Meg	peg	Winnipeg
keg				

-eld

held	weld	hand-held	upheld	withheld
meld	beheld			

Teaching Phonics & Word Study in the Intermediate Grades • Scholastic Professional Books

-elf

elf	shelf	herself	itself	yourself
self	bookshelf	himself	myself	

-ell

bell	sell	yell	gazelle	school bell
cell	shell	bombshell	inkwell	show and tell
dell	smell	dinner bell	jail cell	sleigh bell
dwell	spell	doorbell	misspell	unwell
fell	swell	dumbbell	nutshell	very well
jell	tell	eggshell	oil well	wishing well
Nell	well	farewell	retell	

-elp

help	kelp	yelp

-elt

belt	felt	melt	welt	seat belt
dwelt	knelt	pelt	heartfelt	

-em

gem	hem	stem	them

-en

Ben	Ken	then	amen	mother hen
den	men	when	bullpen	now and then
glen	pen	wren	hang ten	pigpen
hen	ten	yen	lion's den	playpen

-ence

fence	pence	commence	consequence	evidence
hence	whence			

-ench

bench	French	trench	monkey wrench	unclench
clench	quench	wrench	park bench	
drench	stench			

Teaching Phonics & Word Study in the Intermediate Grades • Scholastic Professional Books

-end

bend	spend	attend	dividend	recommend
blend	tend	bitter end	end-to-end	suspend
end	trend	comprehend	extend	transcend
fend	vend	dead end	intend	unbend
lend	amend	defend	offend	upend
mend	apprehend	depend	overspend	wit's end
send	ascend	descend	pretend	

-ength

length	strength

-ense

dense	defense	immense	no-nonsense	self-defense
sense	dispense	incense	nonsense	sixth sense
tense	expense	intense	offense	suspense
common sense	false pretense	make sense	pretense	
condense	good sense			

-ent

bent	spent	content	frequent	misspent
cent	tent	descent	heaven sent	percent
dent	vent	discontent	implement	present
gent	went	dissent	indent	prevent
Kent	air vent	event	intent	repent
lent	cement	evident	invent	represent
rent	circus tent	experiment	lament	resent
scent	compliment	extent	malcontent	torment
sent	consent	for rent	misrepresent	underwent

-ep

pep	rep	strep	bicep	overstep
prep	step	yep	doorstep	sidestep

-ept

crept	swept	concept	intercept	rainswept
kept	wept	except	overslept	windswept
slept	accept	inept		

-esh

flesh	mesh	enmesh	in the flesh	refresh
fresh	Bangladesh	gooseflesh		

-ess

Bess	access	duress	outguess	regress
bless	address	excess	overdress	repossess
chess	air express	express	pony express	repress
dress	bench-press	full-court press	possess	second-guess
guess	caress	impress	printing press	success
less	confess	more or less	profess	suppress
mess	depress	nevertheless	progress	undress
press	digress	nonetheless	recess	unless
stress	distress	oppress		

-est

best	rest	blood test	hope chest	protest
blest	test	bulletproof vest	hornet's nest	request
chest	vest	conquest	invest	screen test
crest	west	contest	level best	second best
jest	wrest	crow's nest	life vest	suggest
lest	zest	decongest	manifest	treasure chest
nest	arrest	detest	medicine chest	under arrest
pest	beauty rest	fun-fest	next best	Wild West
quest	bird nest			

-et

bet	pet	bassinet	jet set	reset
Chet	set	bayonet	Juliet	safety net
fret	wet	better yet	minuet	Soviet
get	yet	cadet	mosquito net	sunset
jet	abet	clarinet	not yet	teacher's pet
let	all set	dragnet	quartet	Tibet
met	all wet	duet	regret	upset
net	alphabet	forget		

Teaching Phonics & Word Study in the Intermediate Grades • Scholastic Professional Books

-etch

etch	retch	stretch	wretch	homestretch
fetch	sketch			

-ext

next	text	context		

Short-i Phonograms

-ib

bib	fib	rib	prime rib	sparerib
crib	glib	ad lib		

-ick

brick	pick	trick	handpick	sidekick
chick	quick	wick	heartsick	slapstick
click	Rick	airsick	homesick	toothpick
Dick	sick	broomstick	lipstick	yardstick
flick	slick	card trick	lovesick	candlestick
kick	stick	chopstick	nit-pick	dirty trick
lick	thick	drumstick	seasick	
nick	tick			

-id

bid	lid	squid	hybrid	overdid
did	mid	amid	Madrid	pyramid
grid	rid	arachnid	outbid	redid
hid	skid	eyelid	outdid	whiz kid
kid	slid	forbid		

-iff

cliff	sniff	tiff	midriff	scared stiff
miff	stiff	whiff		

-ift

drift	shift	airlift	night shift	snowdrift
gift	sift	face-lift	shoplift	spendthrift
lift	swift	makeshift	ski lift	uplift
rift	thrift			

-ig

big	gig	sprig	wig	oil rig
brig	jig	swig	bigwig	shindig
dig	pig	twig	guinea pig	thingamajig
fig	rig			

-ilk

bilk	ilk	milk	silk	buttermilk

-ill

bill	Jill	thrill	freewill	standstill
chill	kill	trill	fulfill	treadmill
dill	mill	twill	goodwill	uphill
drill	pill	will	ill will	whippoorwill
fill	quill	anthill	instill	windmill
frill	sill	Capitol Hill	Jack and Jill	windowsill
gill	skill	chlorophyll	oil spill	
grill	spill	dollar bill	overkill	
hill	still	downhill	refill	
ill	till	fire drill	run-of-the-mill	

-ilt

built	jilt	lilt	spilt	tilt
hilt	kilt	quilt	stilt	wilt

-im

brim	him	prim	swim	whim
dim	Jim	rim	Tim	sink or swim
grim	Kim	slim	trim	

Teaching Phonics & Word Study in the Intermediate Grades • Scholastic Professional Books

-imp

blimp	crimp	primp	skimp	wimp
chimp	limp	shrimp		

-in

bin	sin	bobby-pin	next of kin	stand-in
chin	skin	bowling pin	pigskin	tailspin
din	spin	break-in	rolling pin	thick and thin
fin	thin	cave-in	Rumpelstiltskin	trash bin
grin	tin	double chin	safety pin	unpin
in	twin	drive-in	sheepskin	violin
kin	win	hairpin	shoo-in	within
pin	begin	mandolin	snakeskin	
shin	Berlin			

-ince

mince	prince	since	wince	convince

-inch

cinch	finch	inch	pinch	inch by inch
clinch	flinch			

-ing

bring	sing	wing	class ring	porch swing
cling	sling	wring	drawstring	shoestring
ding	spring	zing	earring	something
fling	sting	anything	everything	static cling
king	string	bee sting	first-string	wing-ding
ping	swing	Beijing	offspring	
ring	thing	boxing ring	plaything	

-inge

binge	fringe	singe	tinge	infringe
cringe	hinge			

Teaching Phonics & Word Study in the Intermediate Grades • Scholastic Professional Books

-ink

blink	link	slink	hoodwink	rinky-dink
brink	mink	stink	hot pink	roller rink
clink	pink	think	missing link	soft drink
drink	rink	wink	pen and ink	tickled pink
ink	shrink	cuff link	rethink	
kink	sink			

-int

flint	print	tint	footprint	peppermint
glint	splint	blueprint	imprint	shin splint
hint	sprint	fine print	misprint	spearmint
lint	squint	fingerprint	newsprint	U.S. Mint
mint	stint			

-ip

blip	ship	bean dip	fellowship	penmanship
chip	sip	catnip	field trip	potato chip
clip	skip	censorship	fingertip	round trip
dip	slip	championship	friendship	salesmanship
drip	snip	chocolate chip	guardianship	scholarship
flip	strip	citizenship	hardship	spaceship
grip	tip	comic strip	internship	sportsmanship
hip	trip	companionship	kinship	stiff upper lip
lip	whip	courtship	leadership	unzip
nip	zip	dictatorship	membership	
quip	apprenticeship	double-dip	ownership	
rip	battleship	equip	paper clip	

-is

his	is			

-ish

dish	squish	wish	goldfish	jellyfish
fish	swish			

Teaching Phonics & Word Study in the Intermediate Grades • Scholastic Professional Books

-isk

brisk	frisk	whisk	floppy disk	slipped disk
disk	risk	asterisk	high risk	

-isp

crisp	lisp	wisp

-iss

bliss	kiss	Swiss	dismiss	near miss
hiss	miss	amiss	hit or miss	

-ist

fist	twist	checklist	exist	resist
gist	wrist	coexist	insist	shopping list
list	assist	consist	persist	tongue twist
mist	blacklist	enlist	price list	

-it

bit	skit	bit by bit	moonlit	submit
fit	slit	bottomless pit	nitwit	sunlit
flit	spit	close-knit	omit	switch-hit
grit	split	cockpit	outfit	tar pit
hit	wit	commit	outwit	throw a fit
kit	acquit	counterfeit	perfect fit	tight fit
knit	admit	first aid kit	permit	tool kit
lit	armpit	legit	pinch-hit	transmit
pit	baby-sit	lickety-split	smash hit	unfit
quit	banana split	misfit	snake pit	
sit	benefit			

-itch

ditch	itch	switch	bewitch	master switch
glitch	pitch	twitch	fever pitch	unhitch
hitch	stitch	witch	light switch	

-ive				
give	live	forgive	outlive	relive

-ix				
fix	nix	cake mix	quick fix	transfix
mix	six			

Short-o Phonograms

-ob				
blob	job	slob	corn on the cob	hobnob
Bob	knob	snob	corncob	inside job
cob	lob	sob	doorknob	snow job
glob	mob	throb	heartthrob	thingamabob
gob	rob	con job		

-ock				
block	rock	cell block	laughingstock	shamrock
clock	shock	cuckoo clock	livestock	shell shock
crock	smock	culture shock	mental block	Sherlock
dock	sock	deadlock	o'clock	stumbling block
flock	stock	gridlock	out of stock	sunblock
frock	tock	hard rock	padlock	tick-tock
hock	aftershock	headlock	peacock	unlock
knock	alarm clock	Hitchcock	roadblock	woodblock
lock	auction block	knock-knock	round-the-clock	writer's block
mock				

-od				
clod	nod	rod	cattle prod	lightning rod
cod	plod	sod	fishing rod	pea pod
God	pod	trod	goldenrod	slipshod
mod	prod	Cape Cod	hot rod	tripod

Teaching Phonics & Word Study in the Intermediate Grades • Scholastic Professional Books

-oft

loft	soft

-og

bog	fog	smog	groundhog	top dog
clog	frog	bulldog	hounddog	underdog
cog	hog	bullfrog	leapfrog	watchdog
dog	jog	catalog	road hog	
flog	log	chili dog	ship's log	

-omp

chomp	pomp	stomp	tromp	whomp
clomp	romp			

-ond

blond	fond	beyond	fishpond	vagabond
bond	pond	correspond	respond	

-op

bop	slop	box top	karate chop	shortstop
chop	sop	bus stop	kerplop	teardrop
cop	stop	coffee shop	lemon drop	tiptop
crop	top	cough drop	lollipop	traffic-stop
drop	Aesop	cream of the crop	mountaintop	treetop
flop	barbershop	doorstop	name-drop	truck stop
hop	bebop	eavesdrop	nonstop	window shop
mop	bellhop	flattop	pawnshop	workshop
plop	belly flop	flip-flop	pit stop	
pop	big top	gumdrop	pork chop	
prop	blacktop	hilltop	raindrop	
shop	body shop	hip hop	rooftop	

-ot

blot	pot	bloodshot	hot shot	parking lot
clot	rot	boiling hot	hot to trot	polka dot
cot	shot	Camelot	inkblot	red-hot
dot	slot	cannot	jackpot	slingshot
got	spot	coffee-pot	Lancelot	snapshot
hot	tot	flowerpot	long shot	teapot
jot	trot	forget-me-not	mascot	thanks a lot
knot	apricot	forgot	melting pot	tie the knot
lot	beauty spot	gunshot	on the dot	tight spot
not	big shot	hit the spot	on the spot	whatnot
plot	blind spot			

-otch

blotch	crotch	notch	hopscotch	topnotch
botch				

-ough

cough	trough

-ox

box	cash box	jack-in-the-box	outfox	soap box
fox	chatterbox	lunchbox	paradox	toy box
lox	chickenpox	mailbox	sandbox	unorthodox
ox	detox	music box	shadowbox	Xerox
pox	Fort Knox	orthodox		

Short-u Phonograms

-ome

come	some	become	outcome	overcome

-on

son	ton	won	grandson

140

-ough

rough	tough	fair enough	rough and tough	sure enough
slough	enough			

-ove

dove	shove	labor of love	puppy love	turtledove
glove	above	none of the above	self-love	
love	boxing glove			

-ub

club	hub	snub	bathtub	hubbub
cub	nub	stub	billy club	lion cub
dub	rub	sub	fan club	nightclub
flub	scrub	tub	hot tub	ticket stub
grub	shrub	backrub		

-uch

much	such	not much	pretty much	such and such

-uck

buck	puck	beginner's luck	lame duck	stagestruck
Chuck	struck	dumbstruck	lovestruck	starstruck
cluck	stuck	fire truck	moonstruck	thunderstruck
duck	suck	good luck	out of luck	tough luck
luck	truck	hockey puck	pass the buck	tow truck
muck	tuck	horror-struck	potluck	woodchuck
pluck	awestruck	lady luck	sitting duck	

-ud

bud	dud	spud	thud	stick in the mud
crud	mud	stud	rosebud	taste bud
cud				

-udge

budge	grudge	sludge	trudge	misjudge
drudge	judge	smudge	hot fudge	prejudge
fudge	nudge			

-uff

bluff	gruff	scuff	blindman's bluff	kid stuff
buff	huff	sluff	cream puff	overstuff
cuff	puff	snuff	handcuff	powder puff
fluff	ruff	stuff	huff and puff	rebuff

-ug

bug	lug	slug	bedbug	humbug
chug	mug	smug	chugalug	jitterbug
drug	plug	snug	doodlebug	ladybug
dug	pug	thug	earplug	litterbug
hug	rug	tug	fireplug	unplug
jug	shrug	bear hug		

-ulk

bulk	hulk	skulk	sulk

-ull

cull	gull	lull	skull	sea gull
dull	hull	mull	numskull	

-um

bum	hum	slum	bubble gum	fee-fie-fo-fum
chum	mum	strum	chewing gum	ho-hum
drum	plum	sum	chrysanthemum	humdrum
glum	rum	yum	eardrum	yum-yum
gum	scum	beach bum		

-umb

crumb	plumb	cookie crumb	green thumb	succumb
dumb	thumb	deaf and dumb	rule of thumb	Tom Thumb
numb				

Teaching Phonics & Word Study in the Intermediate Grades • Scholastic Professional Books

-ump

bump	grump	pump	trump	speed bump
chump	hump	rump	broad jump	stomach pump
clump	jump	slump	city dump	trash dump
dump	lump	stump	goose bump	tree stump
frump	plump	thump	ski jump	triple jump

-un

bun	shun	begun	home run	rerun
fun	spun	blowgun	homespun	shotgun
gun	stun	dog run	honeybun	top gun
pun	sun	hamburger bun	jump the gun	trial run
run	Attila the Hun	hit-and-run	outrun	

-unch

brunch	hunch	punch	honeybunch	school lunch
bunch	lunch	scrunch	out to lunch	whole bunch
crunch	munch	fruit punch		

-ung

clung	rung	stung	wrung	high-strung
flung	sprung	sung	egg foo yung	iron lung
hung	strung	swung	far-flung	unsung
lung				

-unk

bunk	flunk	shrunk	stunk	kerplunk
chunk	hunk	skunk	sunk	preshrunk
drunk	junk	slunk	trunk	slam dunk
dunk	plunk	spunk	chipmunk	

-unt

blunt	grunt	punt	stunt	treasure hunt
bunt	hunt	runt	manhunt	witch hunt

-up

cup	buildup	dress up	mix-up	shut up
pup	buttercup	foul-up	paper cup	stickup
sup	checkup	giddy-up	pick-me-up	teacup
all shook up	close-up	grown-up	pickup	throw up
backup	coffee cup	hang-up	roundup	toss-up
blowup	cover-up	hiccup	runner-up	touch-up
breakup	crackup	lineup	setup	washed-up
buckle up	cutup	makeup		

-us

| bus | pus | us | nonplus | school bus |
| plus | thus | make a fuss | | |

-ush

blush	gush	plush	bum's rush	hairbrush
brush	hush	rush	cheek blush	hush-hush
crush	lush	slush	gold rush	toothbrush
flush	mush	thrush		

-ust

bust	rust	coal dust	entrust	sawdust
crust	thrust	combust	gold dust	stardust
dust	trust	crop dust	mistrust	unjust
gust	adjust	disgust	pie crust	wanderlust
just	bite the dust	distrust	robust	
must	brain trust			

-ut

but	nut	clear-cut	King Tut	uncut
cut	rut	coconut	open and shut	undercut
glut	shut	haircut	precut	uppercut
gut	strut	halibut	rebut	
hut	catgut	in a rut	shortcut	
jut	chestnut			

-utch

| clutch | crutch | Dutch | hutch | rabbit hutch |

Teaching Phonics & Word Study in the Intermediate Grades • Scholastic Professional Books

-utt

butt	mutt	putt	scuttlebutt

Variant Vowel /âr/ Phonograms

-air

air	pair	dentist chair	midair	repair
chair	stair	despair	millionaire	rocking chair
fair	affair	fresh air	no fair	solitaire
flair	billionaire	high chair	on the air	unfair
hair	county fair	impair	questionnaire	wheelchair
lair	debonair			

-are

bare	mare	stare	compare	prepare
blare	pare	ware	declare	silverware
care	rare	airfare	Delaware	threadbare
dare	scare	aware	fair and square	Times Square
fare	share	beware	fanfare	unaware
flare	snare	bus fare	intensive care	warfare
glare	spare	child care	nightmare	welfare
hare	square			

-ear

bear	swear	outerwear	underwear	wash and wear
pear	wear	teddy bear		

Variant Vowel /ûr/ Phonograms

-earn

earn	learn	yearn	live and learn

-erb

herb	verb	adverb	proverb	superb

-erge

merge	verge	diverge	emerge	submerge
serge	converge			

-erk

jerk	clerk	perk	berserk

-erm

germ	term	long-term	midterm	pachyderm

-ern

fern	stern	concern	intern

-erve

nerve	brown-and-serve	deserve	preserve	self-serve
serve	conserve	observe	reserve	unnerve
swerve				

-ir

fir	stir	whir	astir	yes sir
sir				

-ird

bird	early bird	jailbird	lovebird	one-third
third	hummingbird	ladybird	mockingbird	songbird
blackbird				

-irk

quirk	shirk	smirk

-irl

girl	twirl	awhirl	cover girl	dream girl
swirl	whirl			

-irst

first	thirst	die of thirst	feet-first	headfirst

Teaching Phonics & Word Study in the Intermediate Grades • Scholastic Professional Books

-irt

dirt	skirt	miniskirt	pay dirt	stuffed shirt
flirt	squirt	nightshirt	redshirt	undershirt
shirt	hula skirt			

-irth

| birth | girth | mirth | childbirth | rebirth |

-ur

| fur | slur | concur | demur | occur |
| blur | spur | | | |

-urb

| curb | disturb | news blurb | perturb | suburb |
| blurb | do not disturb | | | |

-urge

| urge | purge | splurge |

-url

| curl | furl | hurl | unfurl |

-urn

burn	urn	out of turn	sojourn	toss and turn
churn	downturn	overturn	sunburn	upturn
spurn	heartburn	return	tax return	U-turn
turn	nocturne	slow burn		

-urk

| lurk | murk |

-urse

| curse | nurse | purse | reimburse |

-urt

| curt | blurt | spurt | Frankfurt | unhurt |
| hurt | | | | |

Variant Vowel /är/ Phonograms

-ar

bar	scar	boxcar	falling star	salad bar
car	spar	cable car	guitar	seminar
char	star	candy bar	handlebar	snack bar
czar	tar	caviar	jaguar	so far
far	ajar	cigar	movie star	streetcar
jar	all-star	cookie jar	near and far	superstar
mar	bazaar	costar	registrar	Zanzibar
par	bizarre	disbar		

-ard

card	backyard	boulevard	disregard	regard
guard	barnyard	coast guard	flash card	report card
hard	baseball card	credit card	graveyard	safeguard
lard	birthday card	crossing guard	junkyard	scorecard
yard	blowhard	cue card	leotard	shipyard
armed guard	bodyguard	diehard	lifeguard	St. Bernard
avant-garde	bombard	discard	postcard	vanguard

-arge

barge	large	enlarge	recharge	take charge
charge	discharge	overcharge		

-ark

bark	park	baseball park	disembark	remark
Clark	shark	birthmark	double-park	skylark
dark	spark	bookmark	earmark	theme park
hark	stark	Central Park	landmark	trademark
lark	aardvark	check mark	postmark	
mark	ballpark	Denmark	question mark	

-arm

arm	harm	disarm	fire alarm	lucky charm
charm	alarm	false alarm	firearm	underarm
farm	arm in arm			

Teaching Phonics & Word Study in the Intermediate Grades • Scholastic Professional Books

-arn

barn	darn	yarn

-arp

carp	harp	sharp	tarp

-art

cart	start	eye chart	impart	restart
chart	tart	fall apart	jump-start	running start
dart	à la carte	false start	martial art	shopping cart
mart	apart	folk art	mini-mart	street smart
part	counterpart	go cart	Mozart	upstart
smart	depart	golf cart	outsmart	work of art

Variant Vowel /ô/ Phonograms

-all

all	appall	curtain call	know it all	shopping mall
ball	baseball	downfall	meatball	snowball
call	basketball	enthrall	nightfall	snowfall
fall	birdcall	eyeball	oddball	spitball
hall	blackball	football	off-the-wall	stonewall
mall	butterball	free fall	overall	study hall
small	cannonball	free-for-all	phone call	toll call
squall	city hall	goofball	pinball	volleyball
stall	close call	gum ball	pitfall	wake-up call
tall	cotton ball	handball	rainfall	wall-to-wall
wall	crystal ball	install	recall	waterfall

-alk

balk	back talk	fast-talk	outtalk	small talk
chalk	beanstalk	girl talk	pep talk	space walk
stalk	boardwalk	jaywalk	sidewalk	sweet talk
talk	crosswalk	nature walk	sleepwalk	
walk	double talk			

-alt

halt	malt	salt	asphalt	exalt

-aught

caught	naught	taught	distraught	self-taught
fraught				

-aunch

haunch	launch	paunch	staunch

-aunt

daunt	gaunt	haunt	jaunt	taunt
flaunt				

-ault

fault	assault	default	pole-vault	somersault
vault				

-aw

caw	gnaw	raw	straw	outlaw
claw	jaw	saw	hem and haw	seesaw
draw	law	slaw	jigsaw	southpaw
flaw	paw	squaw	last straw	withdraw

-awl

bawl	crawl	drawl	scrawl	shawl
brawl				

-awn

brawn	fawn	pawn	yawn	overdrawn
dawn	lawn	prawn	crack of dawn	withdrawn
drawn				

-ong

bong	tong	belong	hop-a-long	sarong
dong	prong	folk song	lifelong	sing-along
gong	strong	headlong	oblong	so long
long	wrong	headstrong	Ping-Pong	tagalong
song	along	Hong Kong	prolong	

Teaching Phonics & Word Study in the Intermediate Grades • Scholastic Professional Books

-oss

boss	loss	across	double-cross	memory loss
cross	moss	crisscross	hearing loss	Red Cross
floss	toss	dental floss	lip gloss	ring toss
gloss				

-ost

cost	lost	at any cost	defrost	low-cost
frost				

-oth

broth	froth	sloth	chicken broth	three-toed sloth
cloth	moth			

-ought

bought	fought	sought	afterthought	store-bought
brought	ought	thought	food for thought	

/ô/ with r

-oar

boar	roar	soar	uproar

-oor

door	door-to-door	next-door	outdoor	trapdoor
floor	indoor			

-orch

porch	torch	scorch

-ord

chord	lord	discord	record	smorgasbord
cord	sword	harpsichord	rip cord	spinal chord
fjord	afford	landlord	slumlord	tape-record
ford				

-ore

bore	snore	apple core	explore	outscore
chore	sore	ashore	eyesore	restore
core	spore	Baltimore	folklore	seashore
fore	store	before	forevermore	Singapore
gore	swore	carnivore	galore	sophomore
more	tore	cold sore	ignore	Theodore
pore	wore	drugstore	nevermore	therefore
score	adore	encore	no more	underscore
shore	anymore	evermore		

-ork

cork	pork	York	New York	pitchfork
fork	stork			

-orm

dorm	barnstorm	deform	misinform	snowstorm
form	brainstorm	duststorm	perform	thunderstorm
norm	co-ed dorm	free-form	platform	transform
storm	conform	inform	reform	uniform

-orn

born	torn	ear of corn	Matterhorn	shoehorn
corn	worn	first-born	native-born	timeworn
horn	acorn	foghorn	newborn	unborn
morn	adorn	foreign-born	outworn	unicorn
scorn	airborne	forlorn	popcorn	weatherworn
sworn	bullhorn	greenhorn	reborn	well-worn
thorn	Capricorn	inborn		

-ort

fort	airport	distort	import	seaport
port	bad sport	escort	last resort	spoilsport
sort	cavort	export	passport	support
short	cohort	good sport	report	transport
snort	contort	heliport	resort	
sport	deport			

Teaching Phonics & Word Study in the Intermediate Grades • Scholastic Professional Books

-our

| four | pour | downpour | ten-four | troubadour |

Diphthong /oi/ Phonograms

-oil

boil	foil	spoil	hard-boil	tinfoil
broil	oil	toil	recoil	turmoil
coil	soil			

-oin

| coin | join | Des Moines | purloin | sirloin |
| groin | loin | flip a coin | rejoin | tenderloin |

-oint

joint	ballpoint	focal point	out of joint	viewpoint
point	checkpoint	high point	pinpoint	West Point
appoint	disappoint	needlepoint	starting point	

-oise

| noise | poise | traffic noise | turquoise |

-oist

| foist | hoist | moist |

-oy

boy	Roy	annoy	enjoy	overjoy
buoy	soy	corduroy	killjoy	pride and joy
coy	toy	destroy	life buoy	real McCoy
joy	Troy	employ	oh boy	
ploy	ahoy			

Diphthong /ou/ Phonograms

-ouch

couch	grouch	pouch	slouch	vouch
crouch	ouch			

-oud

cloud	proud	out loud	thundercloud	war cloud
loud	aloud	rain cloud		

-ounce

bounce	ounce	trounce	mispronounce	pronounce
flounce	pounce	announce	ounce for ounce	renounce

-ound

bound	abound	chow hound	inbound	profound
found	aground	compound	lost and found	rebound
ground	all around	dog pound	merry-go-round	runaround
hound	around	dumbfound	muscle-bound	snowbound
mound	astound	earthbound	newfound	solid ground
pound	background	fool around	outbound	spellbound
round	battleground	foreground	outward bound	surround
sound	bloodhound	greyhound	pitcher's mound	undergound
wound	campground	honor bound	playground	year-round

-ount

count	account	bank account	head count	tantamount
mount	amount	discount	paramount	

-our

flour	scour	dinner hour	noon hour	sweet and sour
hour	sour	lunch hour	rush hour	
our	devour			

154

-ouse

blouse	bird house	firehouse	madhouse	powerhouse
douse	cat and mouse	full house	Mickey Mouse	roughhouse
house	church mouse	haunted house	on the house	warehouse
louse	clubhouse	house-to-house	outhouse	White House
mouse	courthouse	lighthouse	penthouse	
spouse	doghouse			

-out

bout	stout	down and out	in and out	shoot-out
clout	tout	dropout	inside out	sold-out
gout	trout	dugout	knockabout	stakeout
out	about	fade-out	knockout	standout
pout	blackout	falling-out	lookout	take-out
rout	blowout	fallout	odd man out	talent scout
scout	brussels sprout	far out	over and out	throughout
shout	campout	handout	pass out	tryout
snout	cookout	hangout	roundabout	without
spout	devout	holdout	runabout	workout
sprout	do without			

-outh

mouth	big mouth	deep south	loudmouth	word of mouth
south	blabbermouth	hand-to-mouth		

-ow

bow	now	allow	here and now	powwow
brow	plow	anyhow	know-how	snowplow
chow	sow	bowwow	kowtow	solemn vow
cow	vow	cat's meow	meow	somehow
how	wow	eyebrow	Moscow	take a bow

-owl

fowl	howl	scowl	on the prowl	wise old owl
growl	prowl			

-own

brown	ballgown	crosstown	letdown	small-town
clown	breakdown	downtown	lowdown	splashdown
crown	broken-down	face-down	meltdown	sundown
down	cap and gown	ghost town	nightgown	touchdown
drown	Chinatown	hand-me-down	out-of-town	trickle-down
frown	circus clown	hoe-down	put-down	up and down
gown	countdown	hometown	renown	upside down
town	crackdown	knockdown	slowdown	wedding gown

Variant Vowel /o͞o/ Phonograms

-ew

blew	grew	threw	curfew	renew
brew	knew	anew	interview	review
chew	mew	bird's-eye view	on view	skeleton crew
crew	new	book review	outgrew	unscrew
dew	pew	brand-new	panoramic view	withdrew
few	screw	cashew	point of view	world-view
flew	stew	corkscrew	quite a few	

-o

do	ado	misdo	redo	well-to-do
to	hairdo	no can do	two by two	whoop-de-do
two	how-to	outdo	undo	
who	into	overdo	unto	

-oo

boo	zoo	bugaboo	hullabaloo	switcheroo
coo	ah-choo	choo-choo	kangaroo	taboo
goo	ballyhoo	cock-a-doodle-doo	kazoo	tattoo
moo	bamboo	cockatoo	peek-a-boo	toodle-oo
shoo	boo-boo	cuckoo	shampoo	voodoo
too	boo-hoo	goo-goo	stinkaroo	yoo-hoo
woo	buckaroo			

Teaching Phonics & Word Study in the Intermediate Grades • Scholastic Professional Books

-ood

brood	mood	dog food	in the mood	seafood
food	baby food	fast food		

-oof

goof	roof	aloof	fireproof	soundproof
proof	spoof	childproof	foolproof	

-ool

cool	school	April fool	Liverpool	tidepool
drool	spool	car pool	nursery school	toadstool
fool	stool	cesspool	preschool	whirlpool
pool	tool	high school	swimming pool	

-oom

bloom	groom	bathroom	elbow room	mushroom
boom	loom	bride and groom	gloom and doom	powder room
broom	room	bridegroom	heirloom	rest room
doom	zoom	classroom	leg room	sonic boom
gloom	baby boom	courtroom	locker room	

-oon

boon	swoon	cocoon	lampoon	raccoon
coon	afternoon	full moon	macaroon	saloon
croon	baboon	harpoon	maroon	spittoon
loon	balloon	high noon	monsoon	too soon
moon	bassoon	honeymoon	platoon	twelve noon
noon	buffoon	hot-air balloon	pontoon	tycoon
soon	Cameroon	lagoon	pretty soon	typhoon
spoon	cartoon			

-oop

coop	hoop	sloop	swoop	hula hoop
droop	loop	snoop	troop	inside scoop
goop	scoop	stoop	alley-oop	nincompoop

-oose

goose	noose	hang loose	on the loose	silly goose
loose	caboose	mongoose	papoose	vamoose
moose	footloose	Mother Goose		

-oot

boot	moot	shoot	outshoot	troubleshoot
hoot	root	snoot	overshoot	uproot
loot	scoot	toot	square root	

-ooth

booth	kissing booth	snaggletooth	sweet tooth	voting booth
tooth	phone booth			

-ooze

ooze	snooze

-oup

croup	soup	in-group	pressure group	regroup
group	chicken soup	peer group		

-ube

cube	tube	Danube	ice cube	test tube
lube				

-uce

Bruce	spruce	deduce	introduce	reduce
deuce	truce	induce	produce	reproduce

-ude

crude	allude	elude	include	multitude
dude	altitude	exclude	interlude	protrude
nude	aptitude	exude	latitude	seclude
prude	conclude	gratitude	longitude	solitude
rude	delude			

Teaching Phonics & Word Study in the Intermediate Grades • Scholastic Professional Books

-ue

blue	true	misconstrue	past due	revue
clue	avenue	miscue	postage due	subdue
cue	barbecue	navy blue	pursue	tried and true
due	black-and-blue	on cue	red, white, and blue	true blue
glue	construe	out of the blue	residue	untrue
hue	counter-sue	overdue	revenue	
Sue	curlicue			

-uke

duke	Luke	nuke	puke	rebuke
fluke				

-ule

mule	gag rule	majority rule	module	overrule
rule	golden rule	minuscule	molecule	ridicule
yule	home rule			

-ume

fume	assume	costume	perfume	resume
plume	consume	exhume	presume	

-une

dune	tune	immune	Neptune	out of tune
June	commune	loony tune	opportune	
prune	fine tune			

-ure

cure	assure	ensure	manicure	premature
lure	brochure	immature	mature	reassure
pure	curvature	impure	obscure	secure
sure	demure	insecure	overture	unsure
aperture	endure	insure	pedicure	

-use

fuse	abuse	confuse	excuse	refuse
muse	accuse	defuse	infuse	short fuse
ruse	amuse	effuse	misuse	
use	blow a fuse	enthuse	peruse	

-ute

brute	absolute	deaf mute	ill repute	refute
chute	acute	destitute	institute	repute
cute	astute	dilute	minute	resolute
flute	attribute	dispute	parachute	salute
jute	commute	electrocute	persecute	substitute
lute	compute	execute	pollute	tribute
mute	constitute			

-uth

| Ruth | truth | Baby Ruth | moment of truth | untruth |
| sleuth | youth | half-truth | naked truth | |

Variant Vowel /o͞o/ Phonograms

-ood

good	childhood	Hollywood	neighborhood	Robin Hood
hood	deadwood	likelihood	no-good	sainthood
stood	driftwood	livelihood	pretty good	sisterhood
wood	falsehood	misunderstood	Red Riding Hood	so far so good
brotherhood	fatherhood	motherhood	redwood	understood

-ook

book	look	checkbook	handbook	overlook
brook	nook	comic book	mistook	scrapbook
cook	rook	dirty look	notebook	textbook
crook	shook	fishhook	outlook	unhook
hook	took	gobbledygook		

Teaching Phonics & Word Study in the Intermediate Grades • Scholastic Professional Books

-oot

foot	afoot	Big Foot	tenderfoot	underfoot
soot	barefoot	hotfoot		

-ould

could	should	would

-ull

bull	pull	pit bull	push-pull	Sitting Bull
full	chock-full			

-ush

bush	push	ambush	rosebush

What About Rules?

Use *i* before *e* except after *c*. When two vowels go walking, the first does the talking. Don't hit your sister. Sit up straight, Wiley! These and other rules swim around in my head when I think about my childhood. When it comes to reading, I often wonder how many rules I actually recall and use as a skilled reader and writer. This list is probably quite small.

"Effective decoders see words not in terms of phonics rules, but in terms of patterns of letters that are used to aid in identification" (Stahl, 1992). Through phonics instruction that focuses students' attention on each letter in a word, teaches blending, and highlights common spelling patterns, students will begin to internalize rules, or generalizations, about words. For example, when students encounter words in which the letter *c* stands for either the /s/ sound or the /k/ sound, we want them to be able to generalize the conditions under which each is likely to occur. Rules can be used to help students attend to a specific spelling pattern or organize their thinking about it. As time goes by, and we give students more and more opportunities to review and apply a rule, they'll internalize it.

In addition, teachers of reading need to be aware of rules so that they can verbalize them for students who would benefit from them (Durkin, 1993). However, since few rules are 100% reliable, they should never be taught as absolutes. That's why I prefer the term *generalization*, rather than *rule*.

Guidelines for Using Rules/Generalizations

- **Don't make rules/generalizations the emphasis of phonics instruction.** Instead, use them as one tool to help students focus on important spelling patterns and recognize unfamiliar words.

- **Teach only those rules/generalizations that are most useful.** For example, teaching students that the spelling pattern *-ough* can stand for up to six sounds is wasteful. In addition, avoid generalizations that are wordy or full of technical language.

- **Emphasize applying the rules/generalizations rather than verbalizing them.** Remember that once students can apply the generalizations, there's no need to spend instructional time on them.

- **Don't teach the rules/generalizations too soon or too late.** Teach them at a point when students can best understand and apply them.

- **Never teach rules as absolutes.** Since students tend to think of rules as absolutes, it's better to use the term *generalization*. And be sure to make the students aware of exceptions to the generalizations.

Teaching Phonics & Word Study in the Intermediate Grades • Scholastic Professional Books

The classic study on generalizations and their utility was conducted in 1963 (Clymer). Clymer examined 45 generalizations (rules) taught by basal reading programs. He found that many of the generalizations commonly taught were of limited value. In fact, less than half of the rules worked as much as 75% of the time. The chart below shows the generalizations he examined. I've updated the wording of some of them so that they're consistent with the language used in today's basals.

	Consonant Generalizations	Example	Exception	% Utility
1.	When two of the same consonants appear side by side in a word, only one is heard.	berry	suggest	99
2.	When the letter c is followed by the letter o or a, the c stands for the /k/ sound.	cat		100
3.	The digraph ch is usually pronounced /ch/ as in watch and chair, not /sh/.	batch	machine	95
4.	When the letters c and h appear next to each other in a word, they stand for only one sound.	rich		100
5.	The letter g often has a sound similar to that of the letter j in jump when it comes before the letter i or e.	ginger	give	64
6.	When the letter c is followed by the letter e or i, the /s/ sound is likely to be heard.	cent	ocean	96
7.	When a word ends in the letters ck, it has the /k/ sound as in book.	sick		100
8.	When the letters ght appear together in a word, the letters gh are silent.	fight		100
9.	When a word begins with the letters kn, the letter k is silent.	know		100
10.	When a word begins with the letters wr, the letter w is silent.	write		100

Vowel Generalizations	Example	Exception	% Utility
11. If there is one vowel letter in an accented syllable, it has a short sound.	city	lady	61
12. When a word has only one vowel letter, the vowel sound is likely to be short.	lid	mind	57
13. When two vowels appear together in a word, the long sound of the first one is heard and the second is usually silent. Note: This is the old "when 2 vowels go walking, the first does the talking" rule.	seat	chief	45
14. When a vowel is in the middle of a one-syllable word, the vowel is short.	best	gold	62
15. The letter *r* gives the preceding vowel a sound that is neither long nor short.	torn	fire	78
16. When there are two vowels, one of which is final *e*, the first vowel is long and the *e* is silent.	hope	come	63
17. The first vowel is usually long and the second silent in the digraphs *ai, ea, oa,* and *ui*.	nail/said 64% bead/head 66% boat/cupboard 97% suit/build 6%		66
18. When words end with silent *e*, the preceding *a* or *i* is long.	bake	have	60
19. When the letter *y* is the final letter in a word, it usually has a vowel sound.	dry	tray	84
20. When the letter *y* is used as a vowel in words, it sometimes has the sound of long *i*.	fly	funny	15
21. When *y* or *ey* appears in the last syllable that is not accented, the long *e* sound is heard.		baby	0
22. The letter *a* has the same sound as /ô/ when followed by *l, w,* and *u*.	fall	canal	48
23. The letter *w* is sometimes a vowel and follows the vowel digraph rule.	snow	few	40
24. When there is one *e* in a word that ends in a consonant, the *e* usually has a short sound.	pet	flew	76
25. In many two- and three-syllable words, the final *e* lengthens the vowel in the last syllable.	invite	gasoline	46

Teaching Phonics & Word Study in the Intermediate Grades • Scholastic Professional Books

Vowel Generalizations cont.		Example	Exception	% Utility
26.	Words having double *e* usually have the long *e* sound.	feet	been	98
27.	The letters *ow* stand for the long *o* sound.	own	town	59
28.	When the letter *a* follows the letter *w* in a word, it usually has the sound that *a* stands for *as in was*.	watch	swam	32
29.	In the vowel spelling *ie*, the letter *i* is silent and the letter *e* has the long vowel sound.	field	friend	17
30.	In *ay* the *y* is silent and gives *a* its long sound.	play	always	78
31.	If the only vowel letter is at the end of a word, the letter usually stands for a long sound.	me	do	74
32.	When the letter *e* is followed by the letter *w*, the vowel sound is the same as represented by *oo* (/o͞o/).	blew	sew	35
33.	When the letter *a* is followed by the letter *r* and final *e*, we expect to hear the sound heard in *care*.	dare	are	90
34.	When the letter *i* is followed by the letters *gh*, the letter *i* usually stands for its long sound and the *gh* is silent.	high	neighbor	71

Syllable Generalizations		Example	Exception	% Utility
35.	If the first vowel sound in a word is followed by two consonants, the first syllable usually ends with the first of the two consonants.	bullet	singer	72
36.	If the first vowel sound in a word is followed by a single consonant, that consonant usually begins the second syllable.	over	oven	44
37.	In a word of more than one syllable, the letter *v* usually goes with the preceding vowel to form a syllable.	cover	clover	73
38.	If the last syllable of a word ends in *le*, the consonant preceding the *le* usually begins the last syllable.	tumble	buckle	97
39.	When the first vowel in a word is followed by *th*, *ch*, or *sh*, these symbols are not broken when the word is divided into syllables, and they may go with either the first or second syllable.	dishes		100
40.	In most two-syllable words, the first syllable is accented.	famous	polite	85
41.	When the last syllable is the sound /r/, it is unaccented.	butter	appear	95
42.	In most two-syllable words that end in a consonant followed by *y*, the first syllable is accented and the last is unaccented.	baby	supply	96
43.	If *a*, *in*, *re*, *ex*, *de*, or *be* is the first syllable in a word, it is usually unaccented.	above	insect	87
44.	When *tion* is the final syllable in a word, it is unaccented.	nation		100
45.	When *ture* is the final syllable in a word, it is unaccented.	picture		100

Teaching Phonics & Word Study in the Intermediate Grades • Scholastic Professional Books

Syllabication

Guidelines:

- A syllable is a unit of pronunciation. Each syllable contains only one vowel sound. Finding the vowels in a word is an important starting point for breaking it apart by syllables. However, each syllable may have more than one vowel. For example, the word *boat* contains one vowel sound, therefore one syllable. However, the vowel sound is represented by the vowel digraph *oa.*

- Whether a group of letters forms a syllable depends on the letters that surround it (Adams, 1990). For example, the letters *par* form a syllable in the word *partial*, but not in the word *parade.*

- One syllable in a multisyllabic word receives more emphasis or stress. The vowel sound in this syllable is heard most clearly. Stress is indicated in dictionary pronunciation keys by accent marks. In addition to one primary accent, some words also have one or more secondary accents. Vowels in unstressed syllables become schwas (/ə/). Generally, in words with prefixes and suffixes, the prefix or suffix forms a separate syllable and the accent falls on the root (base) word. In compound words, the accent generally falls on or within the first word. The accent in most two-syllable words falls on the first syllable.

- To decode multisyllabic words, students must be able to divide words into recognizable chunks. Some readers develop a sense of syllabication breaks independently through their exposures to print; others have great difficulty and need instruction (Just & Carpenter, 1987). Some students' phonics skills break down when confronted by multisyllabic words because they can't readily identify syllable boundaries (Eldredge, 1996).

- Children need training in dividing words according to syllables. They must (1) understand how to figure out the vowel sound in one-syllable words [teach them common one-syllable spelling patterns such as CVC and CVCe], and (2) understand that a syllable has only one vowel sound, but that the vowel sound may be spelled using more than one vowel.

- Children can use syllabication strategies to approximate a word's pronunciation. This approximation is generally close enough for the reader to recognize the word if it's in his speaking or listening vocabularies. This demonstrates how important it is to help students develop their speaking and listening vocabularies and to combine building their background knowledge with vocabulary instruction.

- Some words can be divided in more than one way. For example: treat-y, trea-ty, tr-ea-ty. The fewer chunks into which a word is divided, the easier it is to decode the word.

- Traditional syllabication strategies can be ineffective. Clapping syllables in words, for example, doesn't work because the child must already know the word before she can clap the syllables (Johnson & Bauman, 1984). Similarly, memorizing countless syllabication rules has little effect on a child's ability to decode multisyllabic words. (Note: *Syllabication* and *syllabification* are synonymous.)

- Few syllabication generalizations are very useful to children, but some are worth pointing out (Chall & Popp, 1996). State them in simple, clear terms. Focus on applying them, not reciting them:

  - If the word is a compound word, divide the word between the two words that comprise it. If either or both of these words has more than one syllable, follow the syllabication generalizations below.

  - Inflectional endings such as *ing, er, est*, and *ed* often form separate syllables. The remaining portion of the word is the root (base) word. Looking for these and other meaning units in words is known as morphemic analysis. A morpheme is a meaning unit. There are free morphemes—whole words that can stand alone and cannot be divided into other meaning units (i.e., root words). There are also bound morphemes—word parts that can't stand alone and must be combined with a free morpheme (i.e., suffixes and prefixes). Bound morphemes alter the meaning of the free morphemes to which they are attached (example: *un + happy = unhappy*).

  - When two or more consonants appear in the middle of a word, divide the word between them (CVC + CVC words). Then try the short sound for the vowel in the first syllable. This generalization doesn't apply if the two consonants form a digraph such as *ch, tch, ck, ph, sh,* or *th.* These digraphs cannot be separated across syllable boundaries.

  - When only one consonant appears between two vowels, divide the word before the consonant. Then try the long sound of the first vowel (examples: *tiger, pilot*). This works about 55% of the time. If a recognizable word is not formed using the long sound, divide the word after the consonant and try the short sound for the first syllable (examples: *exit, second*). This works about 45% of the time.

168

- When a two-syllable word ends in a consonant plus *le*, the consonant and *le* form the last syllable. If the preceding syllable ends in a consonant, try the short sound of the vowel (examples: *wiggle*, *sample*). If the preceding syllable ends with a vowel, try the long sound of the vowel (examples: *table*, *bridle*).

- When a two-syllable word ends in a consonant plus *re*, the consonant and *re* form the last syllable. If the preceding syllable ends with a vowel, try the long sound of that vowel (example: *acre*).

- Never break apart vowel digraphs or diphthongs across syllable boundaries.

Tips for Teaching Syllabication

- **Begin syllabication instruction in grade 1** by pointing out compound words, words with double consonants, and words with common prefixes and suffixes such as *un*, *re*, *s*, *es*, *ing*, and *ed*. In later grades, additional prefixes and suffixes, as well as common root words can become the focus of instruction. In addition, practice in recognizing common syllabic units is beneficial.

- **Teach syllabication strategies using known words,** then provide ample opportunities for students to apply the strategy in context.

- **Use dictionaries with caution.** Most dictionaries divide words according to how the word should be broken across lines. This sometimes has little to do with the division of the word into its syllables for the purpose of pronunciation.

Sample Pronounciations

/rēd/

/rit/

/fon´iks/

Teaching Phonics & Word Study in the Intermediate Grades • Scholastic Professional Books

Six Basic Syllable Spelling Patterns

(Moats, 1995)

1. closed: These syllables end in a consonant. The vowel sound is generally short (examples: *rabbit, napkin*).

2. open: These syllables end in a vowel. The vowel sound is generally long (examples: *tiger, pilot*).

3. vowel–silent *e* (VCe): These syllables generally represent long-vowel sounds (examples: *compete, decide*).

4. vowel team: Many vowel sounds are spelled with vowel digraphs such as *ai, ay, ea, ee, oa, ow, oo, oi, oy, ou, ie,* and *ei*. The vowel digraphs appear in the same syllable (examples: *boat, explain*).

5. *r*-controlled: When a vowel is followed by *r*, the letter *r* affects the sound of the vowel. The vowel and the *r* appear in the same syllable (examples: *bird, turtle*).

6. consonant + *le*: Usually when *le* appears at the end of a word and is preceded by a consonant, the consonant + *le* form the final syllable (examples: *table, little*).

Teaching Phonics & Word Study in the Intermediate Grades • Scholastic Professional Books

Syllabication Lessons

Begin teaching syllabication by providing explicit, multisensory lessons on the concept of a syllable.

Sample Lesson

What Is a Syllable?

Phonic Principle: A syllable is a unit of pronunciation. A word can be divided into syllables.

1. Distribute small mirrors to your students or have them find a partner to watch as he or she pronounces words.

2. Together, say aloud a series of words of varying lengths as students look in the mirrors. Have students count the number of times their mouths open when saying the word. Explain that this is the number of syllables in the word. Another way to count the syllables is to have them count the number of times their jaw drops when they say a word.

3. Ask students to identify which part of the word causes their mouth to open (the vowel sound). Point out to students that a syllable has one vowel sound.

4. Conclude by choosing one or all of the following activities:

- Ask students to generate a list of short words, then a list of long words. Write the words on the chalkboard and compare them. Most long words contain more letters and more syllables.

- Ask students to repeat a series of words you say. As they pronounce each word, have students clap or tap the number of syllables. Start with compound words, progress to two-syllable words, then to three- and four-syllable words.

- Ask students to repeat a series of words you say. As they pronounce each word, have them move a counter for each syllable they hear. Have them count the number of counters moved. Provide modeling as necessary.

- Ask students to repeat a series of words you say. For each word, have them delete the first syllable. For example, "Say *sunflower* without the *sun*," or "Say *robot* without the *ro*." Go on to have them delete the ending syllables.

Lessons for the Most Common Syllable Spelling Patterns

Once students have mastered the concept of the syllable, you can begin teaching the six most common syllable spelling patterns. Learning these common patterns will give students insight into how words are put together. In a series of intervention studies, Shefelbine (1990) found that when students were taught how to pronounce common syllables and then practiced reading multisyllabic words with these syllables, their ability to read multisyllabic words in general improved. Since closed syllables are the most frequent, begin instruction there (Stanback, 1992). I suggest the following sequence: closed syllables, open syllables, VCe (final e, VCe), vowel team, *r*-controlled, consonant + *le*. I've included a sample lesson and a reteach lesson for each syllable type.

Sample Lesson

Closed Syllables
Syllabication Spelling Pattern

Key Concept: Explain to your students that every syllable in a word has only one vowel sound. Write *napkin* and *subject* on the chalkboard. Divide the words syllable by syllable. Point out that the first syllable in each word ends in a consonant and explain that this is called a **closed syllable**. Most closed syllables have a short vowel sound.

Teacher Model: Write the word *fabric* on the chalkboard. Do not say the word, but give your students time to examine its parts. Then model how to use syllabication strategies to read the word.

Think-Aloud: I know that each syllable has one vowel sound. I see two vowels in this word separated by two consonants. If I divide the word between the consonants I get *f-a-b* and *r-i-c*. Both of these syllables are closed syllables since they end in a consonant. Therefore, I will try the short vowel sound when pronouncing each syllable: /fab/ /rik/. When I put these two syllables together, I get *fabric*.

Blending Practice: Write the following words on the chalkboard. Have students chorally read each word. Provide modeling as necessary.

absent	atlas	comet
husband	kitten	fossil
velvet	zigzag	plaster
habit	sunset	tidbit

Teaching Phonics & Word Study in the Intermediate Grades • Scholastic Professional Books

Reteach Lesson: Closed Syllables

1. Write the following words on the chalkboard: *sat, run, lid, nest*. Say: *Look at these words. How many vowels do you see in each?*

2. Then ask: What does each word end with? (One consonant.)

3. Have students read the words aloud, noting their pronunciation. Ask: *How did you pronounce the words at the end?* (Tongue, teeth, or lips closed.)

4. Ask: *What would be a good name for this syllable?* (Closed, since the mouth is closed at the end.)

5. Define closed syllable for students. (A closed syllable ends in at least one consonant; the vowel sound is short.)

6. Write the following sentences on the chalkboard for students to complete: A closed syllable ends in at least one _____. The vowel sound is _____.

7. Extend the lesson by writing two-syllable words with a closed first syllable (e.g., *napkin, candid, subject*). Help students blend each syllable to read the words.

Teacher note: Short vowel sounds in unaccented syllables, particularly before *m, n,* or *l,* may be distorted and sound like a schwa. Also, short vowel sounds before the nasal sounds /m/, /n/, and /ng/ may seem distorted (e.g., *ram, ant, sank, sing*).

Closed Syllable Word List

absent	contest	hatbox	pasture	submit
active	context	hectic	pencil	sudden
admit	cosmic	helmet	picnic	suffix
album	cottage	hiccup	picture	summit
anklet	cotton	hidden	pigment	sunset
antic	crimson	hostel	plaster	suntan
atlas	culprit	husband	plastic	sunup
attic	custom	index	plumber	suspect
axis	cutlet	inlet	pocket	tablet
basket	dapple	insect	pollen	tactic
beggar	denim	instinct	practice	tandem
beverage	dental	insult	pregnant	tantrum
blanket	dentist	jacket	pretzel	tendon
blister	dismal	jogger	princess	tennis
bobbin	distant	kingdom	problem	ticket
bonnet	dollar	kitchen	public	tidbit
budget	eggnog	kitten	publish	timid
button	engine	lesson	pumpkin	tonsil
cabin	exit	limit	puppet	tractor
cactus	fabric	litmus	rabbit	transit
campus	falcon	madcap	random	tremor
cancer	fasten	magnet	ransom	tunnel
candid	fatten	manner	rapid	until
cannot	fender	mantel	ribbon	upset
canvas	fidget	mascot	robin	valid
canyon	figment	mental	rotten	velvet
catnap	filter	metric	rustic	victim
catnip	fossil	midget	sadden	vivid
channel	frantic	mishap	sandwich	vulture
chicken	gallon	mitten	satin	welcome
cluster	goblet	muffin	septic	witness
comet	goblin	napkin	signal	zigzag
comic	gospel	nectar	socket	
common	gossip	nostril	splendor	
contact	habit	padlock	splinter	
content	hangar	panic	subject	

Teaching Phonics & Word Study in the Intermediate Grades • Scholastic Professional Books

Open Syllables
Syllabication Spelling Pattern

Key Concept: Explain to your students that every syllable in a word has only one vowel sound. Write *favor* and *tiger* on the chalkboard. Divide the words syllable by syllable. Point out that the first syllable in each word ends in one vowel. Explain that this is called an **open syllable**. Most open syllables have a long vowel sound.

Teacher Model: Write the word *secret* on the chalkboard. Don't say the word, but give students time to examine its parts. Then model how to use syllabication strategies to read the word.

Think-Aloud: I know that each syllable has one vowel sound. I see two vowels in this word separated by two consonants. If I divide the word between the consonants, I get *s-e-c* and *r-e-t*. Both of these syllables are closed syllables since they end in a consonant. Therefore,

I will try the short vowel sound when pronouncing each syllable: /sek/ /ret/. When I put these two syllables together, I don't get a word I know. So, I'll separate the word between the letters *e* and *c*. The first syllable becomes an open syllable since it ends in a vowel. The vowel sound will be long. When I pronounce the syllables, I get /sē/ /kret/— *secret*. This is a real word.

Blending Practice: Write the following words on the chalkboard. Have students chorally read each word. Provide modeling as necessary.

baby	cedar	cider
diver	frozen	female
hijack	human	lady
motor	prefix	social

Reteach Lesson: Open Syllables

1. Write the following words on the chalkboard: *me, hi, no, she*. Ask students: *How many vowels do you see in each word?*

2. Then ask: *What does each word end with?* (One vowel.) *Can these be closed syllables?* (No, a closed syllable ends in a consonant.)

3. Have students read the words, paying attention to the way each is pronounced. Ask: *How are the words pronounced at the end?* (The mouth is open.)

4. Ask: *What would be a good name for the syllable?* (Open, since the mouth is open at the end.)

5. Define open syllable for students. (An open syllable ends in a vowel; the vowel sound is long.)

6. Write the following sentences on the chalkboard for students to complete: An open syllable ends in a _____. The vowel sound is _____.

7. Extend the lesson by writing two-syllable words with an open first syllable (e.g., *tiger*, *lady*, *secret*). Help students blend each syllable to read the words.

Open-Syllable Word List

agent	donate	irate	oval	sinus
baby	donor	iris	ozone	siren
bacon	donut	item	penal	slogan
bagel	edict	label	phony	social
basal	ego	lady	photo	solo
basic	equal	latent	pilot	spinal
basin	even	latex	pliers	spiral
basis	evil	lazy	polo	stamen
biceps	fatal	legal	pony	table
bison	favor	lethal	prefix	tidal
blatant	feline	lilac	primate	tidy
bogus	female	local	probate	tiger
bonus	final	locate	profile	tirade
butane	finite	locust	program	titan
cedar	focal	major	propane	token
cider	focus	migraine	pupil	total
cobalt	fragrant	minus	raven	totem
cobra	frequent	mogul	rebate	tribal
cogent	frozen	moment	recent	unit
colon	future	motor	regal	vacant
cozy	global	mucus	rhino	vagrant
cradle	gracious	museum	rival	vinyl
crazy	gravy	music	rodent	virus
crisis	grocery	mutate	saber	vital
cubic	halo	nasal	sacred	vocal
cupid	helix	nature	secret	yo-yo
data	hijack	naval	senile	zebra
decent	holy	navy	sequence	
demon	human	obese	sequin	
depot	humid	odor	silent	
diver	idol	open	silo	

176

Final *e* (VCe)
Syllabication Spelling Pattern

Key Concept: Explain to students that every syllable in a word has only one vowel sound. Write *compete* and *inflate* on the chalkboard. Divide the words syllable by syllable. Point out that the last syllable in each word ends in vowel, consonant, final *e*. Explain that this is called a **Final *e*, or VCe**, syllable. The final *e* is silent and the vowel sound before it is long.

Teacher Model: Write the word *female* on the chalkboard. Don't say the word, but give students time to examine the word's parts. Then model how to use syllabication strategies to read the word.

Think-Aloud: I know that each syllable has one vowel sound. I see three vowels in this word. However, the word ends in an *e*.

Therefore, I will keep the *e* and the vowel before it in the same syllable. This syllable will have a long vowel sound. If I divide the word between the *e* and *m*, I get an open syllable (*f-e*) and a VCe syllable (*m-a-l-e*). When I pronounce these two syllables, I get /fē/ /māl/— *female*.

Blending Practice: Write the following words on the chalkboard. Have students chorally read each word. Provide modeling as necessary.

alone	amuse	complete
delete	expose	hopeless
invade	refine	shameful
stampede	suppose	unmade

Reteach Lesson: Final *e* (VCe)

1. Write the following words on the chalkboard: *make, bike, cute, hope*. Ask students: *How many vowels do you see in each word?*

2. Then ask: *What does each word end with?* (The letter *e*.) *What comes between the vowel and the final* e*?* (A consonant.)

3. Have students read the words, paying particular attention to the vowel sound. Ask: *What happens to the final* e*?* (It's silent.) *How are the vowels pronounced?* (Each has a long sound.)

4. Say: *Each of these words ends in a vowel, a consonant, and a final* e. *What would be a good name for this syllable?* (VCe or final *e*.)

5. Define VCe syllable for students. (It ends in a vowel, a consonant, and *e*; the vowel sound is long.)

6. Write the following sentences on the chalkboard for students to complete: A VCe syllable ends in a ____, a ____, and an ____. The vowel sound is ____.

7. Extend the lesson by writing two-syllable words with VCe final syllable (e.g., *alone*, *debate*, *invite*). Help students blend each syllable to read the words.

VCe Word List

abuse	cyclone	excuse	inside	refine
accuse	debate	explode	insulate	refuse
advice	deflate	explore	invade	regulate
advise	degrade	expose	invite	relate
alone	delete	extreme	iodine	remote
amaze	describe	fanfare	locate	replete
amuse	desire	feline	lonesome	reptile
athlete	despite	female	membrane	retire
blockade	dethrone	finely	mistake	sapphire
boneless	device	finite	negate	secrete
calcite	devote	franchise	ninety	severe
captivate	dictate	fructose	notebook	shameful
cascade	diffuse	frustrate	obscene	sidewalk
collide	disclose	galore	octane	sincere
combine	disgrace	graphite	oppose	stampede
commode	dispose	hopeless	ozone	sublime
commune	dispute	humane	phoneme	subscribe
compare	divine	ignite	pomade	subside
compete	donate	imbibe	prepare	suppose
compile	efface	immune	profane	supreme
complete	empire	impede	profile	tadpole
concise	entice	impose	propose	textile
concrete	erase	incite	provide	translate
confuse	erode	incline	rebate	trombone
connote	escape	inflate	rebuke	unmade
console	estate	innate	recede	widespread
convene	excite	insane	recite	xylophone

178

Teaching Phonics & Word Study in the Intermediate Grades • Scholastic Professional Books

Vowel Digraphs (Vowel Teams)
Syllabication Spelling Pattern

Key Concept: Explain to your students that sometimes two letters together stand for one vowel sound. Write the words *met, meat,* and *metal* on the chalkboard. Say each word and ask the students how many syllables they hear. Explain that every syllable in a word has only one vowel sound. Point out that the **vowel digraph** (or **vowel team**) *ea* stands for the long *e* sound in *meat*. Explain that when two vowels appear in a long word, such as *meat-eater,* they often stay in the same syllable. This is called a vowel digraph, or vowel team, syllable.

Teacher Model: Write the word *beanbag* on the chalkboard. Don't say the word, but give students time to examine its parts. Then model how to use syllabication strategies to read the word.

Think-Aloud: I know that every syllable has one vowel sound. In this word I see two vowels side-by-side, *ea*. I know that when two vowels team up in a word, I need to keep them in the same syllable. Therefore, I can divide this word into two parts: *bean* and *bag*. The letters *ea* stand for the long *e* sound. When I put these two parts together, I get the word *beanbag*.

Blending Practice: Write the following words on the chalkboard. Have students chorally read each word. Provide modeling as necessary. Remind students that the letters *y* and *w* can stand for a vowel sound in vowel teams such as *ay* and *ow*.

mailbox	maintain	midday
paycheck	freedom	seaweed
sleepless	highway	soaking
railroad	oatmeal	leaving

Reteach Lesson: Vowel Digraphs (Vowel Teams)

1. Write the following words on the chalkboard: *pea, zoo, rain, boat, leaf.* Ask students: *How many vowels do you see in each?* (Two.)

2. Ask: *What does each word end with?* (Some with a consonant, some with two vowels.) Then ask: *Can these be closed syllables?* (No, a closed syllable has only one vowel and must end in a consonant.) *Can these be open syllables?* (No, an open syllable must end in only one vowel.)

3. Have students read the words. Ask: *What is the same about the vowel sound in each word?* (It's long.) *What is the same about the way the vowel sound is written?* (It is always written with a vowel pair or team.)

4. Next ask: *What would be a good name for this syllable?* (Vowel team or vowel pair.)

5. Define a vowel-team syllable for students. (A vowel-team syllable contains two vowels next to each other; the vowel sound is long.) Explain to students that when they're looking at a long word, they should put the vowel team in the same syllable.

6. Write the following sentences on the chalkboard for students to complete: A vowel-team syllable contains _____. The vowel sound is _____.

7. Extend the lesson by writing two-syllable words with a vowel-team syllable (e.g., *trainer*, *bookbag*, *repeat*). Help students blend each syllable to read the words.

Vowel-Team (Vowel-Digraph) Word List

abound	canteen	essay	mistreat	shallow
about	cartoon	esteem	Monday	spoilage
account	chimney	exclaim	monkey	subway
affair	classroom	exhaust	moonbeam	Sunday
agree	cocoon	explain	mushroom	tattoo
agreed	coffee	exploit	oatmeal	textbook
airfare	complain	fellow	obtain	thirteen
allow	complaint	fingernail	overpaid	trainer
aloud	compound	follow	pedigree	turmoil
amount	contain	fourteen	pillow	unafraid
annoy	convey	freeload	poison	unclear
appeal	cuckoo	galley	prevail	unfair
appear	decay	halfway	proceed	unreal
appoint	devour	handbook	raccoon	valley
approach	discount	hockey	railroad	viewpoint
assault	display	holiday	raincoat	volunteer
away	donkey	impeach	release	window
baboon	dugout	indeed	remain	withdraw
ballgown	elbow	mermaid	repeat	yellow
balloon	emcee	midair	retreat	
beneath	employ	midweek	reveal	
blackmail	enjoy	mislead	seesaw	

Teaching Phonics & Word Study in the Intermediate Grades • Scholastic Professional Books

r-Controlled Vowels
Syllabication Spelling Pattern

Key Concept: Explain to your students that when the letter *r* follows a vowel, it affects the sound the vowel usually stands for. When dividing a word into syllables, the vowel plus the *r* usually stay in the same syllable.

Teacher Model: Write the word *snorkel* on the chalkboard, but don't say the word aloud. Ask students to identify the vowel that precedes the letter *r*. Then model how to use that information to figure out how to pronounce the word.

Think-Aloud: I see two vowels in the word, so it probably has two syllables. I see an *r* following an *o* as in the word *or*. I can put these sounds together with *s-n* to get *snor-*. If I combine that with the second syllable, *-kel*, I say the word *snorkel.*

Blending Practice: Write the following words on the chalkboard. Have students chorally read each word. Provide modeling as necessary.

circus	**barber**	**charter**
dirty	**floral**	**forty**
garlic	**hermit**	**marshal**
perfect	**target**	**thirsty**

Reteach Lesson: *r*-Controlled Vowels

1. Write the following words on the chalkboard: *red, men, hen, her*. Ask: *How many vowels do you see in each?* (Two.)

2. Then ask: *What does each word end with?* (One consonant.) *What kind of syllable ends in one consonant?* (A closed syllable.)

3. Have students read the words, paying particular attention to the vowel sound in each. Ask: *How are they pronounced?* (All with a short vowel sound, except the last word.) Ask: *Why can't the last word be read with a short vowel sound?* (The *r* controls the vowel sound.)

4. Ask: *What would be a good name for this syllable?* (An *r*-controlled syllable.)

5. Define *r*-controlled syllable for students. (An *r*-controlled syllable contains a vowel plus *r*; these two letters are kept in the same syllable.)

6. Write the following sentences on the chalkboard for students to complete. An *r*-controlled syllable contains _____. The vowel sound is affected by the letter _____.

7. Extend the lesson by writing two syllable words with an *r*-controlled vowel (e.g., *harvest, circus, normal*). Help students blend each syllable to read the words.

r-Controlled Vowel Words

aboard	chairperson	enter	hornet	nearby
absorb	chapter	entire	hunger	never
adhere	charcoal	error	ignore	normal
admire	charter	expert	immerse	northwest
adore	cheerful	explore	import	number
adorn	cherish	fairway	infer	nurture
afford	chorus	favor	inspire	offer
after	circus	filter	invert	otter
airplane	clover	finger	jargon	parcel
alarm	clutter	fireman	kernel	pardon
anger	color	flirtatious	labor	pattern
appear	comfort	floral	ladder	pearly
ardent	concert	formal	lantern	peering
arson	confer	fortress	laser	pepper
artist	consort	forty	lemur	perfect
assert	copper	fourteen	letter	peril
barber	courtship	further	litter	person
batter	cursor	galore	liver	plaster
before	curtain	garden	lumber	platter
berry	dairy	garlic	lunar	portal
better	desert	garnish	manner	porthole
birthday	differ	gerbil	margin	pouring
blister	dinner	girded	market	prairie
blizzard	dirty	glimmer	marshal	purchase
border	discard	glory	master	razor
burden	distort	guitar	matter	rebirth
burlap	disturb	hairbrush	member	rehearse
butter	doctor	hammer	merchant	resource
cancer	dollar	harness	merit	restore
carbon	dormant	harvest	merriment	return
carton	dreary	herald	mister	revere
cashmere	duration	herbal	modern	rubber
cellar	earache	hereby	monster	rumor
center	earliest	hermit	morning	scarlet
certify	effort	hoarding	mortal	scatter
certain	endurance	hopper	murmur	scoreless

Teaching Phonics & Word Study in the Intermediate Grades • Scholastic Professional Books

searchlight	slipper	sterling	thirsty	urgent
servant	snorkel	suburb	thunder	vapor
severe	soared	summer	timber	varnish
shelter	soccer	supper	torture	vendor
sheriff	solar	target	tractor	vertical
silver	sordid	tearful	tumor	virtue
sincere	spider	temper	turkey	whether
sister	splinter	tender	turnip	whirlwind
skipper	spurious	terrace	under	whisker
skirmish	stairway	terrible	unstirred	winter
slender	stardom	thermos	urban	yearling

Sample Lesson

Words with Consonant + *-le, -al, -el*

Syllabication Spelling Pattern

Key Concept: Explain to your students that every syllable in a word has only one vowel sound. Write *dimple, colossal,* and *counsel* on the chalkboard. Review that *-le, -al,* and *-el* all stand for the same sounds: /ə + l/. Explain that these letter pairs and the consonant that precedes them usually form the last syllable in a word.

Teacher Model: Write the word *rumble* on the chalkboard. Don't say the word, but give students time to examine the word's parts. Then model how to use syllabication strategies to read the word.

Think-Aloud: I know that *-le* and the consonant before it forms the last syllable in a word. Therefore, the last syllable in *r-u-m-b-l-e* is *ble*. That stands for /b ə l/. This leaves *r-u-m*, which is pronounced /rum/. When I put the two word parts together, I get *rumble*.

Blending Practice: Write the following words on the chalkboard. Have students chorally read each word. Provide modeling as necessary.

table	**bundle**	**sparkle**
sizzle	**pickle**	**little**
mantle	**middle**	**global**
hospital	**model**	**chapel**

Reteach Lesson: Words Ending with -le, -al, -el

1. Write the following words on the chalkboard: *table, bridle, puzzle, middle*.

2. Ask students: *What is the same in each of these words?* (They end in a consonant + *-le*.)

3. Have students read the words. Ask: *How many syllables do you hear?* (Two.)

4. Say: *The second syllable is spelled with the consonant +* le. *What sound does the* e *stand for?* (It's silent.)

5. Ask: *What would be a good name for this syllable?* (Consonant + *le*.)

6. Define consonant + *le* syllable for students. (A consonant + *le* syllable ends in a consonant + *le*. Whenever you see a consonant + *le* in a long word, keep them together in the same syllable.)

7. Write the following sentence on the chalkboard for students to complete: A consonant + *le* syllable ends in _____.

8. Extend the lesson by writing two-syllable words with a consonant + *le* final syllable (e.g., *table, bridle, puzzle*). Help students blend each syllable to read the words.

Teacher note: The consonant + *le* syllables (along with the syllables *-ture, -age, -sion,* and *-tion*) are stable final syllables. These are good syllables to include in instruction from grade 3 on up. Directly teach the sounds that each consonant + *le* syllable represents. For example, list on the chalkboard these spelling patterns: *tle, ple, zle, ble, gle, dle*. Read aloud each syllable [e.g., /d ? l/]. Then have students chorally repeat.

Consonant + -*le* Words

able	cable	enable	incurable	pebble
assemble	crumble	fable	jumble	quibble
babble	curable	fumble	kibble	resemble
bauble	disable	gobble	marble	rubble
bible	double	grumble	mumble	rumble
bobble	dribble	hobble	nibble	sable
bubble	durable	humble	noble	scramble

184

scribble	bundle	grapple	cackle	throttle
securable	coddle	maple	chuckle	title
squabble	cuddle	pimple	crackle	turtle
stubble	curdle	purple	fickle	whittle
stumble	dawdle	quadruple	freckle	muffle
table	diddle	ripple	heckle	ruffle
thimble	doodle	sample	honeysuckle	scuffle
timetable	dwindle	scruple	knuckle	shuffle
treble	fiddle	simple	pickle	snuffle
tremble	girdle	steeple	pinochle	truffle
trouble	griddle	temple	ramshackle	bristle
tumble	handle	triple	shackle	bustle
unable	huddle	ankle	sickle	castle
unstable	hurdle	crinkle	spackle	gristle
wobble	kindle	periwinkle	swashbuckle	hustle
angle	meddle	sparkle	tackle	muscle
beagle	middle	sprinkle	tickle	rustle
boggle	muddle	twinkle	trickle	thistle
bugle	needle	wrinkle	Aristotle	tussle
bungle	noodle	dazzle	battle	whistle
eagle	paddle	drizzle	beetle	
giggle	peddle	fizzle	belittle	
goggle	piddle	guzzle	bottle	
jiggle	poodle	muzzle	brittle	
jingle	puddle	nuzzle	cattle	
joggle	riddle	puzzle	gentle	
jungle	saddle	sizzle	hurtle	
mingle	skedaddle	bicycle	kettle	
ogle	spindle	chronicle	little	
shingle	straddle	circle	mantle	
single	swindle	debacle	prattle	
squiggle	toddle	icicle	rattle	
struggle	twiddle	tabernacle	scuttle	
tingle	waddle	tricycle	Seattle	
wiggle	apple	uncle	settle	
befuddle	cripple	vehicle	shuttle	
bridle	dimple	buckle	tattle	

Consonant + -al or -el Words

accidental	focal	mental	chisel
acquittal	fraternal	metal	drivel
bifocal	fundamental	monumental	duffel
brutal	global	nocturnal	kernel
coincidental	hospital	ornamental	label
committal	illegal	parental	mislabel
conical	incidental	paternal	model
continental	instrumental	pedal	mussel
cymbal	internal	petal	nickel
dental	ironical	regal	strudel
detrimental	jackal	rental	pumpernickel
dismissal	journal	sentimental	rebel
environmental	judgmental	temperamental	shrivel
eternal	legal	transcendental	snivel
experimental	local	transmittal	swivel
external	maternal	vocal	yokel
feudal	medal	chapel	

Helping Students Recognize Common Syllables

As students develop in their reading ability, they begin to notice larger word parts, or orthographic chunks (Moats, 1999). "Once a reader perceives a syllable, he begins searching the memory for a word that matches those letters, simultaneously beginning to sound out the letter combinations" (Hall and Moats, 1999). Instead of sounding out each letter, students can more easily sound out and blend larger portions of the word, making decoding more efficient. "As whole words, morphemes, and print patterns become increasingly familiar, knowledge of these larger units of print allows students to read efficiently and spend less and less attention on sounding out words letter by letter" (Share, 1995). For some students this is quite easy and natural, for others it is a daunting task.

There's a great deal teachers can do to help students learn to focus on larger parts of longer words and thus struggle less with decoding. Unfortunately, little is done in most classrooms to build this orthographic awareness that is so critical to reading multisyllabic words. In several studies, Shefelbine (1989, 1990) examined students' (a) ability to read common syllables by sight, (b)

Teaching Phonics & Word Study in the Intermediate Grades • Scholastic Professional Books

flexible identification of multisyllabic word patterns (open and closed syllables), and (c) oral vocabularies. His studies revealed that through systematic, focused instruction on, and flexible use of, common syllable patterns, students' ability to read longer words can be improved. However, he notes that students' oral vocabularies must be well developed so that many words they encounter while reading are already in their speaking and listening vocabularies. As teachers, we can help students sound out words, but if they don't know the words' meanings or have no way of figuring them out, we've only partially done our job of developing skilled readers.

Read aloud at least two nonfiction books a week to expand student's vocabulary and world knowledge.

Shefelbine's research provides a powerful argument for developing a strong nonfiction, read-aloud component in every reading curriculum, beginning in the earliest grades. The more words we can expose our students to, the better off they'll be when they begin to read more complex, vocabulary-laden texts in the upper elementary grades. Thus phonics and vocabulary instruction go hand in hand. Not only can we increase students' oral vocabularies through reading aloud to them and discussing novel words, we can also highlight orthographic regularities among these words to make students aware of how words are similar. For example, when you're reading a text about ocean life, you might point out that all the words beginning with *aqua* have something to do with water, or that all the words beginning with *sub* have something to do with the concept of under. Write a few of these words on the chalkboard and have students comment on the spelling patterns common to the words. Moats (1999) contends that "attention to the internal structure of words, *in both speech and spelling*, supports whole-word identification; it is linguistic awareness, not rote visual memory, that underlies memory for sight words. . . ." Research has shown that learning the structure of words at the syllable and morpheme levels supports word recognition, spelling, and vocabulary development (Nagy and Anderson, 1984).

Cunningham and Stanovich (1998) suggest that teachers can help students become "word detectives" and notice common spelling and pronunciation patterns among related words. The activities that follow are designed to achieve that goal. Since word parts, such as prefixes and suffixes, are much easier to recognize, point these out first. Leave other spelling patterns, such as long-vowel spellings, which are harder to recognize visually, until later. Remember, in order to read multisyllabic words easily, students must be able to (CORE, 2000):

- quickly recognize as "chunks" the phonic patterns they learned in single-syllable words

- understand the concept of a syllable and how to identify vowels and consonants

- recognize various syllable types and their pronunciations

- know where syllables divide (syllable patterns)

- recognize common prefixes, suffixes, and base words

- break apart a word and arrive at an approximate pronunciation, then use context to resolve ambiguity and confirm the word

To help students learn to read multisyllabic words, display a chart like this one on a classroom wall and model the process. Encourage students to refer to the chart as they read independently.

188

READING BIG WORDS

1. Look for the word parts (prefixes) at the beginning of the word.

2. Look for the word parts (suffixes) at the end of the word.

3. In the base word, look for familiar spelling patterns. Think about the six syllable-spelling patterns you have learned.

4. Sound out and blend together the word parts.

5. Say the word parts fast. Adjust your pronunciation as needed. Ask yourself: *"Is it a real word?" "Does it make sense in the sentence?"*

Use the following procedure with students who struggle to identify syllables. Model it frequently with important multisyllabic words from selections your students will be reading.

Model Lessons for Dividing Words

	Routine	Teacher-Student Dialogue
1.	Select a word with recognizable word parts according to the six common syllable-spelling patterns.	Teacher writes the word *fantastic* on the chalkboard.
2.	Underline, loop your finger under, or reveal the first syllable of the word. Help students pronounce the syllable.	**Teacher:** Let's look at the first part of this word: *f-a-n.* How would you pronounce this syllable? **Students:** fan **Teacher:** That's right. This is a closed syllable, since it ends in a consonant. Closed syllables usually have a short vowel sound.
3.	Continue syllable by syllable for the rest of word.	**Teacher:** Let's look at the next syllable: *t-a-s.* How would you pronounce this syllable? **Students:** tas **Teacher:** Great! How is this syllable like the first syllable in the word? **Students:** They are both closed syllables; they both have short vowel sounds. **Teacher:** Super! Now let's read the last syllable in the word: *t-i-c.* It's a closed syllable, too. **Students:** tic
4.	When you have finished working through every syllable, have students blend the syllables together to pronounce the word. During reading, finish the model by asking: "Is that a real word? Does it make sense in the sentence?"	**Teacher:** You read *fan-tas-tic.* Let's put these syllables together to read the whole word. **Students:** fantastic **Teacher:** That's right. The word is *fantastic.*

Teaching Phonics & Word Study in the Intermediate Grades • Scholastic Professional Books

Syllabication Activities

The following quick, fun activities can heighten students' awareness of syllable divisions (Carreker, 1999). Use the Common Syllable Frequency Charts on pages 196–199 to select syllables for the activities.

Research Behind the Common Syllable Frequency Charts

One chart contains the **100 Most Common Non-word Syllables**. The other contains the **322 Most Frequent Syllables in the 5,000 Most Common Words in English**. Of these syllables, 222 or 69% are non-word syllables and 100 or 31% are word syllables. These syllables account for over 70% of the syllables used in these 5,000 words. Sakiey and Martin (1980) have shown that 92% of the syllables found in primary-grade basal readers have no more than two pronunciations; 66% of the syllables have only one pronunciation. Therefore, because these syllables are so regular and are used so often, knowing them will give students great flexibility and agility in reading multisyllabic words.

---

1. Separated-Syllables Read: Write words on the chalkboard syllable by syllable, leaving enough space between the word parts for students to see syllable divisions. Ask students to use their knowledge of common syllable spelling patterns (e.g., closed syllables, open syllables, consonant + *-le*) to read each word. Model blending as necessary by discussing syllable generalizations. When there's a question about a syllable's pronunciation, be sure to have students explain why they pronounced it as they did. It is critical that students be able to verbalize all six syllable-spelling patterns. When they've read each syllable in a word, have students read the word at a natural pace (Gillingham and Stillman, 1997).

fan tas tic	fa ble	ab sent
pump kin	ad ven ture	croc o dile

2. Related-Syllables Read: Write on the chalkboard a series of related open and closed syllables, such as *re, rem, em*. Have students use their knowledge of open and closed syllables to read each. *Alternative:* Create syllable lists using all prefixes, all suffixes, all consonant + *-le* syllables, or some other grouping.

| re | rem | em | | lo | lom | om |
| fi | fim | im | | bo | bot | ot |

3. Multisyllabic Words Manipulation: Divide words you've selected from upcoming reading selections into syllables. Write each syllable on a note card. Display the syllables that make up one of the words in jumbled order (e.g., *tas fan tic*). Have students arrange the syllables to form the word. When necessary, discuss the pronunciation and spelling generalizations of any confusing syllables.

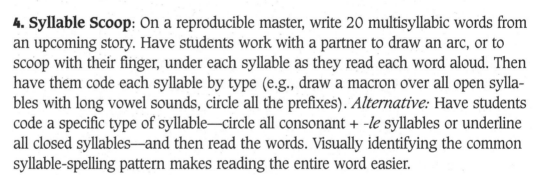

4. Syllable Scoop: On a reproducible master, write 20 multisyllabic words from an upcoming story. Have students work with a partner to draw an arc, or to scoop with their finger, under each syllable as they read each word aloud. Then have them code each syllable by type (e.g., draw a macron over all open syllables with long vowel sounds, circle all the prefixes). *Alternative:* Have students code a specific type of syllable—circle all consonant + *-le* syllables or underline all closed syllables—and then read the words. Visually identifying the common syllable-spelling pattern makes reading the entire word easier.

table

5. Speed Drills: These quick-paced, timed drills (see pages 193–194 for samples) are fun. One drill contains 20 common syllables in random order. The other contains words with a specific syllable-spelling pattern (consonant + *-le*). Before timing students, give them a chance to practice reading the syllables or words on the drill. Then, give them one minute to read as many syllables or words as they can. This must be done one-on-one with each student. I suggest selecting five students each day to test. On a copy of the drill, mark the syllables or words the students mispronounce. Have students count the number of syllables or words read correctly and mark this on a progress chart. Students find it highly motivating to track their own progress.

Sample Syllable Speed Drill

ing	un	ture	ex	dis	com	un	im	ter	ment
er	der	ing	dis	un	ver	er	ble	ble	tion
ter	num	ment	ver	ing	bout	der	ex	er	ple
tion	ble	er	ple	ple	re	dis	num	re	est
re	ment	bout	re	ble	der	ing	com	un	ver
ver	ture	un	ble	er	em	bout	tion	ing	ture
ex	est	ter	im	num	ex	ter	re	fi	com
bout	dis	com	tion	est	tion	ture	ver	dis	ex
com	im	est	num	ter	ment	ment	fi	der	bout
ple	fi	der	fi	ture	fi	est	ple	num	im

Sample Consonant + le Word Speed Drill

bubble	circle	giggle	pebble	steeple	wiggle	fable	middle	sample	simple
battle	crinkle	handle	little	sparkle	puddle	bottle	steeple	rattle	settle
angle	fable	purple	shingle	stubble	uncle	angle	marble	needle	saddle
bridle	cattle	fizzle	middle	rattle	wrinkle	title	apple	uncle	single
apple	eagle	noble	simple	struggle	title	cattle	gentle	pebble	struggle
ankle	fiddle	kettle	puzzle	puddle	saddle	eagle	rumble	vehicle	ankle
double	maple	jungle	rumble	temple	vehicle	circle	giggle	purple	stubble
bottle	dazzle	kindle	mantle	sprinkle	bubble	fiddle	tumble	jungle	puzzle
bugle	marble	sample	single	tumble	double	bundle	maple	little	wrinkle
bundle	gentle	muzzle	needle	settle	battle	handle	kettle	bridle	wiggle

Teaching Phonics & Word Study in the Intermediate Grades • Scholastic Professional Books

102 Most Common Non-Word Syllables

ing	der	la	coun
er	tle	el	mon
i	ber	n't	pe
y	ty	si	lar
ter	num	ent	por
al	peo	ven	fi
ed	ble	ev	bers
es	af	ac	sec
e	ers	ca	ap
tion	mer	fol	stud
re	wa	ful	ad
o	ment	na	tween
oth	pro	tain	gan
ry	ar	ning	bod
de	ma	col	tence
ver	ri	par	ward
ex	sen	dis	hap
en	ture	ern	nev
di	fer	ny	ure
bout	dif	cit	mem
com	pa	po	ters
ple	tions	cal	cov
u	ther	mu	ger
con	fore	moth	nit
per	est	pic	
un	fa	im	

322 Most Common Syllables
in the 5,000 Most Frequent English Words

1.	ing	36.	ment	71.	ger	106.	light	141.	age
2.	er	37.	or	72.	low	107.	ob	142.	ba
3.	a	38.	tions	73.	ni	108.	of	143.	but
4.	ly	39.	ble	74.	par	109.	pos	144.	cit
5.	ed	40.	der	75.	son	110.	tain	145.	cle
6.	i	41.	ma	76.	tle	111.	den	146.	co
7.	es	42.	na	77.	day	112.	ings	147.	cov
8.	re	43.	si	78.	ny	113.	mag	148.	da
9.	tion	44.	un	79.	pen	114.	ments	149.	dif
10.	in	45.	at	80.	pre	115.	set	150.	ence
11.	e	46.	dis	81.	tive	116.	some	151.	ern
12.	con	47.	ca	82.	car	117.	sub	152.	eve
13.	y	48.	cal	83.	ci	118.	sur	153.	hap
14.	ter	49.	man	84.	mo	119.	ters	154.	ies
15.	ex	50.	ap	85.	on	120.	tu	155.	ket
16.	al	51.	po	86.	ous	121.	af	156.	lec
17.	de	52.	sion	87.	pi	122.	au	157.	main
18.	com	53.	vi	88.	se	123.	cy	158.	mar
19.	o	54.	el	89.	ten	124.	fa	159.	mis
20.	di	55.	est	90.	tor	125.	im	160.	my
21.	en	56.	la	91.	ver	126.	li	161.	nal
22.	an	57.	lar	92.	ber	127.	lo	162.	ness
23.	ty	58.	pa	93.	can	128.	men	163.	ning
24.	ry	59.	ture	94.	dy	129.	min	164.	n't
25.	u	60.	for	95.	et	130.	mon	165.	nu
26.	ti	61.	is	96.	it	131.	op	166.	oc
27.	ri	62.	mer	97.	mu	132.	out	167.	pres
28.	be	63.	pe	98.	no	133.	rec	168.	sup
29.	per	64.	ra	99.	ple	134.	ro	169.	te
30.	to	65.	so	100.	cu	135.	sen	170.	ted
31.	pro	66.	ta	101.	fac	136.	side	171.	tem
32.	ac	67.	as	102.	fer	137.	tal	172.	tin
33.	ad	68.	col	103.	gen	138.	tic	173.	tri
34.	ar	69.	fi	104.	ic	139.	ties	174.	tro
35.	ers	70.	ful	105.	land	140.	ward	175.	up

Teaching Phonics & Word Study in the Intermediate Grades • Scholastic Professional Books

322 Most Frequent Syllables
in the 5,000 Most Frequent English Words

176.	va	211.	cir	246.	tra	281.	lead	316.	tract
177.	ven	212.	cor	247.	tures	282.	lect	317.	tray
178.	vis	213.	coun	248.	val	283.	lent	318.	us
179.	am	214.	cus	249.	var	284.	less	319.	vel
180.	bor	215.	dan	250.	vid	285.	lin	320.	west
181.	by	216.	dle	251.	wil	286.	mal	321.	where
182.	cat	217.	ef	252.	win	287.	mi	322.	writ
183.	cent	218.	end	253.	won	288.	mil		
184.	ev	219.	ent	254.	work	289.	moth		
185.	gan	220.	ered	255.	act	290.	near		
186.	gle	221.	fin	256.	ag	291.	nel		
187.	head	222.	form	257.	air	292.	net		
188.	high	223.	go	258.	als	293.	new		
189.	il	224.	har	259.	bat	294.	one		
190.	lu	225.	ish	260.	bi	295.	point		
191.	me	226.	lands	261.	cate	296.	prac		
192.	nore	227.	let	262.	cen	297.	ral		
193.	part	228.	long	263.	char	298.	rect		
194.	por	229.	mat	264.	come	299.	ried		
195.	read	230.	meas	265.	cul	300.	round		
196.	rep	231.	mem	266.	ders	301.	row		
197.	su	232.	mul	267.	east	302.	sa		
198.	tend	233.	ner	268.	fect	303.	sand		
199.	ther	234.	play	269.	fish	304.	self		
200.	ton	235.	ples	270.	fix	305.	sent		
201.	try	236.	ply	271.	gi	306.	ship		
202.	um	237.	port	272.	grand	307.	sim		
203.	uer	238.	press	273.	great	308.	sions		
204.	way	239.	sat	274.	heav	309.	sis		
205.	ate	240.	sec	275.	ho	310.	sons		
206.	bet	241.	ser	276.	hunt	311.	stand		
207.	bles	242.	south	277.	ion	312.	sug		
208.	bod	243.	sun	278.	its	313.	tel		
209.	cap	244.	the	279.	jo	314.	tom		
210.	cial	245.	ting	280.	lat	315.	tors		

50 Sample Two-Syllable Words for Instruction

absent	dessert	inspect	paper	sandbox
action	exclaim	jolly	pencil	special
applaud	excuse	joyous	planet	stubborn
balloon	fastest	kicking	plastic	subtract
because	flavor	laughing	pocket	surprise
before	grassy	louder	pretzel	table
center	hammer	magic	pumpkin	turtle
contest	helpful	mitten	puzzle	unlock
cricket	insect	monster	question	valley
dinner	insist	notebook	railroad	water

50 Sample Three-Syllable Words for Instruction

activate	Chihuahua	fabulous	kangaroo	normally
adventure	committee	factory	labyrinth	poisonous
advisor	crocodile	fantastic	listening	popular
banana	cucumber	forever	magnify	terrible
bicycle	cumulus	gigantic	marshmallow	tornado
butterfly	curious	habitat	marvelous	underneath
cantaloupe	different	honestly	magical	vacation
capable	difficult	however	millionaire	watery
caravan	discotheque	icicle	mosquito	whichever
carousel	elephant	invention	multiply	wonderful

50 Sample Four-Syllable Words for Instruction

absolutely	conceptual	escalator	kindergarten	populated
acceptable	considerate	especially	librarian	refrigerate
activity	conversation	exaggerate	magnificent	regularly
adorable	dedicated	fortunately	material	reversible
adversary	dependable	graduation	misunderstood	spectacular
affectionate	demonstration	hysterical	motorcycle	stationery
alligator	differences	independent	mysterious	tarantula
calculator	energetic	information	necessary	transformation
caterpillar	enjoyable	interested	operation	unusual
competitive	entertainment	interrupted	pepperoni	watermelon

Teaching Phonics & Word Study in the Intermediate Grades • Scholastic Professional Books

Five-Syllable Words

abracadabra	choreography	inexcusable	representative	unacceptable
academia	claustrophobia	intellectual	schizophrenia	uncontrollable
administration	hippopotamus	irreplaceable	tonsillectomy	underachiever
auditorium	indestructible	paraphernalia	transcontinental	underdeveloped
bibliography	indisputable	reprehensible	transfiguration	Yugoslavia

Six-Syllable Words

authoritarian	encyclopedia	onomatopoeia	undereducated
autobiography	incomprehensible	paleontology	unimaginable
disciplinarian	octogenarian	Tyrannosaurus Rex	unsatisfactory

Just for Fun! 14 Syllables

supercalifragilisticexpialidocious

Word Study (Structural Analysis)

When they begin reading increasingly complex texts, students will encounter growing numbers of multisyllabic words. Teaching students word analysis gives them additional strategies they need to tackle those longer, more difficult words. The following pages provide guidelines and word lists for the following word-study skills:

1. Compound Words

2. Prefixes

3. Suffixes (including plurals and inflectional endings)

4. Homophones

5. Greek and Latin Roots

Word-Study Research

"The term word study refers to the process of learning everything about words, including their spelling, meaning, pronunciation, historical origin, and relationship with other words" (Moats, 2000). Skilled readers use phonics to determine a word's pronunciation, context clues to infer a word's meaning, and structural analysis, or knowledge of word parts, to determine both a word's meaning and pronunciation. Nagy and Anderson (1984) estimated that as many as 60% of English words have meanings that can be predicted from the meanings of their parts. For another 10% of English words, word parts may give useful, though incomplete, information. This is critical when you consider that the average fifth-grader reads 1 million words of text a year (Anderson, Wilson, and Fielding, 1998). Of these 1 million words, they'll see 10,000 only once—1,000 are truly novel words not related to words they've previously encountered. Therefore, the majority of the words are related to known words, and structural analysis can play a key role in figuring out their pronunciations and meanings. For example, 4,000 of the words are derived from more frequent words (e.g., *romantic/unromantic, debt/indebtedness*) and 1,300 are inflections (*merit/merited, merge/merges*).

In a study by Henry (1988), on-level students knew far too little about the major structures of words, including syllable and morpheme patterns. Below-level students knew virtually nothing about word structure. As Henry states: "Unfortunately, decoding instruction largely neglects syllable and morpheme patterns, perhaps because these techniques are primarily useful for the longer words found in literature and subject matter text beyond grade 2 or 3, at which point decoding instruction becomes virtually nonexistent in most schools. Without recognizing the value of syllabic and morphological patterns, the student is constrained from using clues available to identify long, unfamiliar words." Although some on-level students can use knowledge of structural analysis to determine the meanings of new words (Tyler and Nagy, 1989), many fail to apply their knowledge of word parts where it would be helpful (White, Power, and White, 1989; Wysocki and Jenkins, 1987). Therefore, instruction in structural analysis, or key word parts, can improve students' ability to interpret, remember the meanings of, and spell new multisyllabic words.

Teaching Phonics & Word Study in the Intermediate Grades • Scholastic Professional Books

How to Teach Word Study/
<u>Structural Analysis</u>:

- **Introduce, or reinforce, the concept that words can be made up of several elements.** Define these elements, such as prefixes, suffixes, and roots, for students, but focus primarily on how students can use word parts to sound out a word and figure out its meaning. The word part *un*, for example, is very common; students should be able to recognize it immediately in unfamiliar words. Teach children to recognize the word part and explain that its meaning affects the meaning of the whole word. Some examples include *unhappy, unsuccessful,* and *unable.* Contrast these words with non-examples such as *uncle* and *until.*

- **Be sure your instruction is explicit.** Tell students why they are learning a specific skill, show when they can use it, and provide many opportunities for them to practice using it.

- **During instruction, rely more on concrete, known examples, rather than abstract rules, principles, or definitions.** Illustrate all generalizations with countless examples. During reading, focus students' attention on the relationship between a word's internal structure and its role in a sentence. For example, although it's not particularly useful to teach the meanings of suffixes, knowing that a particular suffix changes a word from an adjective to a noun can be important in understanding a word's role in a sentence.

- **Alert students to the diversity of English words.** Provide instruction in Anglo-Saxon, Greek, and Roman roots and clarify the differences among them. Also, teach prefixes and suffixes differently. For example, although learning the meanings of prefixes is important, learning the meanings of suffixes has less value.

- **Be sure students are aware of the limitations of structural analysis.** For example, not all words that begin with *un* begin with a prefix (e.g., *unhappy* vs. *under*). Remind students that after they analyze a word to determine its pronunciation and meaning they should check to see if it makes sense in the sentence.

- **Apply! Apply! Apply!** Use all reading experiences as an opportunity for students to use their knowledge of word parts to pronounce and determine the meanings of unfamiliar words.

Teaching Phonics & Word Study in the Intermediate Grades • Scholastic Professional Books

Compound Words

Guidelines:

- A compound word is a word made up of two smaller words. Often its meaning can be derived from the meaning of the two smaller words that comprise it: a *doghouse* is a "house for a dog." However, there are notable exceptions such as *butterfly*.

- There are three types of compound words: open (*fire drill*), closed (*doghouse*), and hyphenated (*by-pass*).

- Encourage students to look for smaller words in larger words to help them pronounce and, sometimes, figure out the meanings of the larger words. Compound-word instruction serves as an introduction to this concept. However, it's important to encourage children to look for words with more than two or three letters in a larger word. Identifying a two-letter word in a larger word isn't always useful. For example, finding the word *to* in *town* or *tornado* is useless for both determining pronunciation and meaning.

- Point out that when a compound word is divided, each remaining smaller word must be able to stand on its own.

Teaching Phonics & Word Study in the Intermediate Grades • Scholastic Professional Books

Compound Words

after all	baseball	broomstick	downhill	firefly
afternoon	basketball	bulldog	downstairs	firehouse
aftershave	bath mat	bullfrog	downtown	firelight
air bag	bathrobe	butterfly	dragonfly	fireplace
air boat	bathroom	buttermilk	dressmaker	firewood
air hole	bathtub	by-pass	driveway	fireworks
airmail	bathwater	campfire	drumstick	flowerpot
air mattress	beanbag	campground	dugout	football
airplane	beanpod	candlelight	eardrum	footbridge
airsick	beanpole	candlemaker	earthquake	footpath
airtight	bed rest	candlestick	electric guitar	footprint
anteater	bedroll	cardboard	everybody	footrest
anthill	bedroom	cheerleader	everyday	footstep
anybody	bedside	classroom	everyone	footstool
anyhow	bedspread	clothespin	everything	give-and-take
anyone	bedspring	clubhouse	everywhere	goldfish
anything	bedtime	coal mine	eyeball	grapevine
anywhere	beehive	collarbone	eyeglasses	grasshopper
applesauce	beeline	cookbook	eyelid	greenhouse
armchair	birdbath	cornbread	eyesight	grownup
armrest	birdcall	corncob	faraway	headstand
back away	birdcage	cornfield	farmhouse	hairbrush
backboard	bird dog	countdown	father-in-law	haircut
backbone	birdhouse	cowboy	finger bowl	hairnet
backdoor	birdseed	crossword	finger hole	hairpiece
backfield	birthday	cupcake	fingernail	hairpin
background	blackbird	daydream	fingerpaint	hairstyle
backpack	blackboard	daylight	fingerprint	hand-feed
back room	blindfold	diving board	fingertip	handbag
backseat	blueberry	doghouse	fire drill	handball
backstage	bluebird	dollhouse	fire engine	handbook
backstop	blueprint	doorbell	fire escape	handmade
backstroke	boathouse	doorknob	fire station	handpick
backyard	bookbag	doormat	fire truck	handsaw
bagpipe	bookcase	doorstep	fire-eater	handshake
bandleader	bookmark	doorway	fireboat	handstand
barnyard	bottonhole	double-header	firefighter	handwrite

Compound Words (continued)

headache	mailbox	raincoat	smokestack	teaspoon
headband	masterpiece	raindrop	snapshot	tennis court
headphone	merry-go-round	rainfall	snowball	thunderstorm
henhouse	milkshake	ringmaster	snowfall	tightrope
high chair	moonbeam	roadside	snowflake	toadstool
high jump	moonlight	roof garden	snowman	toenail
high noon	mother-in-law	rooftop	snowplow	toeshoe
high school	motorboat	rosebud	snowshoe	toolbox
high-rise	motorcycle	rosebush	snowstorm	toothache
hilltop	mousetrap	rowboat	snowsuit	toothbrush
home plate	music box	sailboat	somebody	toothpaste
home run	newspaper	sandbox	someday	townspeople
homegrown	nightgown	sandpaper	someone	treetop
homemade	notebook	saucepan	something	tugboat
homeroom	outdoors	sawdust	someway	underground
homesick	outfield	scarecrow	spaceship	underwater
hometown	outside	scrapbook	spacesuit	upstairs
homework	overlook	sea breeze	springtime	wallpaper
horseback	overnight	sea captain	starfish	washcloth
horsefly	overtake	sea gull	starlight	watchdog
horseshoe	pancake	sea horse	starship	waterfall
hotdog	passer-by	seacoast	steamboat	whatever
houseboat	peanut	seafood	stepladder	wheelchair
ice skate	pillowcase	seaport	storehouse	windmill
ice skater	pinecone	seashell	storeroom	windpipe
iceberg	pinwheel	seashore	storyteller	windshield
inside	playground	seaside	sunburn	wintertime
jellyfish	playhouse	seat belt	sunflower	wishbone
keyhole	playpen	seaweed	sunlight	without
lawnmower	pocketbook	send-off	sunrise	workbench
lifetime	poison ivy	shopkeeper	sunset	workday
lighthouse	polar bear	shoreline	sunshine	worktable
living room	popcorn	sidewalk	supermarket	wristwatch
lookout	postcard	sideways	swimming pool	
loudspeaker	railroad	skyline	tablespoon	
lunchroom	rainbow	skyscraper	teacup	

204

Prefixes

Guidelines:

- **A prefix is a group of letters that appears at the front of a word.** A prefix affects the meaning of the root (base) word to which it is attached. To determine whether or not a group of letters is a prefix, remove them from the word. The letters are a prefix if a known word remains. For example, remove the letters *un* from the following words: *unhappy, untie, uncle, uninterested.* In which word are the letters *un* <u>not</u> a prefix? Yes, these letters are not a prefix in the word *uncle.*

- **Make students aware of the following warnings about prefixes.**

  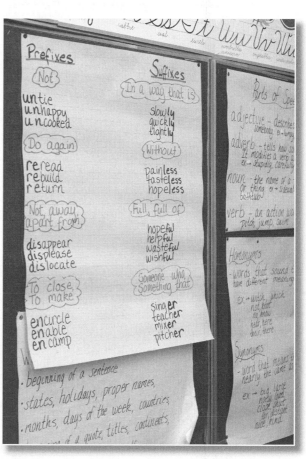

  1. Most prefixes have more than one meaning. For example, the prefix *un* can mean "not" as in *unhappy*, or "do the opposite of" as in *untie*. Teach the multiple meanings of the most common prefixes, and use careful language during lessons such as, "the prefix *un* <u>sometimes</u> means not."

  2. Be careful of letter clusters that look like prefixes, but aren't. For example, when the letters *un* are removed from *uncle*, no recognizable root word is left. In addition, when the letters *in* are removed from *invented*, the word that remains has no relation to the whole word. The prefixes that cause the most difficulty are *re, in,* and *dis.*

  3. Don't rely solely on word-part clues to determine meaning. Use context clues as well to verify a word's meaning. For example, you might think the word *unassuming* means "not assuming/not supposing" instead of its actual meaning "modest." It is estimated that about 15 to 20% of the prefixed words students will encounter share this complexity (White et al., 1989).

- **Teach only the most common prefixes.** The chart that follows shows the most common based on a count of prefixed words appearing in the *Word Frequency Book* (Carroll, Davies, and Richman, 1971). The prefix *un* alone accounts for almost one-third of the total. The top three on the list account for over half.

Rank	Prefix	%		Rank	Prefix	%
1.	un (not, opposite of)	26		11.	pre (before)	3
2.	re (again)	14		12.	inter (between, among)	3
3.	in, im, ir, il (not)	11		13.	fore (before)	3
4.	dis (not, opposite of)	7		14.	de (opposite of)	2
5.	en, em (cause to)	4		15.	trans (across)	2
6.	non (not)	4		16.	super (above)	1
7.	in, im (in or into)	4		17.	semi (half)	1
8.	over (too much)	3		18.	anti (against)	1
9.	mis (wrongly)	3		19.	mid (middle)	1
10.	sub (under)	3		20.	under (too little)	1

All other prefixes (about 100) accounted for only 3% of the words.

Teaching Phonics & Word Study in the Intermediate Grades • Scholastic Professional Books

Prefixes
Word Study

Key Concept: Explain that a prefix is a group of letters added to the beginning of a word, changing its meaning.

Teacher Model: Write the word *unhappy* on the chalkboard. Don't say the word, but give students time to examine its parts. Then model how to use knowledge of prefixes to decode the word and figure out its meaning.

Think-Aloud: I know that sometimes a base word contains parts added to it, such as a prefix. In this word I see the prefix *un,* meaning not. The rest of the word is *happy.* I can put the two word parts together to get the word *unhappy.* Since *un* means not, this word means "not happy." Looking for common word parts, such as prefixes, is a good way to read an unfamiliar word and figure out its meaning.

Blending Practice: Write the following words on the chalkboard. Have students chorally read each word. Provide modeling as necessary.

unafraid	**uncover**	**unheard**
unpleasant	**unprotected**	**unhurt**
unreal	**unroll**	**uneven**
unstuck	**uncap**	**unwrap**

Point Out Non-Examples: Explain to students that just because a word begins with the letters *un* (or any other letters for a prefix) doesn't mean it's a prefix. They must look at what's left over when removing the prefix to see if it's a real word. For example, write the words *unable, unplug, uncle,* and *under* on the chalkboard. Ask students to identify which words begin with a prefix and why.

Prefix Word Lists

un

unable	unclip	unfamiliar	unlawful	unrest
unaccustomed	uncombed	unfasten	unlike	unrestrained
unafraid	uncomfortable	unfelt	unlikely	unroll
unanswered	uncommon	unfinished	unlit	unruly
unathletic	unconscious	unfit	unload	unsafe
unattractive	uncontrollably	unfold	unlock	unsatisfactory
unaware	uncooked	unfortunate	unloved	unscrew
unbearable	uncover	unfriendly	unlucky	unseen
unbelievable	uncrate	unglue	unmade	unsnap
unbend	uncrowded	unhappy	unmake	unsold
unbind	uncut	unharmed	unmarked	unspoiled
unblock	undamaged	unhealthy	unmarried	unsteady
unborn	undecided	unheard	unmistakable	unstick
unbound	undo	unhook	unmoved	unstring
unbroken	undone	unhurt	unnamed	unsuccessful
unbuilt	undress	unidentified	unnatural	unsure
uncanny	unearth	unimaginable	unpack	untangle
uncap	uneasy	unimportant	unpaid	unthinkable
uncertain	unequal	unimpressed	unpleasant	untie
unchain	uneven	uninhabited	unprotected	untouched
unchanged	uneventful	uninteresting	unplug	unwanted
unchecked	unexpected	unkind	unravel	unwind
unclean	unexplored	unknown	unreal	unwise
unclear	unfair	unlatch	unreasonable	unwrap

Teaching Phonics & Word Study in the Intermediate Grades • Scholastic Professional Books

re

reappear	redraw	remix	reread	retrace
reapply	refigure	remove	rescore	return
rearrange	refill	rename	respond	retype
reassure	reform	renew	reseal	reunite
reattach	refreeze	reoil	resell	reuse
rebuild	refuse	reopen	resew	reveal
recall	regain	repack	reshoot	reverse
recheck	regrade	repaid	restack	revise
recook	regroup	repave	restate	rewash
recopy	rehang	repay	restuff	rewind
recount	rehearse	replace	resume	rewrite
recover	reheat	replan	retag	rewrap
recut	relearn	replenish	retie	
recycle	release	reproduce	retire	
rediscover	reload	request	retold	

in, im, ir, il

illegal	impatient	inappropriate	indirect	insane
illegible	imperfect	inboard	indistinct	insatiable
illiterate	impersonal	inbounds	indoors	inseparable
imbalance	impetuous	incapable	inefficient	insight
immaterial	impolite	incase	inevitable	invaluable
immature	impossible	incompetent	inexpensive	invisible
immodest	impractical	incomplete	inexperienced	irrational
immortal	improper	inconvenient	infinite	irregular
immovable	impure	incorrect	infrequent	irresistible
impartial	inaccurate	indefinite	ingrown	irresponsible
impassable	inadequate	indignant	injustice	irrevocably

dis

disable	disarray	disengage	dislodge	displeasure
disadvantage	disbelief	disgrace	dismantle	dispute
disagree	discard	disgust	dismiss	disqualify
disagreeable	discolor	dishearten	disobey	distort
disallow	discomfort	dishonest	disorder	distract
disappear	disconnect	disintegrate	disown	distrust
disappoint	discourage	disjoin	displace	disturb
disapprove	disdain	dislike	displease	

en, em

embark	encage	encounter	enjoy	entangle
embarrass	encamp	encourage	enlarge	entitle
embattle	encase	endear	enlighten	entrust
embedded	enchant	endure	enlist	envelop
emblazon	encircle	enfold	enrage	envision
embrace	enclose	enforce	enrich	enwind
employ	encode	engage	enroll	
enable	encompass	engulf	ensure	

non

nonabrasive	nonchalant	nondrip	nonrealistic
nonabsorbent	nonchallenged	noneffective	nonremovable
nonacademic	noncombustible	nonequivalent	nonreflecting
nonacceptance	noncommittal	nonexplainable	nonresponsive
nonactive	nonconditional	nonfactual	nonsimilar
nonadjustable	nonconsecutive	nonfiction	nonslip
nonaquatic	noncontagious	nongraded	nonsmoker
nonathletic	noncreative	nonhistoric	nonspecific
nonattached	noncritical	nonindustrial	nonsticky
nonbeing	noncurrent	noninfected	nonstop
nonbinding	nondeductible	nonliving	nonsupporter
nonbreakable	nondigestible	nonpaying	nonwashable
noncentral	nondissolved	nonperfect	
noncertified	nondrinkable	nonqualified	

Teaching Phonics & Word Study in the Intermediate Grades • Scholastic Professional Books

over

overact	overcast	overflow	overplan	overstep
overbake	overclean	overjoyed	overpowering	oversweet
overbeat	overcoach	overlap	overrate	overtake
overbill	overcome	overlarge	override	overthin
overboard	overcook	overlength	oversalt	overtight
overbook	overcrowded	overload	overshadow	overtip
overbusy	overdo	overnice	oversized	overuse
overcame	overdry	overpay	overslept	overwhelm

mis

misact	miscalculate	misdo	mislocate	misread
misaddress	mischoose	misfile	misname	mistreat
misadjust	misconnect	misguide	misnumber	mistype
misadvise	misdefine	misjudge	misorder	misunderstood
misarrange	misdiagnose	mislead	mispronounce	

sub

subaquatic	subdivide	sublease	submerge	subterranean
subclass	subgroup	submarine	substandard	subway
subconscious				

pre

preadult	predinner	prelunch	preplan	prestamp
prearrange	pregame	premeasure	prequalify	pretrial
precool	preharvest	premix	prerinse	pretrim
precut	preheat	prenoon	presale	prewash
predawn	prejudge	preorder	preseason	prework

inter

interact	intercommunity	interlock	intersect
interchange	interconnect	intermix	interspace
intercollegiate	intergroup	international	interstate

fore

forearm	foreground	forereach	foreshadow	forethought
forecast	forehead	forerun	foreshock	forewarn
forecheck	forejudge	foresaid	forespeak	
forego	foreknow	foresail	foretaste	
foregone	forename	foresee	foretell	

de

debug	deface	deform	deplane	dethrone
declaw	defang	defrost	derail	detrain
decompose	deflate			

trans

transatlantic	transfer	transmit
transborder	translocate	transplant

super

superable	superdifficult	superman	supersize
superabsorbent	superfast	supernatural	supersoft
superabundant	superheat	superpower	superspeed
supercharge	superhighway	supersafe	superthin
superclean	superhuman	supersensitive	superwide

semi

semiactive	semidome	semiopen	semistiff
semiautomatic	semidry	semipeaceful	semiweekly
semiclosed	semifinal	semipro	
semidangerous	semifinished	semiskilled	

Teaching Phonics & Word Study in the Intermediate Grades • Scholastic Professional Books

anti

antibacterial	anticrime	antigravity	antisocial

mid

midafternoon	midland	midsize	midweek
midcourse	midnight	midterm	midwinter
midday	midrange	midway	midyear

under

underachieve	undercover	underfeed	undershirt
underage	underdeveloped	underground	undersize
underbake	underdo	undergrown	understudy
underbrush	underdog	underpay	undertake
undercharge	underdress	underperform	underwater
underclothes	underemploy	underrate	underway
undercoat	underestimate	undersea	underwear
undercook	underexpose	undersell	

Suffixes

Guidelines:

- **A suffix is a letter, or group of letters, that is added to the end of a root (base) word. Common suffixes include *s, ed, ing, ly,* and *tion*.** A suffix changes the meaning of the root or base word. Therefore, children, need to understand the meanings of suffixes and how they affect the words they're attached to. By helping children quickly identify a suffix and visually remove it to identify the base word, you'll help them figure out the meaning of the whole word.

- **Adding a suffix sometimes changes the spelling of a base word,** and children need to be directly taught the suffixes that cause changes. The three most common spelling changes resulting from the addition of suffixes are:

   1. *Consonant doubling* (*runner, running*): The consonant is doubled so that the first syllable will form a CVC pattern. Most CVC words contain a short vowel sound. Therefore, the second consonant acts as a diacritical mark, ensuring that the short vowel sound of the root word is maintained.

   2. *Changing* y *to* i (*flies, happiest, loneliness*): Words that end in *y* change the *y* to *i* before adding a suffix. The letter *y* at the beginning of a word or syllable acts as a consonant and stands for the /y/ sound. However, the letter *y* at the end of a word either stands for a vowel sound (*fly*) or is part of a vowel digraph (*play*). The change from *y* to *i* ensures that the vowel sound the *y* stands for in the word is maintained.

   3. *Deleting the silent* e (*making*): When a word ends in silent *e,* the letter is removed before adding the suffix (except *s*). Most of the common suffixes begin with vowels and vowel doubling in this case would cause confusion; it would create a vowel digraph.

- **Teach only the most commonly used suffixes.** The chart on page 215 shows the 20 most frequent suffixes appearing in words in the *Word Frequency Book* (Carroll, Davies, and Richman, 1971). The suffixes *s, es, ed,* and *ing* account for almost two-thirds of the words. The suffixes *s* and *es* are used to form the plurals of most nouns. The suffixes *ed* and *ing* are inflectional endings added to verbs to change their tense. These suffixes are generally introduced to children in grade one. The word lists included here are for those suffixes that need to be formally taught in the primary grades.

Teaching Phonics & Word Study in the Intermediate Grades • Scholastic Professional Books

Rank	Suffix	%
1.	s, es (plurals)	31
2.	ed (past-tense verbs)	20
3.	ing (verb form/present participle)	14
4.	ly (characteristic of)	7
5.	er, or (person connected with)	4
6.	ion, tion, ation, ition (act, process)	4
7.	ible, able (can be done)	2
8.	al, ial (having characteristics of)	1
9.	y (characterized by)	1
10.	ness (state of, condition of)	1

Rank	Suffix	%
11.	ity, ty (state of)	1
12.	ment (action or process)	1
13.	ic (having characteristics of)	1
14.	ous, eous, ious (possessing the qualities of)	1
15.	en (made of)	1
16.	er (comparative)	1
17.	ive, ative, itive (adjective form of a noun)	1
18.	ful (full of)	1
19.	less (without)	1
20.	est (comparative)	1

All other suffixes (about 160) accounted for only 7% of the words.

Noun suffixes: *age, al, ance, ant, ate, ee, ence, ent, er, or, ar, ese, ess, hood, ice, ism, ist, ment, ness, sion, tain, tion, ure*

Suffixes that form adjectives: *able, al, er, est, ette, let, ful, fully, ible, ic, ical, ish, ive, less, ous, some, worthy*

Suffixes that form adverbs: *ly, wards, ways, wide, wise*

Suffixes that create a verb form: *ate, ed, en, ing, ise, ize, yze*

Suffixes
Word Study

Key Concept: Explain that a suffix is a word part added to the end of a base word, changing its meaning. Common suffixes include *s*, *es*, *ed*, *ing*, *ly*, and *ful*.

Teacher Model: Write the word *softly* on the chalkboard. Don't say the word, but give students time to examine the word's parts. Then model how to use knowledge of suffixes to decode the word and figure out its meaning.

Think-Aloud: I know that sometimes a base word contains parts added to it, such as a suffix. In this word I see the suffix *ly*. The rest of the word is *soft*. I can put the two word parts together to get the word *softly*. Looking for common word parts, such as suffixes, is a good way to read an unfamiliar word and figure out its meaning.

Blending Practice: Write the following words on the chalkboard. Have students chorally read each word. Provide modeling as necessary.

brightly	**clearly**	**closely**
correctly	**costly**	**quickly**
quietly	**repeatedly**	**sadly**
safely	**sickly**	**delicately**

Suffix Word Lists

-es

arches	catches	kisses	reaches
ashes	circuses	latches	riches
axes	classes	mashes	rushes
batches	coaches	matches	sizes
beaches	dashes	misses	sketches
benches	dishes	mixes	smashes
bosses	dresses	passes	splashes
boxes	fishes	patches	teaches
breezes	fixes	peaches	touches
brushes	flashes	presses	washes
buses	gases	prizes	watches
bushes	glasses	pushes	wishes
buzzes	grasses	quizzes	
cashes	inches	ranches	

216

-s

bags	cakes	dates	kites	plays	tests
beads	capes	days	lakes	plums	toads
beans	caps	dimes	masks	pots	toes
beds	cats	dots	mats	queens	toys
bees	caves	dreams	mitts	rakes	trains
bells	cents	eggs	moms	rats	trays
belts	chains	flakes	mugs	roads	trees
bibs	clocks	gifts	notes	ropes	trucks
bikes	coats	globes	oats	sacks	vans
blocks	cones	hams	paints	sinks	weeks
boats	cots	hats	pans	skates	
bones	cubes	hens	pies	skunks	
boys	cubs	jeans	pigs	socks	
braids	cups	jeeps	pits	sticks	
cabs	dads	jobs	plants	streets	

-ed /d/

bagged	closed	fined	nabbed	robed	snagged
banged	crammed	framed	named	ruled	staged
blabbed	craved	fumed	phoned	sagged	tamed
blamed	cubed	gazed	phrased	scanned	throbbed
bombed	dazed	glazed	planned	schemed	timed
boned	dined	grabbed	poled	scrammed	toned
bragged	doled	holed	prized	shamed	tugged
buzzed	domed	hummed	probed	shaved	tuned
caged	dozed	jammed	raged	sized	used
canned	dragged	jogged	rammed	slammed	
chimed	fanned	lined	rhymed	slugged	
cloned	filed	longed	robbed	smiled	

-ed /ed/

acted	drafted	handed	matted	quoted	squinted
added	drifted	hated	melted	rated	stated
banded	ended	hinted	mended	rested	stranded
batted	faded	hunted	muted	rusted	tempted
blasted	fitted	jaded	nodded	sanded	tended
budded	frosted	jotted	noted	sculpted	tilted
busted	funded	jutted	petted	shaded	toted
ceded	gifted	kidded	planted	shifted	traded
chanted	gilded	knotted	plodded	shredded	trotted
chatted	glided	landed	plotted	sided	trusted
coded	graded	lasted	printed	skated	voted
crated	granted	lifted	prodded	skidded	waded
dated	grunted	listed	prompted	slanted	
dotted	guided	mated	quilted	spotted	

-ed /t/

asked	chomped	guessed	paced	sloped	taped
axed	clapped	helped	passed	smacked	taxed
backed	clashed	hiked	pecked	smoked	thanked
baked	clipped	hoped	picked	snaked	traced
based	coped	hopped	pinched	sniffed	trapped
biked	cracked	iced	placed	spiked	tricked
blinked	crunched	inched	poked	spliced	tripped
boxed	dipped	itched	priced	spruced	tucked
braced	draped	joked	puffed	staked	typed
brushed	dressed	kicked	quaked	stamped	wiped
bumped	dropped	knocked	raked	stepped	wished
bussed	faced	liked	ripped	stitched	zipped
capped	fished	locked	roped	stopped	
cased	fixed	milked	rushed	strapped	
chased	flapped	missed	scraped	striped	
checked	flipped	mixed	shaped	stroked	
choked	griped	napped	sliced	swiped	

Teaching Phonics & Word Study in the Intermediate Grades • Scholastic Professional Books

-ing

acting	drawing	helping	planning	smashing	waiting
beating	eating	keeping	planting	soaking	walking
blocking	ending	landing	playing	speaking	washing
boating	fainting	leaking	reaching	speeding	watching
boxing	feeding	mashing	resting	sticking	winking
brushing	fishing	matching	ringing	swaying	wishing
catching	fixing	meeting	running	sweeping	
cleaning	flashing	painting	saying	teaching	
covering	floating	painting	sinking	training	
draining	heating	parking	sleeping	treating	

-er

banker	closer	heater	player	sweeper
blocker	cooker	jogger	reader	simmer
boxer	dreamer	jumper	robber	teacher
builder	eater	leader	runner	user
caller	farmer	logger	singer	washer
catcher	flier	maker	sleeper	worker
cleaner	fryer	packer	speaker	wrapper
climber	gardener	painter	splasher	writer

-or

actor	collector	director	inventor	senator
advisor	conductor	governor	sailor	survivor
auditor	creator	investigator	sculptor	visitor

-ion, -tion

abbreviation	comprehension	education	plantation
addition	computation	elevation	pollution
admiration	concentration	eruption	population
admission	concoction	evaporation	precaution
adoption	concussion	exaggeration	production
ambition	condition	exception	profusion
animation	confirmation	excursion	pronunciation
anticipation	congratulation	exhibition	qualification
application	congregation	expectation	quotation
appreciation	consolation	explanation	radiation
association	consultation	explosion	reaction
assumption	contemplation	expression	reception
attention	conversation	fascination	recollection
attraction	coordination	graduation	recreation
audition	corporation	hesitation	reflection
aviation	creation	humiliation	registration
calculation	declaration	identification	rejection
carnation	decoration	illumination	relation
celebration	definition	illustration	reproduction
champion	delusion	implication	reservation
circulation	demonstration	institution	restriction
civilization	depression	investigation	salutation
collection	description	mansion	speculation
collision	destination	meditation	subscription
commission	destruction	motivation	suggestion
communication	determination	multiplication	superstition
companion	devotion	notation	termination
compassion	digestion	obligation	tradition
compensation	dimension	occasion	vegetation
competition	direction	operation	
completion	distraction	passion	
complication	diversion	perspiration	

Teaching Phonics & Word Study in the Intermediate Grades • Scholastic Professional Books

-al, -ial

accidental	continental	illegal	psychological
ancestral	conventional	impractical	quizzical
architectural	criminal	industrial	recital
artificial	crucial	ineffectual	removal
astronomical	cylindrical	internal	rhythmical
biblical	disapproval	judicial	sacrificial
bifocal	disposal	magical	seasonal
biographical	economical	mathematical	spiritual
biological	editorial	memorial	supernatural
centrifugal	educational	musical	survival
ceremonial	environmental	mythical	technological
chemical	essential	national	territorial
classical	exceptional	nautical	theatrical
clinical	federal	neutral	traditional
coastal	financial	normal	tribal
colonial	general	original	universal
comical	gradual	pastoral	withdrawal
commercial	guttural	physical	
confidential	historical	political	
conspiratorial	hysterical	potential	

-y

bloody	gloomy	leaky	oily	shifty	teary
bouncy	goofy	leery	patchy	slimy	thirsty
catchy	grainy	liquidy	peachy	snoopy	toasty
chubby	grassy	lofty	peppery	spidery	toothy
clingy	gusty	lucky	perky	squeaky	tricky
cooky	hairy	meaty	pesky	squirmy	twisty
crazy	hefty	messy	picky	steamy	twitchy
dingy	huffy	minty	pointy	stocky	weighty
easy	humpy	misty	pushy	stormy	woody
fluffy	inky	moldy	rainy	stringy	wormy
foxy	itchy	mossy	rubbery	stuffy	
frosty	jerky	musty	rusty	sugary	
glassy	jumpy	needy	savory	summery	
glittery	leafy	nosy	scanty	sweaty	

-er (comparative)

bigger	faster	lesser	nicer	slower
brighter	fewer	lighter	older	smaller
busier	fresher	littler	poorer	smoother
cleaner	fuller	longer	prettier	softer
clearer	funnier	louder	quicker	sooner
colder	happier	lower	rounder	straighter
darker	higher	madder	sadder	taller
deeper	hotter	meaner	safer	thicker
earlier	kinder	narrower	shorter	warmer
fairer	larger	nearer	sicker	wider

-est (comparative)

biggest	fastest	largest	oldest	smallest
brightest	fewest	lightest	poorest	smoothest
busiest	freshest	longest	prettiest	softest
cleanest	fullest	loudest	quickest	soonest
clearest	funniest	lowest	roundest	stillest
coldest	happiest	maddest	saddest	straightest
darkest	healthiest	meanest	softest	tallest
deepest	highest	narrowest	shortest	thickest
earliest	hottest	nearest	sickest	warmest
fairest	kindest	nicest	slowest	widest

-ful

armful	doubtful	healthful	playful	tasteful
beautiful	fearful	helpful	restful	thankful
bowlful	forceful	hopeful	roomful	thoughtful
careful	forgetful	joyful	skillful	truthful
cheerful	frightful	mouthful	spoonful	useful
colorful	graceful	painful	successful	willful
cupful	handful	peaceful	tankful	wonderful

Teaching Phonics & Word Study in the Intermediate Grades • Scholastic Professional Books

-ity, -ty

agility	felicity	loyalty	parity	spontaneity
amnesty	honesty	mediocrity	regularity	unity
civility	humidity	necessity	safety	
falsity	inferiority	obesity	specialty	

-ic

academic	atmospheric	fanatic	hysteric	sarcastic
acrobatic	autistic	frantic	magnetic	scientific
aeronautic	ballistic	galactic	manic	specific
alcoholic	caloric	generic	mathematics	strategic
allergic	civic	geographic	mythic	sympathetic
angelic	cosmetic	graphic	optimistic	theatrics
antiseptic	economic	gymnastic	pacific	volcanic
artistic	electric	heroic	rhythmic	
astronomic	enthusiastic	hieroglyphic	romantic	
athletic	exotic	historic	rustic	

-ous, -eous, -ious

adventurous	disastrous	incredulous	officious	subconscious
ambitious	enormous	infectious	precarious	superstitious
anonymous	expeditious	marvelous	presumptuous	tenacious
boisterous	fabulous	miraculous	pretentious	tremendous
cautious	flirtatious	momentous	raucous	vacuous
cavernous	furious	monotonous	repetitious	vigorous
conscientious	glorious	monstrous	scrumptious	zealous
continuous	gorgeous	nauseous	semiconscious	
curious	grievous	numerous	serious	
delicious	impetuous	nutritious	spontaneous	

-en

barren	darken	frozen	hidden	quicken	stiffen
bitten	deepen	glisten	loosen	sharpen	straighten
blacken	enlighten	harden	madden	shorten	thicken
brazen	fasten	hasten	oaken	soften	woven
broken					

-ive, -ative, -itive

adaptive	digestive	ineffective	negative	representative
additive	disruptive	informative	objective	respective
captive	effective	insensitive	positive	secretive
cognitive	executive	instructive	prescriptive	sensitive
comparative	exhaustive	inventive	preventive	subjective
competitive	festive	locomotive	primitive	suggestive
consecutive	fugitive	lucrative	productive	talkative
conservative	hyperactive	massive	radioactive	tentative
deceptive	inactive	motive	reactive	
definitive	inattentive	narrative	receptive	
descriptive	incentive	native	repetitive	

-able, -ible

abominable	comfortable	erasable	inconceivable
acceptable	controllable	exchangeable	inconsolable
affordable	coverable	fixable	indescribable
agreeable	crushable	flammable	indispensable
allowable	deferrable	formidable	indisputable
answerable	delectable	hospitable	inescapable
applicable	despicable	immeasurable	inexcusable
appreciable	disposable	immovable	inexplicable
beatable	drinkable	impassable	innumerable
bendable	durable	impeccable	inoperable
breakable	enforceable	impenetrable	insatiable
capable	enjoyable	inadvisable	inseparable
charitable	enviable	incalculable	insurmountable
cleanable	equitable	incomparable	intolerable

Teaching Phonics & Word Study in the Intermediate Grades • Scholastic Professional Books

-able, -ible continued

invaluable	regrettable	compatible	incomprehensible
irreplaceable	replaceable	convertible	incorrigible
irritable	salvageable	corruptible	incredible
knowledgeable	sinkable	credible	indefensible
liable	sociable	deducible	indelible
lovable	thinkable	deductible	indestructible
malleable	traceable	digestible	inedible
manageable	transferable	discernible	inflexible
memorable	unbelievable	divisible	invincible
movable	uncontrollable	edible	irresistible
navigable	undeniable	fallible	irresponsible
nonflammable	unforgettable	feasible	irreversible
nonnegotiable	usable	flexible	negligible
noticeable	valuable	forcible	plausible
peaceable	washable	gullible	possible
permeable	workable	horrible	reproducible
pliable	accessible	illegible	reversible
probable	audible	implausible	sensible
programmable	coercible	impossible	tangible
questionable	collapsible	inaccessible	visible
readable	collectible	inadmissible	
redeemable	combustible	inaudible	

-ness

badness	fairness	quickness	smoothness
baldness	fondness	roughness	sourness
blackness	goodness	roundness	sweetness
brightness	greatness	sadness	thinness
closeness	happiness	shyness	tightness
dampness	illness	sickness	ugliness
darkness	kindness	silliness	unhappiness
dimness	lightness	slowness	weakness
dryness	nearness	smallness	wildness

Teaching Phonics & Word Study in the Intermediate Grades • Scholastic Professional Books

-ment

advertisement	contentment	entertainment	placement
agreement	detachment	equipment	puzzlement
amazement	development	government	settlement
announcement	employment	improvement	statement
appointment	engagement	movement	treatment
argument	enjoyment	pavement	
arrangement	entanglement	payment	

-less

ageless	hairless	nameless	spotless
blameless	harmless	painless	sunless
careless	headless	penniless	thoughtless
childless	helpless	pointless	timeless
cloudless	homeless	rainless	useless
colorless	hopeless	seamless	waterless
doubtless	lifeless	shapeless	weightless
endless	loveless	shirtless	windless
faceless	meatless	shoeless	worthless
fearless	mindless	sleepless	

Teaching Phonics & Word Study in the Intermediate Grades • Scholastic Professional Books

Homophones

Guidelines:

- Homophones are words that sound the same, but have different meanings and spellings.

- Each homophone contains the same number of phonemes, but different graphemes. The spellings of homophones are critical because they provide clues to the word's meaning.

- You can teach homophones at all grades. Some of the simplest homophones children will encounter are provided on the list below. Children will improve their skills when they read and write homophones in a variety of contexts.

Homophone Word List

accept/except	brews/bruise	desert/dessert
ad/add	by/buy	gate/gait
adds/ads/adz	capital/capitol	grease/Greece
affect/effect	carat/caret/carrot	great/grate
aisle/I'll/isle	caught/cot	groan/grown
aloud/allowed	ceiling/sealing	guessed/guest
altar/alter	cell/sell	hail/hale
ant/aunt	cellar/seller	hair/hare
arc/ark	cent/sent/scent	hall/haul
ate/eight	cents/scents/sense	hay/hey
bail/bale	cereal/serial	heal/heel/he'll
ball/bawl	chalk/chock	hear/here
based/baste	cheap/cheep	heard/herd
be/bee	chews/choose	here/hear
beach/beech	choral/coral	hi/high
bear/bare	clause/claws	higher/hire
beat/beet	close/clothes	him/hymn
been/bin	core/corp	hoarse/horse
berry/bury	creak/creek	hoes/hose
billed/build	cymbal/symbol	hole/whole
blew/blue	days/daze	horse/hoarse
board/bored	deer/dear	hour/our
brake/break	dense/dents	I/eye

Teaching Phonics & Word Study in the Intermediate Grades • Scholastic Professional Books

in/inn	right/rite/write	ware/wear/where
its/it's	ring/wring	dew/do/due
Jim/gym	road/rode/rowed	die/dye
knead/need	roll/role	doe/dough
knew/new/gnu	rose/rows	dual/duel
knight/night	tacks/tax	earn/urn
knot/not	tail/tale	ewe/yew/you
know/no	tea/tee	eye/I
knows/nose	team/teem	fare/fair
lead/led	teas/tease/tees	fairy/ferry
leak/leek	their/there/they're	feat/feet
lessen/lesson	theirs/there's	find/fined
lie/lye	threw/through	fir/fur
loan/lone	throne/thrown	flair/flare
made/maid	thyme/time	flea/flee
mail/male	tide/tied	flew/flu/flue
main/Maine/mane	to/too/two	flour/flower
pause/paws	toad/towed	for/fore/four
peace/piece	tow/toe	forth/fourth
peak/peek	tale/tail	foul/fowl
peal/peel	undo/undue	Mary/marry/merry
pear/pair/pare	vain/vane/vein	meat/meet
pedal/peddle	waist/waste	might/mite
plain/plane	way/weigh	mind/mined
pole/poll	weak/week	missed/mist
poor/pour/pore	wear/where	moose/mousse
praise/prays/preys	weight/wait	muscle/mussel
presence/presents	which/witch	none/nun
prince/prints	whole/hole	oar/or/ore
principal/principle	who's/whose	oh/owe
quarts/quartz	wood/would	one/won
rain/reign/rein	wrap/rap	our/hour
raise/rays/raze	vain/vane/vein	overdo/overdue
rap/wrap	vary/very	paced/paste
read/reed	wade/weighed	pail/pale
real/reel	waist/waste	pain/pane
red/read	wait/weight	past/passed

228

Teaching Phonics & Word Study in the Intermediate Grades • Scholastic Professional Books

patience/patients	shear/sheer	straight/strait
root/route	shoe/shoo	suite/sweet
rote/wrote	shone/shown	sundae/Sunday
rough/ruff	side/sighed	wave/waive
rung/wrung	sight/cite	we'd/weed
sail/sale	some/sum	we/wee
scene/seen	son/sun	weather/whether
sea/see	stare/stair	weave/we've
seam/seem	steal/steel	you'll/yule
seas/sees/seize	stake/steak	you/ewe
sew/so/sow	stationary/stationery	your/you're

Greek and Latin Roots

Background

English words are derived from three primary origins—Anglo-Saxon, Romance (Latin), and Greek (see chart; Moats, 1999). About 60% of the words in English text are of Latin and Greek origin (Henry, 1997). Words with Greek roots are common in science and social studies textbooks (Bear et al., 1996; Henry, 1988). Words with Latin roots are common in technical, sophisticated words found in literature and upper-elementary textbooks. Words with Anglo-Saxon roots are common in everyday speech; these words are found in primary-level texts. The following lists contain some of the most common Greek and Latin roots.

Common Latin Roots

audi:	auditory, audience, audit, auditorium, audible, inaudible, audition
dict:	dictate, predict, dictator, edict, contradict, dictation, indict, prediction
ject:	reject, inject, projection, interjection, eject, objection, dejection
port:	transport, transportation, import, export, porter, portable, report, support
rupt:	rupture, erupt, eruption, interrupt, interruption, disruption
scrib/ script:	scribe, describe, manuscript, inscription, transcript, description, prescription
spect:	spectator, inspect, inspector, respect, spectacle, spectacular
struct:	structure, construct, construction, instruct, destruction, reconstruction
tract:	tractor, traction, attract, subtraction, extract, retract, attractive
vis:	vision, visual, visit, supervisor, invisible, vista, visualize, visionary

Common Greek Roots

auto:	automatic, autograph, autobiography, automobile, autocracy
bio:	biology, biosphere, biography, biochemistry, biometrics, biophysics
graph:	graphite, geography, graphic, photograph, phonograph
hydro:	anhydrous, dehydration, hydrogen, hydrant, hydrostatic, hydrophobia, hydrotherapy, hydroplane
meter:	speedometer, odometer, metronome, thermometer, chronometer, perimeter, hydrometer
ology:	geology, theology, zoology, meteorology, phonology
photo:	photography, photocopy, photosynthesis, phototropism, photostat, photogenic
scope:	periscope, stethoscope, telescope, microscope, microscopic
tele:	telephone, telepathy, telegraph, television
therm:	thermos, thermodynamics, thermostat, thermophysics

Teaching Phonics & Word Study in the Intermediate Grades • Scholastic Professional Books

English Word Origins (Moats, 1999)			
Layer of Language	**Sound**	**Syllable**	**Morpheme**
Anglo-Saxon	**consonants:** single, blends, digraphs **vowels:** short, long (VCe), teams, diphthongs, *r*-control	closed open VCe *r*-control C + -*le* vowel team (schwa)	compounds (highlight) inflections (*ed, s, ing, er, est*)
Romance (Latin)			prefixes (*mis, in*) suffixes (*ment, ary*) roots (*fer, tract*) plurals (*a, ae,* as in *curricula, alumnae*)
Greek	/i/ = y (*gym*) /k/ = ch (*chorus*) /f/ = ph (*photo*)		combining forms (*biography, micrometer*) plurals (*es,* as in *crises, metamorphoses*)

Guidelines:

Teach common Greek and Latin roots in Grades 4–8 to give students access to a larger number of words. These roots provide clues to word meanings and help students cognitively group related words.

Teach Greek and Latin roots in categories, such as those related to number, size, or the body. Such grouping will help students efficiently sort and cluster words in their memory.

Use the following lists of related roots and sample words for instruction. However, keep in mind that it isn't necessary or reasonable to teach the meanings of all the roots and their corresponding words. What's important is to teach children key words that they can use to analyze unfamiliar words. Focus on the most common, high-utility roots shown in the lists provided.

Number Roots

Root	Meaning	Words for Instruction
monos (Greek)	one	monologue, monarch, monarchy, monogram, monopoly, monopolize, monolith, monolithic, monastery, monk, monorail, monotonous, monochromatic, monocle, monogamy, monograph, monolingual, monomania, mononucleosis, monophonic, monoplane, monosyllable, monotone
unus (Latin)	one	unanimous, unanimity, unanimously, unilateral, unilaterally, inch, onion, ounce, unicorn, unicycle, uniform, unify, unique, unit, universal, union, unite, universe, university, unicameral, unicellular, unisex, unison, unitary, univalent
duo (Latin) duplex (Latin)	two, twofold	duplicate, double, doublet, doubloon, duplicity, duplex
bi (Latin)	two	bilateral, bilaterally, bipartisan, bisect, bisection, biceps, bicultural, bicycle, bifocals, bilingual, billion, bimonthly, binoculars, biracial, biweekly, biannual, bicameral, bicarbonate, bicentennial, bicuspid, biennial, bifurcate, bigamy, binomial, biped, biplane, bipolar, bivalve
tri (Greek) tres (Latin)	three	trilogy, trisect, trisection, trisector, triumvirate, tricycle, trillion, trimester, trio, triple, triplet, triplicate, tricentennial, trident, triennial, trinity, tripartite, triplex, triptych
quartus (Latin) quatuor (Latin)	fourth four	quadrant, quartet, quatrain, quadrangle, quadruple, quadruplet, quart, quarter, squad, square, quadraphonic, quadrennial, quadrille, quadripartite, quarry, quarto, quatrefoil
decem (Latin)	ten	decimate, decathlon, decade, December, decimal, decagram, Decalogue, deciliter, decimeter, duodecimal
centum (Latin)	hundred	bicentennial, centenary, cent, centennial, centimeter, centipede, century, percent, centavo, centenarian, centiliter, centime, centigrade

Teaching Phonics & Word Study in the Intermediate Grades • Scholastic Professional Books

Body-Parts Roots

Root	Meaning	Words for Instruction
caput, capitis (Latin)	head	cap, capital, capital letter, capitalize, capitol, captain, chapter, chief, kerchief, mischief, recap, cap-a-pie, capitation, per capita, capitalist, capitalism, capitalize, capitulation, capitulate, decapitate, precipice, precipitate, precipitation, precipitous, recapitulation, recapitulate
cerebrum (Latin)	brain	cerebral, cerebrum, cerebration, cerebrate, cerebellum, cerebral cortex, cerebral palsy
facies (Latin)	face, form, shape	deface, defacement, face, face-off, face-saving, facial, surface, typeface, facing, prima facie, efface, façade, facet
frons, frontis (Latin)	front, forehead, face	front, frontage, frontal, frontier, affront, confront, frontispiece, confrontation, effrontery
gurges, gurgitis (Latin)	throat, whirlpool	gorge, gargle, gurgle, disgorge, gargantuan, gargoyle, regurgitate
supercilium (Latin)	eyebrow	supercilious
os, oris (Latin) oro, orare, orai, oratum (Latin)	mouth to speak	adore, oral, inexorable, oracle, oratorio, orotund, peroration, oracular, oration, orate, orator, oratorical, oratory, orifice, osculate, osculation
dens, dentis (Latin)	tooth	indentation, indenture, dandelion, dental, dentrifice, dentist, dentistry, denture, indent, dentate, dentin, dentition, indention, trident
odon, odontos (Greek)	tooth	periodontal, orthodontist, orthodontia, orthodontics
caro, carnis (Latin)	flesh	carnage, carnal, carnation, carnival, carnivorous, charnel, crone, incarnadine, carnality, carnally, carrion, incarnate, incarnation

Teaching Phonics & Word Study in the Intermediate Grades • Scholastic Professional Books

Body-Parts Roots continued

Root	Meaning	Words for Instruction
collum (Latin)	neck	collar, accolade, décolletage, décolleté
corpus, corporis (Latin)	body	corporal, corporate, corpse, incorporate, leprechaun, corpus delicti, corpuscle, esprit de corps, corporality, corporally, corporeal, corporeity, corps, corpulent, corpulence, corpus
cor, cordis (Latin)	heart	accord, according, accordingly, corsage, courage, discord, encourage, record, cordial, concordance, concord, concordant
os, ossis (Latin)	bone	ossify, ossification
derma (Greek)	skin	derma, dermal, dermatitis, pachyderm, dermatology, dermatologist, epidermis, epidermal, epidermic
dorsum (Latin)	the back	dorsal, dossier, endorse, endorsee, endorsement, do-si-do, reredos
gaster, gastreros (Greek)	stomach, belly	gastric, gastronome
nervus (Latin)	sinew, nerve	nerve, nerve-racking, nervous, nervy, unnerve, enervate
sanguis, sanguinis (Latin)	blood	sanguine, sanguinary, sanguinity, sangfroid, consanguinity, consanguineous
sedeo, sedere, sedi, sessum (Latin)	to sit, to settle	assess, hostage, preside, president, resident, residue, sediment, session, sewer, siege, subsidize, subsidy, assiduous, assiduity, dissident, dissidence, séance, obsession, presidium, sessile, sedentary, supersede
manus (Latin)	hand	emancipate, emancipation, manacle, mandate, manifest, manifestation, manifestly, manifesto, manipulate, manipulation, manipulative, command, commend, demand, maintain, manage, maneuver, manicure, manner, manual, manufacture, manure, manuscript, amanuensis, countermand, legerdemain, manumission

Teaching Phonics & Word Study in the Intermediate Grades • Scholastic Professional Books

Body-Parts Roots continued

Root	Meaning	Words for Instruction
dextra (Latin)	right hand	dexterity, dexterous, ambidextrous, ambidexterity, digitalis, digitigrade, prestidigitation
digitus (Latin)	finger	digital, digit
flecto, flectere, flexi, flexum (Latin)	to bend	flex, flexible, inflexible, reflector, reflex, flexure, reflexive, deflect, deflection, genuflect, genuflection, inflection, inflect, inflected, reflection, reflect, reflective
rapio, rapere, rapui, raptum (Latin)	to snatch	enraptured, rape, rapid, rapids, rapture, ravenous, rapacious, rapacity, rapt, raptly, raptness, surreptitious, surreptitiously, rapine, ravine, ravish, surreptitiousness
plico, plicare, plicavi, plicatum (Latin)	to fold	complicity, duplicity, accomplice, apply, complex, comply, display, duplex, duplicate, employ, multiply, pliant, plight, supply, triplicate, explicate, explicable, explication, explicative, deploy, implicate, multiplex, multiplicity, plissé, replicate, explicit, implicit, exploit, exploitable, exploitation, exploiter, imply, implication, ploy, ply, supplicate, suppliant, supplicant, supplication
prehendo, prehendere, prehendi, prehensum (Latin)	to catch, to seize, to grasp	apprehend, apprentice, comprehend, enterprise, prison, prize, surprise, misprision, prehensile, reprise, apprehensible, apprehension, apprehensive, comprise, entrepreneur, impregnable, reprehend, reprehensible, reprehension, reprisal
pes, pedis (Latin)	foot	biped, expedition, moped, pedal, pedestrian, pedicure, pioneer, quadruped, expedient, expediency, expediently, expedite, expeditious, expeditiously, impede, impediment, pedigree, pedometer, peon, peonage, cap-a-pie, expeditionary, millipede, pedicab, pied-á-terre, sesquipedalian
pous, podos (Greek)	foot	octopus, tripod, antipodes, antipodal, antipode, podiatry, podium, chiropody, platypus
gradior, gradi, gressum (Latin)	to step, to walk	aggression, aggressive, aggressiveness, degradation, congress, degree, grade, gradual, graduate, ingredient, progress, transgress, egress, ingress, degrade, degraded, digress, digression, digressive, gradation, gradient, regress, regression, regressive

Body-Parts Roots continued

Root	Meaning	Words for Instruction
ambulo, ambulare, ambulavi, ambulatum (Latin)	to walk around	ambulance, somnambulist, ambulatory, circumambulate, perambulate, perambulator, ambulant, ambulate, preamble
calcitro, calcitrare, calcitravi, calcitratum (Latin)	to kick	recalcitrant, recalcitrance, recalcitrantly
sto, stare, steti, statum (Latin) statio, stationis (Latin) sisto, sistere, steti, statum (Latin)	to stand a standing, a standing position to cause to stand, to put, to place	constituent, desist, destitute, destitution, interstice, obstinate, obstinacy, oust, ouster, prostitute, prostitution, restitution, restive, restiveness, stance, static, subsist, subsistence, arrest, assist, circumstance, consistency, constant, constitute, constitution, contrast, cost, distant, exist, insist, instant, obstacle, persist, resist, rest, stable, stage, stand, state, station, stationary, statistic, statue, status, substance, substitute, superstition, extant, instate, obstetrics, reinstate, stanch, stanchion, statute

Teaching Phonics & Word Study in the Intermediate Grades • Scholastic Professional Books

Other Useful Word Lists

Contractions

I'm	could've	here's	aren't	let's
they're	I've	he's	can't	I'll
we're	might've	it's	couldn't	it'll
you're	should've	she's	didn't	he'll
	they've	that's	doesn't	she'll
	we've	there's	don't	that'll
I'd	would've	what's	hadn't	they'll
it'd	you've	where's	hasn't	we'll
she'd		who's	haven't	you'll
there'd			isn't	
they'd			mustn't	
we'd			needn't	
you'd			shouldn't	
			wouldn't	

Synonyms

add/total	change/swap	fat/chubby
after/following	city/town	fetch/get
all/every	close/shut	find/locate
anger/rage	continue/persist	fix/mend
appear/look	dangerous/hazardous	forgive/excuse
appreciative/thankful	decrease/lessen	fortune/wealth
arrive/reach	delay/postpone	fragile/delicate
ask/question	demonstrate/show	freedom/liberty
baby/infant	different/diverse	frequent/often
back/rear	dislike/detest	giant/huge
before/prior	divide/split	gift/present
begin/start	during/while	give/donate
below/under	earth/world	grab/take
bitter/tart	eat/consume	grow/develop
brave/courageous	end/finish	guide/lead
call/yell	enough/sufficient	happy/glad
car/vehicle	error/mistake	hasten/hurry

heal / cure	omit / delete	thin / slender
high / tall	operate / use	tiny / small
hold / grasp	overdue / late	touch / feel
huge / vast	own / have	trail / path
idea / concept	pack / fill	try / attempt
illegal / wrong	pain / ache	tug / pull
income / earnings	pair / couple	understand / know
injure / hurt	part / piece	undo / untie
insult / offend	peak / summit	unstable / wobbly
job / occupation	perform / act	untamed / wild
jump / leap	pick / choose	untidy / messy
just / fair	praise / applaud	uproar / noise
keep / save	quaint / odd	use / apply
kind / considerate	quake / shake	usual / common
large / big	quick / fast	utter / talk
last / persist	quiet / silent	slam / bang
late / tardy	quit / stop	vacant / empty
leave / depart	quiz / test	vacation / break
like / enjoy	rage / fury	value / worth
listen / hear	rain / shower	vanish / disappear
little / small	raise / increase	vary / change
make / build	record / write	violent / rough
mark / label	relax / rest	vital / necessary
mean / cruel	repeat / echo	wag / wave
messy / sloppy	revise / change	wail / cry
mend / repair	rule / law	walk / stroll
mistake / error	safe / secure	warn / alert
model / example	say / tell	wash / clean
move / transport	scrape / scratch	well / healthy
naughty / bad	scream / shout	whack / hit
near / close	sharp / pointed	whole / entire
neat / tidy	shove / push	yank / pull
need / require	splash / spray	yell / shout
new / fresh	spring / bounce	yummy / tasty
obey / follow	sour / tart	zilch / nothing
odor / smell	tear / rip	zoom / rush
often / frequently	terrify / scare	

Teaching Phonics & Word Study in the Intermediate Grades • Scholastic Professional Books

Antonyms

above/below	buy/sell	exciting/boring
absent/present	cause/effect	fact/fiction
achieve/fail	cheap/expensive	fail/pass
add/subtract	clean/dirty	false/true
admire/dislike	cold/hot	fancy/plain
admit/reject	come/go	far/near
adult/child	cooked/raw	fast/slow
afraid/confident	cool/warm	fat/thin
against/for	coward/hero	female/male
alive/dead	cruel/kind	few/many
all/none	cry/laugh	fiction/fact
allow/forbid	curved/straight	find/lose
alone/together	dangerous/safe	finish/start
always/never	dark/light	first/last
ancient/modern	day/night	flexible/rigid
answer/question	deep/shallow	float/sink
appear/vanish	defend/attack	follow/lead
arrive/depart	different/same	foolish/wise
ask/tell	dim/bright	for/against
asked/told	dirty/clean	forget/remember
asleep/awake	dry/wet	forward/backward
attack/defend	dull/bright	friend/stranger
back/front	dwarf/giant	from/to
backward/forward	eager/lazy	front/back
beautiful/ugly	early/late	frozen/melted
before/after	earn/spend	girl/boy
beginning/end	east/west	give/take
big/little	effect/cause	go/stop
birth/death	easy/difficult	good/bad
black/white	empty/full	guilty/innocent
blame/forgive	ending/beginning	happy/sad
blunt/sharp	enemy/friend	hard/soft
boring/exciting	enjoy/hate	harm/help
bottom/top	enter/exit	hate/love
boy/girl	even/odd	heal/hurt
break/fix	evening/morning	hear/ignore
bright/dim	evil/good	heavy/light

Antonyms continued

high / low	new / old	short / long
hot / cold	night / day	shout / whisper
imaginary / real	no / yes	shut / open
improve / damage	noisy / quiet	silly / serious
icy / warm	north / south	simple / complex
ill / healthy	nothing / everything	sit / stand
illegal / legal	obey / command	slow / fast
in / out	odd / even	small / large
increase / decrease	often / seldom	smooth / rough
inside / outside	old / young	soft / hard
joy / grief	on / off	spend / earn
kind / cruel	open / close	sunrise / sunset
large / small	over / under	start / finish
last / first	pain / joy	stop / start
late / early	pass / fail	sweet / sour
laugh / cry	plain / fancy	tall / short
lead / follow	pleasure / pain	tame / wild
learn / teach	poor / rich	thick / thin
left / right	present / absent	to / from
less / more	private / public	top / bottom
light / dark	push / pull	true / false
long / short	question / answer	ugly / pretty
loose / tight	quick / slow	under / over
lose / find	raise / lower	up / down
lose / gain	real / imaginary	white / black
lose / win	remain / change	whole / part
loud / soft	repair / break	with / without
love / hate	rich / poor	work / play
low / high	right / wrong	yes / no
messy / tidy	rough / smooth	young / old
morning / evening	rude / polite	
most / least	sad / funny	
multiply / divide	sad / glad	
narrow / wide	safe / dangerous	
near / far	same / different	
never / always	shallow / deep	

Teaching Phonics & Word Study in the Intermediate Grades • Scholastic Professional Books

Homographs

Homographs are words that are spelled the same but are different in meaning and origin. When they are pronounced differently, they are called heteronyms.

affect	content	gum	match	root
ball	contest	hatch	mean	row
band	contract	heel	minute	saw
bank	converse	hide	miss	school
bark	count	intern	mole	seal
bass	crow	invalid	object	second
bat	date	jam	palm	sewer
batter	desert	jumper	peaked	slip
bay	does	kind	peck	slug
bill	dove	lap	pen	sock
bit	down	last	pitcher	sow
bow	ear	lead	pool	story
bowl	entrance	left	pop	subject
box	excuse	lie	pound	tear
bridge	fair	light	present	tick
buffet	fan	like	primer	toll
can	file	line	pupils	top
close	fine	loaf	read	use
commune	fit	lock	record	well
compact	flat	long	refuse	wind
conduct	fly	mail	rest	wound
console	ground	mat	ring	yard

Portmaneau Words

Portmaneau words are made of two words that are blended into one.

autobus	automobile + bus	**skylab**	sky + laboratory
brunch	breakfast + lunch	**smash**	smack + mash
clash	clap + crash	**smog**	smoke + fog
hi-fi	high fidelity	**squiggle**	squirm + wiggle
o'clock	of the clock		

Eponyms

Eponyms are words made from the names of people and places.

America . . . . (Amerigo Vespucci)

bikini . . . . (Bikini Atoll in the Pacific Ocean where atomic bombs were tested)

bologna . . . . (city in northern Italy)

bunsen burner . . . . (Robert Bunsen, German chemist)

candy . . . . (French Prince Charles de Condé (con-Day)

cheddar . . . . (village in England where cheese was invented)

Ferris wheel . . . . . (George Washington Ferris, inventor)

frankfurter . . . . . . (city in Germany: Frankfurt)

Geiger Counter . . . (German physicist, Hans Geiger)

hamburgers . . . . . . (Hamburg, Germany)

jeans . . . . (Italian city of Genoa, spelled GENE in middle English)

Levi's . . . . (Levi Strauss, creator)

marathon . . . . (a race named after the Greeks won the battle at Marathon in 490 B.C. and a messenger ran 26 miles to take news to Athens)

sandwich . . . . (English Earl of Sandwich)

teddy bear . . . . . . (President Theodore "Teddy" Roosevelt, who refused to shoot a small bear on a hunting trip)

thug . . . . (gang of professional hoodlums who roamed northern India; comes from the word thag, which means cheat or thief)

Teaching Phonics & Word Study in the Intermediate Grades • Scholastic Professional Books

Spelling Demons

a lot	audience	continuous	every
about	beautiful	correspondence	everybody
abrupt	because	cough	everyone
absence	been	could	exaggerate
accommodate	before	country	excellent
accumulate	beginning	courteous	except
accurate	believe	criticism	excited
ache	benefited	curiosity	existence
acquire	bicycle	cylinder	experience
across	blue	dear	extremely
address	break	decision	familiar
adequate	breathe	definitely	fascinate
adjourn	brilliant	didn't	favorite
advice	built	difference	February
again	bulletin	different	field
all right	business	difficulty	finally
almost	buy	dining	first
also	by	disappear	foreign
always	calendar	disappoint	formally
amateur	campaign	discipline	formerly
among	can't (cannot)	disease	forty
analysis	canceled	dissatisfied	friend
angle	career	division	fulfill
another	cemetery	doctor	fundamental
answer	certain	does	getting
any	chief	doesn't	glimpse
anyone	choose	don't	gorgeous
apologize	close	done	government
apparently	clothes	early	governor
appearance	colonel	easy	grammar
appreciate	color	eighth	groceries
arctic	column	embarrass	guarantee
are	come	enough	guard
argument	coming	environment	guess
arrangement	committee	equipped	guidance
athletic	conscience	especially	half

Spelling Demons continued

handsome	jewelry	mileage	pamphlet
happily	journey	miniature	parallel
have	judgment	minute	particular
having	just	miscellaneous	pastime
he's	khaki	misspell	peaceable
hear	kindergarten	mortgage	people
heard	knead	much	performance
height	knew	muscle	permanent
here	know	myself	personal
heroes	knowledge	naturally	personnel
hoarse	laboratory	necessary	persuade
hole	laid	new	piece
hoping	laugh	nickel	pleasant
hour	leisure	niece	possession
humorous	let's	ninety	precede
hurriedly	library	ninth	privilege
I'd	license	no	probably
illegible	licorice	none	procedure
illustrate	lightning	noticeable	proceed
I'm	likely	nuisance	professor
imaginary	listen	occasion	pronunciation
immediately	livelihood	occur	psychology
incidentally	loneliness	occurred	pumpkin
independence	loose	o'clock	pursue
indispensable	lose	off	quantity
instead	maintenance	often	quarrel
intelligence	making	omission	quite
interesting	maneuver	omitted	raise
interpreted	manufacture	once	read
interrupt	many	one	ready
into	marriage	opinion	realize
irrelevant	mathematics	opportunity	really
it's (it is)	meant	opposite	receive
its	medicine	original	recognize
jealous	might	our	recommend

Teaching Phonics & Word Study in the Intermediate Grades • Scholastic Professional Books

Spelling Demons continued

rehearse	sufficient	unique	won
relevant	sugar	unnecessary	won't
relief	sure	until	would
relieve	surprise	upon	wouldn't
religious	tear	used	write
repetition	temperature	usually	writing
restaurant	temporary	utensil	wrote
rheumatism	tendency	vacancy	yacht
rhubarb	terrible	vacuum	yield
rhythm	that's	vegetable	yolk
ridiculous	their (belongs to)	very	your
right	then	vinegar	you're
safety	there	visible	youth
said	therefore	volume	zealous
says	they	want	
schedule	they're (they are)	was	
school	thorough	wear	
scissors	though	weather	
seems	thought	Wednesday	
seize	threw	week	
separate	through	went	
sergeant	tired	we're	
severely	to	were	
shoes	together	what	
similar	tomorrow	when	
since	tongue	where	
sizable	tonight	whether	
some	too	which	
something	transferred	who	
sometimes	trouble	whole	
souvenir	Tuesday	wholly	
straight	two	who's	
strength	typical	whose	
studying	unanimous	with	
succeed	undoubtedly	women	

Teaching Phonics & Word Study in the Intermediate Grades • Scholastic Professional Books

Shortened Words
(Clipped Words)
These are the result of people shortening words for greater efficiency.

ad	advertisement	lunch	luncheon
auto	automobile	mart	market
bike	bicycle	math	mathematics
burger	hamburger	memo	memorandum
cab	cabriolet	mum	chrysanthemum
champ	champion	phone	telephone
clerk	cleric	photo	photograph
cuke	cucumber	plane	airplane
doc	doctor	ref	referee
dorm	dormitory	specs	spectacles
exam	examination	stereo	stereophonic
fan	fanatic	taxi	taxicab
flu	influenza	teen	teenager
gas	gasoline	tux	tuxedo
grad	graduate	typo	typographical error
gym	gymnasium	vet	veterinarian
lab	laboratory	zoo	zoological gardens
limo	limousine		

Teaching Phonics & Word Study in the Intermediate Grades • Scholastic Professional Books

25 Quick-and-Easy Phonics and Word Analysis Games

M any wonderful educational games and activities providing phonics practice are available from educational supply companies. However, countless simple and engaging activities requiring limited preparation and materials can also be used. Here are some of the easiest and best activities I've collected over the years.

1. **Word-Building from English Roots**: Provide students with a list of base words and a set of prefixes and suffixes. Have them combine the word parts to create and present new words.

2. **Word Webs with Latin and Greek Roots**: On the chalkboard write a root word related to a social studies or science lesson in your curriculum. State the word's meaning and the language it comes from, then have students create a web of related words. Suggest that they search textbooks and dictionaries. Then have them provide definitions for the words on the web. Ask students to present their lists and display them in the classroom.

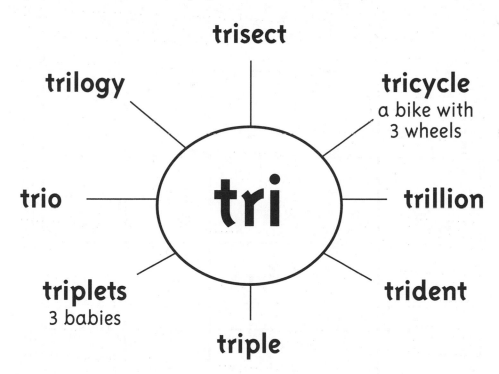

3. **Root Search**: Write a common root on the chalkboard. Provide its meaning and the language it comes from. Have students brainstorm a list of words they think come from this root. Then have them check the dictionary to check their accuracy. Challenge students to find new words related to the root. Use the lists on pages 232–236 to create a Root-Word Dictionary.

4. Beat the Clock: This is a timed word-recognition activity. Provide pairs of students with word lists and have the partners time each other on reading the lists. Have the children monitor and record times at the beginning and end of each week.

5. Word Detective: List key words, syllable patterns, or roots for the week. Give students a point every time they see a words in print, or use one of the words (or another word containing the word, syllable pattern, or root) in speech or writing. Tally points at the end of the week and award prizes (e.g., select the book for oral reading for the week, earn extra recess time).

6. Syllable Bingo: Make copies of a bingo game board and a set of picture cards whose names contain selected syllables. (Choose syllables from the list on pages 196–197.) See the illustration below. Put the syllables in a different order for each game board, and use each syllable at least twice per

Teaching Phonics & Word Study in the Intermediate Grades • Scholastic Professional Books

board. Place the picture cards in a bag. Syllable Bingo is played just like regular bingo. Before the game begins, give each player a game board and ample space markers. The caller (teacher) draws one picture card from the bag and displays it. If a player's game board contains the syllable in the picture's name, he or she places a marker over the space. The first player to get five markers in a row (vertically, horizontally, or diagonally), yells "Syllable Bingo!" The player then states aloud the syllable as the caller checks it against the picture cards drawn from the bag. If these match, the player wins. Players then clear their boards, the picture cards go back in the bag, and a new game begins.

7. **Spin It!:** Cut out three spinners and dials. See example provided. On the outside edge of the first spinner, write the word parts *un* and *re*. On the outside edge of the second spinner, write the word parts *able, apply, cover, born, cap, check, cook, cut, fasten, fold, friend, load, mark, name, pack, paid, safe, sold, tie, wise,* and *wrap*. On the outside edge of the third spinner, write the word part *ed*. Paste the spinners in sequence on a piece of tag board or the inside of a folder. Using a brass fastener, attach the dials to the spinners. Then have each student spin all three spinners. If a word can be formed, the student writes it on a sheet of paper. Each word is worth one point. Students can continue until they have formed five words, or students can challenge one another to see who can form the most words.

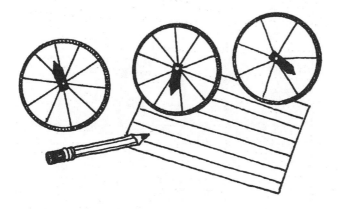

8. **Phonogram Families:** Distribute letter cards to each student. On each card write a consonant, cluster, or digraph. Then display a phonogram card. Students who hold a card that, when combined with the phonogram card, forms a word come to the front of the classroom. They are "members" of this phonogram "family." Invite each student to place a card in front of the phonogram card and blend aloud the word formed.

9. **Build It:** Draw a house or pyramid on a sheet of paper. Divide the house or pyramid into smaller segments, such as squares, rectangles, or triangles. Make a copy of the page and distribute one to each student. Then make a set of word-building cards. On each card write a consonant, cluster, digraph, vowel, or phonogram, depending on the phonics skills you are reviewing. Provide enough cards so that many words can be formed. Divide the class into small groups.

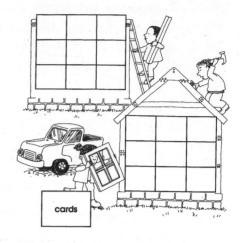

Place a set of cards facedown on the table or floor in front of each group. One at a time, each student in the group draws a set of five cards and builds as many words as possible, and each student writes his or her word in one segment of the house or pyramid, or colors in one segment. The student who builds (completes) the house or pyramid first wins.

10. **Syllable Checkers:** On each square of an old checkerboard, write a word containing a syllable-spelling pattern that you want students to review. The game is played just like checkers, except players must read the word on each space they land on. If a player cannot read the word, he or she returns to the original space.

11. **Word Part Hunt:** Assign each student a syllable, prefix, suffix, or root that you want to review. You might have students work with a partner or in small groups. Then have the children search for objects in the classroom whose names contain the word part. In addition, you might have them search through books, magazines, and newspapers for words that contain the word part. Provide time for students to share their findings.

250

12. Environmental Print Boards: As you teach each syllable spelling pattern or root word, challenge the children to find examples of the word parts in words on signs, cereal boxes, advertisements, junk mail, and other environmental print items. Have them bring these items to class (suggest that they take a photo or draw a picture if it's a large sign) and attach them to an environmental print bulletin board to refer to throughout the week.

13. Graph It: Your students can create graphs that combine language arts with math concepts. For example, instruct students to search a passage for all the words with *-le, -ble, -ple, -zle,* and *-tle* and list them. Have them use their list to create a bar graph showing the number of words found for each.

14. Word Baseball: Divide the class into two teams. One at a time, each team member is "up at bat." Show the student a word card. If the player reads the word card, he or she can go to first base. As players reach home, their team gets a point. If a player can't accurately read the word, the team gets an "out." The team at bat continues until it has three outs. The team that earns more points after nine innings wins. (You might want to limit the game to fewer innings.) To make the game more exciting, level the word cards. Some words are worth a base hit, others are worth a double or triple, and a few are worth the treasured home run. In addition, you might ask the player at bat to read the word, and then state a related word or a word that contains the same syllable, prefix, suffix, or root.

15. Concentration: This classic game can be played by 2–3 students to review almost any skill. Make a set of 12–20 playing cards. On each card write a word. For example, if you are reviewing compound words, you'll write words that, when combined, can form compound words. Place the cards facedown on the table or floor. Each player chooses two cards. If the cards form a compound word, the player keeps them. The player with the most cards at the end of the game wins. When reviewing vowel sounds, make a set of cards in which students can find rhyming word pairs.

16. Password: This game is played by partners. Make a set of word cards with a multisyllabic word on each card. One partner selects a card, then provides clues to his or her partner. For example, if a student draws the word card "sunflower," he or she might say: "My word is a compound word. The first syllable describes something very bright." The student continues providing clues until the partner figures out the word.

17. Bowling for Words: Make a bowling score sheet for each student (see sample). Then make a set of large paper or tagboard bowling pins. On each pin write a word and a number from 1–10. The words with the highest numbers should be the most difficult to read. Divide the class into small teams. Place the bowling pins in a bag or box so that they cannot be seen. One player from each team reaches in and selects a bowling pin. If the player can correctly read the word, the score on the bowling pin is recorded on the score sheet. If the player can't read the word, she receives a "gutter ball," or a score of 0. The game ends when all ten frames of the bowling game have been played and the scores tallied. You might want to have the teams use calculators to tally their scores.

BOWLING FOR WORDS										TOTAL
Max	6	0	7	8	1	0	3	9	0	2	36

18. Word Sort: Provide students with sets of word cards. First have the students sort the cards any way they choose (e.g., by common syllables or roots). Then suggest a specific way for the students to sort the words. Be sure that the words you include can be sorted in more than one way (e.g., multisyllabic words containing *-le, -al*, and *-el*).

19. What's Missing?: Write a brief story or paragraph on a chart. Place self-sticking notes over every fifth or tenth word. Or, select words with target skills you want to review and cover those up. As an alternative, you might write the story or paragraph, leaving blanks for each word you want students to figure out. When you read the story and get to a missing word, have students guess it. Before telling the children whether or not they are correct, write the correct spelling for the first syllable and allow children to modify their guesses. (For example, you would write *ba* for the first syllable in the word *bagel*.) Continue in this fashion until the word is completely spelled.

20. Unscramble It: Divide the class into teams of three to four students. Provide each team with a list of ten scrambled words. Give each team five minutes to unscramble as many words as possible. The team that unscrambles the most words wins. *Alternative*: Provide each team with scrambled sentences.

Teaching Phonics & Word Study in the Intermediate Grades • Scholastic Professional Books

21. **Make a Match:** Make word-part note cards—one for each student. Be sure that all the cards can be combined with at least one other card to form a word. Distribute the cards. You might want to play music while the students circulate and search for their match—the student with another word part that can be combined with their card to form a word. When all the students find their match, provide time for them to share their words with the class. Continue with other word part cards, or challenge students to find another match.

22. **Word Card File:** At the beginning of the year, have students bring in a card file box and blank index cards. Set aside time each week for students to write on one of their cards a word they are having trouble reading or spelling. Have them organize the cards in alphabetical order, and suggest that they add a sentence or picture clue to their cards to help them remember the words. Students should periodically review the cards in their card-file boxes. Point out times when looking at the file cards may help them with reading or writing.

23. **Book Chat:** Divide the class into small groups of four to five students. Ask each student to share a book he has recently read by talking briefly (a few sentences) about it. Students may also enjoy reading aloud a favorite paragraph or page of their book. If the book is fiction, remind students to avoid giving away the ending. Encourage students to read one of the books they heard about in their book chat. These chats honor students' accomplishments and remind them of the purpose of learning phonics—to read great books.

24. Syllable Race: Create a game board such as the one shown. Then make word cards, each containing a two-, three-, or four-syllable word. In turn, each player draws one card and reads the word aloud. If she reads it correctly, she moves forward on the game board as many spaces as there are syllables in the word. Consider writing this number under the word on each card for students to refer to. The game continues, until a player reaches the end.

25. Time It: Make one set of word cards using only base words and another using only prefixes and suffixes. Divide the class into small teams, then mix the cards and give an equal number to each group. Use a three-minute egg timer to time the game as the teams use their cards to form words. Designate one member of each team to record the words. At the end of the game, each team reads aloud the words they formed. The team with the most points (one per correctly formed word) wins.

Teaching Phonics & Word Study in the Intermediate Grades • Scholastic Professional Books

Building Fluency

"*Fluency . . . the neglected goal of reading instruction.*"

—*Richard Allington*

Recently, after several amazing trips to Israel, I began studying Hebrew. Since Hebrew doesn't employ the English alphabet, I was forced to learn a whole new set of symbols and sound-spelling correspondences. At first, these strange-looking squiggles and lines were meaningless to me. I tried everything I use with my students to learn them as quickly as possible. I wrote each letter as I said its sound. I created a set of flash cards and went over the cards several times a day. I even found a computer program that focused on learning the letters and contained mastery tests. After a couple of weeks, I felt ready to tackle my first simple Hebrew text. As I began to read, I struggled through every word, searched my mind for each letter-sound, blended the sounds together, then tried to recall the meaning of the word I had pronounced. Often, by the time I worked my way to the end of a sentence, I had forgotten what was at the beginning. My slow, labored, and inefficient reading was (and still is, unfortunately) characteristic of one who has not acquired reading fluency.

The Tale of Five Balloons by Miriam Roth

What Is Fluency?

According to *A Dictionary of Reading and Related Terms* (Harris and Hodges, 1981), fluency is "the ability to read smoothly, easily, and readily with freedom from word recognition problems." Fluency is necessary for good comprehension and enjoyable reading (Nathan and Stanovich, 1991). A lack of fluency is characterized by a slow, halting pace; frequent mistakes; poor phrasing; and inadequate intonation (Samuels, 1979)—all the result of weak word recognition skills.

Fluent reading is a major goal of reading instruction because decoding print accurately and effortlessly enables students to read for meaning. Fluency begins in Stage 2, the "Confirmation, Fluency, and Ungluing from Print" stage (see Chall's Stages of Reading Development, page 20), around grades 2 to 3 for many students. During this fluency stage, the reader becomes "unglued" from the print; that is, students can recognize many words quickly and accurately by sight and are skilled at sounding out those they don't recognize by sight. A fluent reader can:

Teaching Phonics & Word Study in the Intermediate Grades • Scholastic Professional Books

read at a rapid rate (pace—the speed at which oral or silent reading occurs)

automatically recognize words (smoothness—efficient decoding skills)

phrase correctly (prosody—the ability to read a text orally using appropriate pitch, stress, and phrasing).

Non-fluent readers read slowly and spend so much time trying to identify unfamiliar words that they have trouble comprehending what they're reading.

Automaticity theory, developed by LaBerge and Samuels (1974) helps explain how reading fluency develops. **Automaticity** refers to knowing how to do something so well you don't have to think about it. As tasks become easier, they require less attention and practice. Think of a child learning to play basketball; as initial attention is focused on how to dribble the ball, it's difficult for the child to think about guarding the ball from opponents, shooting a basket, or even running quickly down the court. However, over time, lots of practice makes dribbling almost second nature. The player is ready to concentrate on higher-level aspects of the game.

For reading, automaticity refers to the ability to recognize many words as whole units quickly and accurately. The advantage of recognizing a word as a whole unit is that words have meaning, and less memory is required for a meaningful word than for a meaningless letter. The average child needs between 4 and 14 exposures to a new word to recognize it automatically. However, children with reading difficulties need 40 or more exposures to a new word. Therefore, it's critical that students get a great deal of practice reading stories at their independent reading level to develop automaticity (Beck & Juel, 1995; Samuels, Schermer, & Reinking, 1992).

Three Signs of Automaticity

A child is reading fluently if he can:

1. read with expression

2. read aloud and then retell the story or content of the selection (decode and comprehend at the same time)

3. comprehend equally well a similar passage read if listened to

To commit words to memory, children need to decode many words sound by sound, and then progress to recognizing the larger word chunks. Now, instead of focusing on sounding out words sound by sound, the reader can read whole words, thereby focusing attention on decoding and comprehension simultaneously. In fact, the hallmark of fluent reading is the ability to decode and comprehend at the same time.

Classroom Spotlight

Evaluating Slow Readers

To find out why a student is reading slowly, ask her to read a passage from a book below her reading level. If she reads the passage slowly, her problem is probably poor fluency. If she can read the text easily, she's probably having trouble with decoding or comprehension. One way to determine whether the student's problem is with decoding or with comprehension is to have her read an on-level passage and then ask her a series of questions. If she accurately answers 75% or more of the questions, then the problem is one of weak decoding skills. To help this student with her decoding skills have her read from material at a lower level, involve her in repeated reading or echo readings, and dictate stories to her for reading instruction and practice.

Another way to determine why a student is reading slowly is to give him a running list of the words he will encounter in a text. If he can't recognize 95% of the words, then decoding is likely the issue. If he does recognize 95% or more of the words but has difficulty reading, then comprehension or fluency is the issue. A major reason students experience reading difficulty is that too much is taught too fast. Go back to where they are successful and start again.

Teaching Phonics & Word Study in the Intermediate Grades • Scholastic Professional Books

Although research has shown that fluency is a critical factor in reading development, many teachers and publishers have failed to recognize its importance to overall reading proficiency. Few teachers teach fluency directly, and elementary reading textbooks give fluency instruction short shrift. Consequently, Allington (1983) has called fluency the "neglected goal" of reading instruction. There are many reasons why children fail to read fluently. Allington cites the following:

- **Lack of exposure.** Some children have never been exposed to fluent reading models. These children come from homes in which there are few books and little or no reading.

- **The good-reader syndrome.** In school, good readers are more likely to get positive feedback and more likely to be encouraged to read with expression and make meaning from text. Poor readers receive less positive feedback, and the focus of their instruction is often solely on figuring out words or attending to word parts.

- **Lack of practice time.** Good readers generally spend more time reading during instructional time and therefore become better readers. Good readers also engage in more silent reading. This additional practice stimulates their reading growth. Poor readers spend less time actually reading.

- **Frustration.** Good readers are exposed to more text at their independent reading level, whereas poor readers frequently encounter text at their frustration level. Consequently, poor readers tend to give up because they make so many errors.

- **Missing the "why" of reading.** Good readers tend to view reading as making meaning from text, whereas poor readers tend to view reading as trying to read words accurately.

Measuring Reading Rate

To determine a student's oral reading rate, take a one-minute, timed sampling of his oral reading of a passage at his reading level. Make a copy of the passage for the student and one for yourself so you can record his errors while he reads. As the student reads, follow along and mark on your copy any words he reads incorrectly. Use the guidelines below. For example, if a student stops or struggles with a word for 3 seconds, tell him the word and mark it as incorrect. Place a mark after the last word he reads. Then, tally the results and consult the chart on page 261, which shows national norms for oral reading rates of students in grades 2–5. Using these norms, you can determine how your students rate nationally and which students need more work in developing fluency.

Oral Reading Fluency-Test Scoring Guidelines

Words read correctly. These are words that the student pronounces correctly, given the reading context.

- Count self-corrections within 3 seconds as correct.

- Don't count repetitions as incorrect.

Words read incorrectly. Count the following types of errors as incorrect: (a) mispronunciations, (b) substitutions, and (c) omissions. Also, count words the student doesn't read within 3 seconds as incorrect.

- Mispronunciations are words that are misread: *bell* for *ball*.

- Substitutions are words that are substituted for the correct word; this is often inferred by a one-to-one correspondence between word orders: *dog* for *cat*.

- Omissions are words skipped or not read; if a student skips an entire line, each word is counted as an error.

3-second rule. If a student is struggling to pronounce a word or hesitates for 3 seconds, tell the student the word, and count it as an error.

Teaching Phonics & Word Study in the Intermediate Grades • Scholastic Professional Books

Oral Reading Fluency Norms, Grades 2-5

(Hansbrouck and Tindal, 1992)

Grade	Percentile	WCPM Fall	WCPM Winter	WCPM Spring
2	75%	82	106	124
	50%	53	78	94
	25%	23	46	65
3	75%	107	123	142
	50%	79	93	114
	25%	65	70	87
4	75%	125	133	143
	50%	99	112	118
	25%	72	89	92
5	75%	126	143	151
	50%	105	118	128
	25%	77	93	100

Measuring Oral Reading Fluency

In order to help students develop fluency, you must first know their oral reading accuracy and rate. There are several measurement tools you can use to identify the accuracy and rate, and nationally normed averages exist. Many state standards now include these rates as benchmarks of students' reading progress. The combination of reading accuracy and rate is referred to as a student's oral reading fluency (ORF). It is expressed as "words correct per minute" (WCPM).

It is essential to measure both accuracy and rate. For example, if you measure only accuracy, you wouldn't know that it takes one student twice as long to read the same text as it does another student. Which student is fluent? Likewise, if you measure only rate, you wouldn't know that one student, who could read a text much more quickly than another student, makes significantly more mistakes. Which student is fluent?

Ways to Develop Fluency

Although few reading-textbook teacher manuals contain instruction on building fluency, there are in fact many things you can do to develop your students' fluency. Rasinski (1989) has identified six ways to build fluency.

Books on tape are great for developing a student's listening vocabulary.

1. Model fluent reading

Students need many opportunities to hear texts read. This can include daily teacher read-alouds, books on tape, and books read by peers during book-sharing time. It's particularly critical for poorer readers who've been placed in a low reading group to hear text read correctly because they are likely to hear repeatedly the efforts of other poor readers in their group. They need proficient, fluent models; that is, they need to have a model voice in their heads to refer to as they monitor their own reading. While you read aloud to students, periodically highlight aspects of fluent reading. Point out that you are reading dialogue the way you think the character might have said it, or how you speed up your reading when the text becomes more intense and exciting. Talk about fluency—how to achieve it, and why it's important. Continually remind students that with practice they can become fluent readers. An important benefit of daily read-alouds is that they expose students to a wider range of vocabulary.

Teaching Phonics & Word Study in the Intermediate Grades • Scholastic Professional Books

2. Provide direct instruction and feedback

Direct instruction and feedback in fluency includes, but isn't limited to, independent reading practice, fluent reading modeling, and monitoring students' reading rates. Here are some ways to include lots of this needed instruction in your classroom.

- **Explicitly teach students the sound-spelling correspondences they struggle with, high-utility decoding and syllabication strategies, and a large core of sight words.**

- **Have students practice reading new or difficult words prior to reading a text.**

- **Occasionally time students' reading.** Have students create charts to monitor their own progress. Encourage them to set new reading-rate goals.

- **Include oral recitation lessons.** (Hoffman, 1987; Hoffman and Crone, 1985). With this technique, the focus is on comprehension. Introduce a story and read it aloud. Discuss the content with the class and have the class create a story summary. Then discuss the prosodic (phrasing and intonation) elements of the text (e.g., reading dialogue as if it is spoken; reading all caps louder; the difference between question and statement voices; understanding a character's expressed emotion—anger, sadness, joy, or disgust; reading longer phrases with appropriate pauses). Then have students practice reading sections of the story both on their own and with your guidance. Finally have individual students read sections of the story aloud for the class. Monitor each student's reading rate and word-recognition accuracy.

- **Teach students about "smooshing" the words together.** Some poor readers mistakenly believe that they are supposed to read each word separately; consequently, they always sound like they are reading a list. Model fluent reading by reading a passage without pauses between words. Then read the passage using appropriate pauses and phrasing. Discuss the differences.

- **Explain the return-sweep eye movement.** For some students, return sweeps are difficult. As a result, they lose their place as they read. A common technique to overcome this is to place a sheet of paper or bookmark under the line as one reads and move it down line by line. For many students this is disruptive because it halts the natural return-sweep motion, so some reading specialists suggest placing the bookmark above the line to avoid interfering with the return sweep. To illustrate for students how our eyes move as we read, poke a hole in a sheet of paper and hold it twelve inches away as you read a passage. Have the students comment on the jerkiness of your eyes (and your reading) as you move from word to word and line to line. This observation can result in an "aha moment" for some students.

● **Teach students about the eye-voice span.** When we read aloud, there is a distinct and measurable distance between our eye placement and our voice. Our eyes are one to three words ahead of our oral reading. To illustrate this phenomenon, copy a story or passage onto a transparency. As you are about to finish a paragraph, turn off the transparency. Students will be amazed that you can still say a few words. They'll see how fluent readers phrase appropriate chunks.

Teaching Phonics & Word Study in the Intermediate Grades • Scholastic Professional Books

- **Find alternatives to "round-robin" reading.** Round-robin reading is one of the most harmful techniques for developing fluency. During round-robin reading, students read aloud only a small portion of the text. Although they are supposed to be following along with the other readers, often they don't. It is absolutely essential that students read a lot every day. When they're reading a new story, it is important that they read the entire story—often more than once. One way to avoid round-robin reading every day is to have students read the story silently a few pages at a time and then ask them questions or have them comment on strategies they used. Other appropriate techniques include partner reading, reading softly to themselves while you circulate and "listen in," and popcorn reading, in which students are called on frequently and randomly (often in the middle of a paragraph) to read aloud. If you use any technique in which students have not read the entire selection during their reading group, be sure that they read it in its entirety before or after the reading group.

- **Teach appropriate phrasing and intonation.** Guided oral reading practice and the study of punctuation and grammar can help. To teach appropriate phrasing, see page 269 (#5). For teaching intonation and punctuation, use some or all of the following. Have students:

  ➠ *recite the alphabet as a conversation.*
  ABCD? EFG! HI? JKL. MN? OPQ. RST! UVWX. YZ!

  ➠ *recite the same sentence using different punctuation.*
  Dogs bark? Dogs bark! Dogs bark.

  ➠ *practice placing the stress on different words in the same sentence.*
  I am tired. I am tired. I am tired.

  ➠ *practice reading sentences as if talking to a friend.*

Studying grammar fosters fluency because grammar alerts the reader to natural phrases in a sentence. For example, being able to identify the subject and the predicate of a sentence is one step in understanding phrase boundaries in text. Also, understanding the role of prepositions and conjunctions adds additional clues to phrase boundaries. Try providing students with short passages color-coded according to subject and predicate to assist them in practice reading.

- **Conduct two-minute drills to underline or locate a target word, syllable, or spelling pattern in an array or short passage** (Moats, 1998). This will help students rapidly recognize spelling patterns that are common to many words. And it's a lot of fun.

- **Motivate students to read using incentives, charting, and rewards.** You want to encourage students to practice reading for long enough periods of time to build accuracy and then automaticity in decoding.

3. Provide reader support (choral reading and reading-while-listening)

Readers need to practice reading both orally and silently. Research has shown that oral reading is very important for the developing reader, especially younger children. It appears that young children need to hear themselves read, and they benefit from adult feedback. As well as improving reading, this feedback shows students how highly we adults value the skill of reading. There are several ways to support students' oral reading without evoking the fear and humiliation struggling readers often feel when called on to read aloud. Here are the most popular techniques (always use text at the student's instructional level that models natural language patterns):

- **Reading simultaneously with a partner or small group.** With this technique, students can "float" in and out as appropriate without feeling singled out. For best results, have students practice reading the selection independently before reading it with the partner or group.

- **Echo reading.** As you read a phrase or sentence in the text, the student repeats it. This continues throughout the text. You can also use a tape recording of the text with pauses for the child to echo the reading.

Teaching Phonics & Word Study in the Intermediate Grades • Scholastic Professional Books

Phrase-Cued Text Practice Sessions

Use the following routine for phrase-cued text practice sessions, which should take about 10 minutes a day, several times a week. Select passages on each child's instructional reading level. Make two copies of the passage. On one copy, mark the natural phrase boundaries; leave the other copy unmarked.

Day 1

1. Select, copy, and distribute a marked text passage (approximately 100–250 words) written at the students' reading level. Explain the format, and tell students that good phrasing will improve their comprehension. Assure them that, with practice, they will get used to reading from marked text.

2. Model reading the marked text aloud as students use their copies to follow along silently. Do this two or three times. Invite students to comment on what they observed about your phrasing and expression.

3. Have students use the marked text to read aloud chorally. They will have additional opportunities to practice throughout the week.

Day 2

1. Once again, model reading aloud the marked text.

2. Have students chorally read aloud from copies of their marked text two or three times. Encourage students to comment on their reading and give them your feedback. Also discuss the content of the passage.

3. Have students practice reading aloud the marked text in pairs or small groups. Encourage them to exchange constructive feedback.

Day 3

1. Have students use the marked text to read aloud chorally.

2. Follow up by having students practice reading aloud in pairs or small groups.

3. You may wish to have students tape record themselves so they can assess their own reading.

4. Encourage students to find opportunities during the day to practice reading their marked text.

Day 4

1. Distribute the unmarked version of the text.

2. Ask each student to read aloud the passage without the phrases marked. Give each reader feedback on his or her reading.

3. Have students practice reading the unmarked text in pairs. They may also tape record themselves and compare their various readings.

Day 5

1. Meet with each student individually. Ask him or her to read the unmarked version of the text. Note phrasing, appropriate pauses, expression, and reading rate. Give the student positive feedback.

2. Encourage students to take the passage home and read it to an adult.

- **Reader's theater.** Students choose a favorite part of a book, reading it aloud independently until they're confident, and then read it aloud to the class. This reading can be primarily for class enjoyment or it can be part of the student's oral book report.

- **Choral reading.** Reading together as a group is great for poetry and selections with a distinct pattern.

- **Paired repeated readings** (Koskinen and Blum, 1986). A student reads a short passage three times to a partner and gets feedback. Then the partners switch roles. To avoid frustration, it works best to pair above-level readers with on-level readers and on-level readers with below-level readers.

- **Books on tape.** Select and place appropriate books on tape in a classroom listening center. Have students follow along as the book is read, reading with the narrator where possible. An excellent books-on-tape collection is *Read 180 Audiobooks* (Scholastic, 2000). These books contain audio models that periodically help students work through comprehension difficulties.

4. Repeated readings of one text

Repeated reading, a popular technique developed by Samuels (1979), has long been recognized as an excellent way to help students achieve fluency. It has been shown to increase reading rate and accuracy and to transfer to new texts. As a child reads a passage at his or her instructional level, the teacher times the reading. Afterwards, the teacher gives feedback on word-recognition errors and the number of words per minute the child read accurately, then records this data on a graph. The child should practice reading the same selection independently or with a partner. The process is repeated, and the child's progress plotted on the graph until the passage is mastered. This charting is effective because (1) students become focused on their own mastery of the task and competing with their own past performance, and (2) students have concrete evidence that they are making progress. In addition, repeating the words many times helps students build a large sight-word vocabulary.

Students who resist rereading selections need incentives. Besides simply telling the student that rereading is a part of the important practice one does to become a better reader, you might motivate her by having her:

Teaching Phonics & Word Study in the Intermediate Grades • Scholastic Professional Books

➠ read to a friend, family member, or pet

➠ read to a student in a lower grade

➠ read into a tape player to record the session

➠ set a reading-rate goal for a given passage and try to exceed that goal in successive readings

➠ prepare to perform a reader's theater version of a selection.

Note: This technique is NOT recommended for students already reading fluently.

5. Cueing phrase boundaries in text

One of the characteristics of proficient (fluent) readers is the ability to group words together in meaningful units—syntactically appropriate phrases. "Proficient reading is characterized not only by fast and accurate word recognition, but also by readers' word chunking or phrasing behavior while reading connected discourse" (Rasinski, 1989). Students who are having trouble with comprehension may not be putting words together in meaningful phrases or chunks as they read. Their oral reading is characterized by a choppy, word-by-word delivery that impedes comprehension. These students need instruction in phrasing written text into appropriate segments.

One way to help students learn to recognize and use natural English phrase boundaries—and thus improve their phrasing, fluency, and comprehension—is **phrase-cued text** practice. Phrase-cued text is a short passage marked by a slash (or some other visual) at the end of each phrase break. The longer pause at the end of the sentence is marked by a double slash (//). The teacher models good oral reading, and students practice with the marked text. Later students apply their skills to the same text, unmarked. Have students practice the skill orally for 10 minutes daily.

Here's an example:

In the summer/I like/to swim/at the beach.//

Although it's very hot/I like the idea/

of being in the cool water

all day.// Summer truly is/

my favorite time/of the year.//

6. Provide students with easy reading materials

Students need an enormous amount of individualized reading practice in decodable materials that are not too difficult (Shefelbine, 1999; Beck and Juel, 1995; Samuels, Shermer, and Reinking, 1992). I recommend at least 30 minutes of independent reading every day. Some should occur in school, and some can occur at home. Fluency develops through a great deal of practice reading stories in which students can use sound-spelling strategies (as opposed to contextual strategies) to figure out a majority of the unfamiliar words. In the early grades, there must be a match between instruction in phonics and reading practice—hence the need for practice stories that are decodable. This match encourages students to adopt sound-spelling strategies and at the same time, through extensive practice reading story after story after story, leads to fluent reading. It is critical that practice-reading materials not be at a child's frustration level. In other words, the student's reading accuracy (the proportion of words read correctly) should be above 90%. During individualized practice, students may be reading at different levels. They read aloud "quietly" to themselves as the teacher walks around listening to each child for a minute or so while still monitoring the group as a whole. Students need time to figure out unfamiliar words through phonic patterns. Expecting students to read fluently when they are not fluent only encourages guessing and memorization.

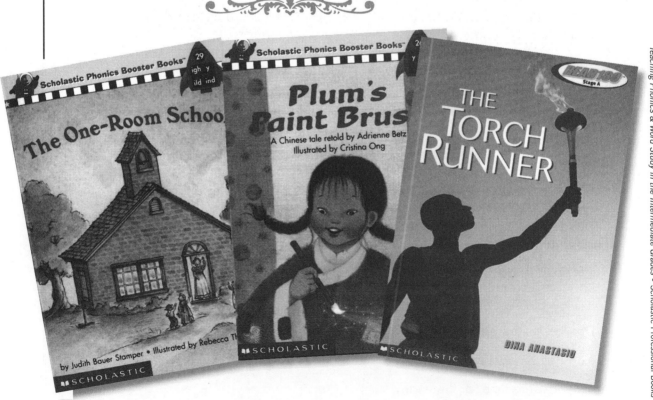

Meeting the Needs of Struggling Readers

" *Reading failure [is] a public health problem with major consequences and costs.* "

—Reid Lyon

What do Thomas Edison, Albert Einstein, Woodrow Wilson, Nelson Rockefeller, Hans Christian Andersen, George Patton, Galileo, Leonardo da Vinci, Michelangelo, Bruce Jenner, Winston Churchill, and Tom Cruise have in common? These notable individuals were all dyslexic. Each struggled in his own way to master the art of reading.

One of the most difficult aspects of teaching is watching a child struggle with learning to read. During one of my early years of teaching, I was given a class of thirty grade 2 and 3 readers who were struggling. My class was designated a Chapter 1 classroom. Most of my students had serious reading difficulties, and a few received additional assistance from the Resource Room teacher. However, many received all their instruction from me and my teaching partner, a highly-skilled veteran instructor. The range of abilities in the class was broad. Matthew was a non-alphabetic reader with almost no sight-word knowledge. Bradley had severe motor-coordination problems that hampered his ability to form letters. Christon couldn't recall the alphabet. Brian had serious behavioral problems. Billy's learned helplessness and lack of motivation were a constant issue. Darlene could read on grade level but couldn't organize her thoughts and ideas logically. Jason had accurate but labored decoding skills. And the list went on.

Teaching Phonics & Word Study in the Intermediate Grades • Scholastic Professional Books

This same situation exists in many classrooms across the country, but with only one full-time teacher in the room. By the time students enter the intermediate grades, the range of abilities is often extremely broad. Certainly, meeting the individual needs of each student in your classroom is perhaps the greatest challenge you will face.

State-of-Reading Statistics

Many sobering statistics regarding the state of reading instruction in this country circulate in the media each year. According to the 1994 National Assessment of Educational Progress, 44% of fourth-graders read at "below basic" levels. Only 5% to 6% of these children can be classified as having severe learning disorders (Lyon, 1996). "The others are likely to be suffering the consequences of inappropriate teaching, low standards, and/or disadvantageous environmental circumstances for learning to read" (Moats, 2000). In addition, Miller (1993) cites the following:

● Approximately 60 million U.S. citizens read below the eighth-grade reading level.

● About 85% of the juveniles appearing in juvenile court are functionally illiterate.

● Approximately 50 to 60% of U.S. prison inmates are functionally illiterate.

● About 75% of the unemployed adults are illiterate.

It is evident that learning to read goes well beyond an educational issue; it is an extremely serious and important social issue. As the researchers at the National Institute of Child Health and Human Development report, "reading failure . . . constitutes not only an urgent challenge for our schools, but a public health problem with major consequences and costs" (Alexander, 1996; Lyon, 1995).

In a country with such tremendous wealth and resources, there is no excuse for the high numbers of children who leave our schools unable to meet the most basic reading demands of adult life. We must do all that we can to reverse these dispiriting statistics. Solutions often cited include improved teacher training, adequate instructional materials, smaller class sizes, family and community support, early preventive measures, and strong intervention programs. These are all important and could help. However, in today's classrooms you face today's reality—a reality that may not come close to these ideals. Who are these below-level readers, and how can you help them given the resources available?

Struggling Readers—They Have a Variety of Problems

We skilled readers read regularly for information and for pleasure. However, for many children reading is neither easy nor enjoyable. While some children seem to learn to read with relative ease, others experience great difficulties. Children with reading difficulties can possess a wide range of language deficits. Those with learning disabilities (dyslexia) have normal or high intelligence and have no problems with vocabulary or understanding English syntax. However, they have trouble with sounds and print. Estimates reveal that 10% to 20% of the student population has this problem. Some estimates say the percentage is even higher. Recent statistics also reveal that as many girls as boys have difficulties learning to read.

Struggling readers might have problems with phonemic awareness, phonics, comprehension, or processing verbal information. They might also lack the auditory and visual skills needed for reading. Often, memory and concentration are a problem. The causes are many—educational, psychological, physiological, and social. Some educational factors that have been cited as causes of reading difficulties include: teaching reading skills too early, instruction that ignores a child's unique needs, inappropriately paced instruction, and large class size.

A child's emotional reaction to these difficulties can compound the problems. Because of their lack of success, struggling readers often view themselves as incapable of learning to read. This "learned helplessness" may cause them to give up and resist making an effort. "Part of teaching children with reading problems is convincing them that they can learn to read, despite their experience to the contrary" (Stahl, 1997).

To help children with reading problems (see "Four Types of Struggling Readers" on the following page), it's critical to assess what they can and cannot do and then plan an intervention program to meet their unique

"Phonics must not be made to carry the whole burden of reading instruction, especially if students have difficulty with it. Although research and experience have demonstrated again and again that phonics knowledge and skill are essential for learning to read, and that they speed up learning to read, there is also considerable evidence that reading development depends on wide reading of connected text, the development of fluency, and the growth of vocabulary, knowledge and reasoning. Thus, it is wise for all students, even those having extreme difficulty with phonics, to read books they find interesting, learn the meanings of ever more difficult words, and continue to acquire knowledge."

—Chall and Popp, 1996

Four Types of Struggling Readers

Non-alphabetic: These children have difficulties during the first stage of reading development. They don't grasp the alphabetic principle. Since their word-recognition skills are extremely poor, in their efforts to read they try to depend on visual clues, such as a word's shape, length, or position on the page. These students need a great deal of phonological awareness training, and benefit most from explicit instruction in recognizing the alphabet and learning sound-spelling relationships.

Compensatory: These children have a limited grasp of the alphabetic principle and weak phonemic-awareness skills. Without a knowledge base of sound-spelling relationships, they have trouble decoding words. As a result, they compensate by relying on context clues and on their sight-word knowledge. These children do okay with easy material, but have serious difficulties when the reading demands increase.

Non-automatic: These readers can accurately sound out words, but with great effort. Since their word-recognition skills are not automatic, decoding requires much of their mental energies, and comprehension suffers. These children need practice and repetition to build fluency. They may also have motivational problems.

Delayed: These readers have automatic word-recognition skills, but acquired them much later than their peers. They lack comprehension skills because they were still concentrating on decoding when they were taught those skills. Therefore, when the reading materials became more complex—with many more multisyllabic words— they weren't ready for the increased comprehension demands. These children need a great deal of instruction on learning and using comprehension strategies. They might also benefit from further instruction in phonics and spelling.

instructional needs. What these children need may not be a different reading program or method, but rather adjustments to their existing program that include more time, more instructional support, and more practice reading connected text. All four types of struggling readers generally suffer from low motivation, low levels of practice, and low expectations. These have to be taken into consideration, too.

Ways to Help Your Strugglers Succeed

When you note that a student has a reading problem, and have diagnosed it, it's time to intervene and turn things around. Effective interventions are generally characterized by the following:

- They are applied as early as possible (as soon as a problem is diagnosed).

- They involve well-trained, highly skilled teachers and specialists.

- They are intensive.

- They can close the reading gap for poor readers.

- They are short lived, lasting only as long as needed.

- They help children overcome "learned helplessness."

- They connect in terms of instructional strategies and content to the reading instruction occurring in the classroom with the "general student population."

In addition to these characteristics, the following techniques will support intervention instruction:

Prompting. While students read a passage, provide prompts that help them focus attention on reading strategies. For example, when a student encounters an unfamiliar word, use prompts such as, "What letter sounds do you know in the word?" or "Are there any word parts you know in the word?" You can also create and display Strategy Picture Cards for students to refer to when they're reading independently. These cards provide written and illustrated cues to help overcome reading stumbling blocks. For example, one card might remind students to "reread a confusing sentence or passage."

Teaching Phonics & Word Study in the Intermediate Grades • Scholastic Professional Books

Assisted Reading. Give students a chance to read with assistance from you or with an audiocassette. Gradually decrease the assistance until the student is reading independently. Assisted readings are particularly helpful for text that is at a student's frustration level.

Supported Contextual Reading. This technique, developed by Stahl (1997), is designed to help students use their phonics knowledge. The assumption is that students with reading difficulties often do possess phonics knowledge, but are unable to use it effectively. First, read aloud to the student the text of some material one or two years above her instructional level and ask comprehension questions to make sure she understands the passage. This takes advantage of the student's oral listening skills and promotes concept development. Next, do an echo reading of the text with the student. Then send the text home with guidance for the family to help the student practice reading it. Finally, have the student reread the text multiple times in class until she has mastered the passage.

Cloze Passages. Select a passage that the student has previously read or that has been read to him. Leaving out every fifth or tenth word, write the passage on a chart. (You can insert blank lines in place of the words or cover them with self-sticking notes.) Now ask the student to use his background knowledge and understanding of English syntax to fill in the missing words. I like to provide the first letter or cluster of letters in each word to help the student use phonics cues, too.

Teacher Read-Alouds. Oral reading is critical for developing a student's listening and speaking vocabularies and world knowledge. Since students with reading difficulties are not developing these through their reading, they must be read to a lot.

Word-Family Construction. Building words belonging to the same word family can help students' reading and spelling by focusing their attention on common word parts. Use letter cards, pocket charts, magnetic letters, or any other type of manipulatable available. You might use the word families to create lists for a Word Wall in your classroom.

Teaching Phonics & Word Study in the Intermediate Grades • Scholastic Professional Books

Read Aloud Tests. When I give content area tests, say in science or social studies, I read aloud the tests to my struggling readers. This enables me to assess more accurately their content knowledge rather than their ability to read the test.

Four Principles of Effective Intervention

As I reflect on my years of teaching and the mountain of reading research on intervention, many theories and guidelines emerge regarding meeting the individual needs of students. I will focus on four principles that I have found to be most useful:

Four Basic Principles of Effective Intervention

PRINCIPLE 1

Begin instruction at the level students need it most. Treat the cause, not just the symptoms of reading difficulties. This requires looking at deficits in prerequisite skills.

PRINCIPLE 2

Assess, assess, assess. Effective diagnosis and ongoing assessment are critical.

PRINCIPLE 3

Select the appropriate literature for instructional and independent uses. Be careful to avoid providing literature that is always at students' frustration level.

PRINCIPLE 4

Maintain consistency. Using multiple instructional methods can confuse students. Use one clearly designed method of instruction, not a multitude of methods and techniques that may be at odds with one another.

Teaching Phonics & Word Study in the Intermediate Grades • Scholastic Professional Books

*B*egin intervention at the level students need it most.

Sometimes we tend to treat the symptoms of reading difficulties, rather than the causes. For example, I recently encountered a teacher who was spending a lot of time reteaching sound-spelling relationships to one of her students. She commented that this didn't seem to be having much effect. When I asked her if the student had weak phonemic awareness skills, she didn't know. We did a phonemic awareness assessment and discovered that his skills were quite weak. He couldn't orally blend words effectively and had little knowledge of how words work. I suggested the student receive phonemic awareness training. It helped.

This anecdote illustrates the need to determine a student's lowest deficit skill and begin instruction there. To do otherwise is like building a house on sand. Without a strong foundation, the house is sure to collapse. Skills prerequisite for phonics instruction include phonemic awareness and alphabet recognition. I should point out that simply treating a lower-deficit skill isn't necessarily enough to correct the reading problem. It will indeed remove a reading road block, but more must be done. "The lowest level deficit should be identified and repaired, followed by a reevaluation of the reader for additional problems, and by further instructional intervention to repair newly identified problems" (Royer and Sinatra, 1994).

> " **P**rovisions must be made for the student's continued conceptual and informational development while the reading issues are dealt with. If not, the reader will lose out on the knowledge, vocabulary, and concepts needed for further education and also as background information for reading in [later stages] and beyond (Chall, 1996). "

Although intervention techniques might not differ much from regular classroom instructional methods, once you determine where to start, be sure that you:

- begin your intervention right away.

- teach only one skill at a time and teach it until it is over-learned.

- adjust the pace at which you introduce skills. Allow students time to master each skill before moving on.

- continually review and reinforce learning.

- continually apply the learning to real reading and writing. Reading in context is critical.

Since I will not attempt to cover the scope that is intervention, I direct you to the following excellent resources for further information on meeting individual needs in your classroom:

Complete Reading Disabilities Handbook by W.H. Miller (The Center for Applied Research in Education, 1993)

No Quick Fix: Rethinking Literacy Programs in America's Elementary Schools by R.L. Allington and S.A. Walmsley (Teachers College Press, 1995)

Off Track: When Poor Readers Become "Learning Disabled" by L. Spear-Swerling and R.J. Sternberg (Westview Press, 1996)

Reading With the Troubled Readers by M. Phinney (Heinemann, 1988)

PRINCIPLE 2

Assess, *assess, assess.*

When students enter the intermediate grades, their phonic decoding abilities vary significantly. To provide effective and purposeful instruction, it's important to assess each student's phonics skills and develop differentiated instruction based on the results. A comprehensive diagnosis of each student is necessary. Both formal and informal assessments can assist you. Using your findings, frequently monitor the student's progress to determine the causes of reading difficulties and the success of your teaching strategies. I am constantly reminded of the old saying, "An ounce of prevention is worth a pound of cure." Certainly the best way to prevent reading difficulties is properly designed instruction and early detection of difficulties. However, even with these safeguards, some students will persist in struggling with decoding, and continual assessment will be necessary.

You can assess students in many ways, including the following (Teaching Reading, 1996):

Screening assessments for phonics, phonemic awareness, and writing/spelling

Checklists for phonics, phonemic awareness, and reading and writing attitudes

Miscue analysis (running records) for assessing reading accuracy, identifying and analyzing consistent reading errors, and determining instructional and independent reading levels

Individual and group-administered tests including formal assessments, basal reading program tests, and reading inventories

Portfolios containing students' work throughout the year

Formal assessments for decoding abilities are listed on pages 290-304. These are generally administered by specialists and possess greater reliability and validity than other forms of assessment. However, many informal assessments such as observation and miscue analysis can provide you with enough vital information to guide instruction and determine what a student already knows. It's important to collect diagnostic information daily, weekly, and monthly.

Standardized diagnostic test batteries, with tests or subtests measuring word recognition, include the Stanford Diagnostic Reading Test (Karlsen, Madden, and Gardner, 1985), the Woodcock Reading Mastery Test–Revised (Woodcock, 1998), the Decoding Skills Test (Richardson and DiBenedetto, 1985), and the CORE Phonics Survey (CORE, 1999). All have good reliability and validity. In addition, I have provided the six quick assessments for you to use.

Frequent and systematic observations of students' reading abilities will also help you in modifying instruction to meet individual needs. To be sure you observe your students regularly, establish a system or observation schedule. For example, you might choose one student to observe per school day, keeping the dated record and analysis in the students' files to monitor their progress during the year. Select a time when you can hear the student read without interruptions. Repeat observations more often for students for who need intervention.

Six Quick Word-Recognition Tests

The **Nonsense Word Test** was developed so that children's sight-word knowledge wouldn't interfere with an assessment of their decoding abilities.

The **Names Test** (Cunningham, 1990) was developed for teachers who are less comfortable with nonsense-word assessments. Having the students read names (not sight words, but not nonsense words) has these advantages over other decoding tests:

- On other tests, some children are able to recognize words not because they can decode them, but because they know them as sight words. These tests tell you little about the students' phonics skills.

- Some children find reading nonsense words (an alternative to the above problem) confusing and attempt to make real words out of nonsense words.

- Name reading provides a context and purpose for reading isolated words.

- Most names are familiar and, therefore, in the student's listening vocabulary.

The **San Diego Quick Assessment** (Lapray and Ross, 1969) contains words common to children's reading materials at each of the grade levels included.

The **TOWRE** (Test of Word Reading Efficiency) was developed by Torgeson, Wagner, and Rashotte (1999) and is distributed by PRO-ED. These easily-administered tests take only 45 sec-onds each (I've included two parts of the test—one to measure phonemic decoding ability and one to measure sight-word ability). They test a student's ability to sound out words accurately and rapidly as well as recognize familiar sight words.

The **Sight Word Proficiency and Automaticity Assessment** checks a student's ability to accurately and effortlessly read the 150 most frequent words in English text. Reading these words proficiently is critical to fluent reading.

The **Phonological Awareness Assessment** identifies students who need phonological awareness training before they can benefit from phonics instruction. The following commercial training programs can help students with weak phonological awareness skills:

- **Auditory Discrimination in Depth**: Developed by C.H. Lindamood and P.C. Lindamood. 1984. Allen, TX. DLM/Teaching Resources Corporation.

- **Phonological Awareness Training** for Reading: Developed by Joseph K. Torgesen and Brian R. Bryant. 1994. Austin, TX. PROD-ED, Inc.

- **Scholastic Phonemic Awareness Kit**: Written by Wiley Blevins. Program Consultants: Louisa Cook Moats and John Shefelbine. 1997. New York, NY. Scholastic, Inc.

- **Sound Foundations**: Developed by B. Byrne and R. Fielding-Barnsley. 1991. Artarmon, New South Wales, Australia. Leyden Educational Publishers.

Teaching Phonics & Word Study in the Intermediate Grades • Scholastic Professional Books

*S*elect the appropriate literature for instructional and independent uses.

Not only do students need to be reading successfully during formal reading instruction, they need to have successful independent reading opportunities each day. Students need to read text with which they have a sense of control and comfort. The relationship between silent reading (and out-of-school reading) and reading growth has been well documented (Rosenshine and Stevens, 1984). As Allington (1984) pointed out, good first-grade readers read about 1,900 words a week, whereas their poor-reader counterparts read only about 16 words a week. By the middle grades, an average reader reads approximately 1,000,000 words a year, whereas a poor reader may read only 10,000 words. You can't become a skilled reader if you rarely read. The following guidelines highlight the differences among a student's independent, instructional, and frustration reading levels.

> "To encourage optimal progress with the use of any of these early reading materials, teachers need to be aware of the difficulty level of the text relative to a child's reading level. Regardless of how well a child already reads, high error rates are negatively correlated with growth; low error rates are positively linked with growth. A text that is too difficult, then, not only serves to undermine a child's confidence and will but also diminishes learning itself." (*Teaching Reading*, 1996)

Levels of Reading

Independent or free reading level: The level at which a student can read a text without the teacher's assistance. Comprehension should average 90% or better, and word recognition should average 95% or better.

Instructional reading level: The level at which a student should receive reading instruction. The student reads with teacher guidance, and is challenged enough to continue reading growth. Comprehension should average 75% or better, and word recognition should average 90% or better.

Frustration reading level: The level at which a student cannot read a text adequately. At this level, the student frequently shows signs of discomfort. Comprehension averages 50% or less, and word recognition averages less than 90%.

To determine a student's independent, instructional, and frustration reading levels, use an individual reading inventory. During an individual reading inventory, a student is asked to read a passage or series of passages and then given sight-word tests, graded word lists, or comprehension questions. The following are commercially available reading inventories:

- Scholastic Reading Inventory (Scholastic, 1997)

- Analytical Reading Inventory (Woods and Moe, 1989/Merrill Publishing Company)

- Basic Reading Inventory (Johns, 1991/Kendall/Hunt Publishing Company)

- Classroom Reading Inventory (Silvaroli, 1990/William C. Brown Publishing Company)

- Ekwall/Shanker Reading Inventory (Ekwall and Shanker, 1993/Allyn and Bacon)

- Burns/Roe Informal Reading Inventory (Burns and Roe, 1993/Houghton Mifflin)

- New Sucher-Allred Reading Placement Inventory (1986/McGraw-Hill)

Teaching Phonics & Word Study in the Intermediate Grades • Scholastic Professional Books

You can also use a readability formula such as the Spache, Dale-Chall, or Fry to determine reading levels. Another popular level assessment system is the Lexile system, developed by MetaMetrics Inc., which is currently being used to level trade books. Each book is assigned a level (for example, 100–400 = grade 1), and a student's scores on a reading inventory are used to help the teacher match a student to an appropriate text.

You can create your own informal reading inventories by selecting 100-word passages from various-level books (you might use the Lexile-system levels). Ask a student to read a passage at each level, count the errors, and ask a series of comprehension questions. Of course, matching students to text requires more than a readability formula or test. A student's background knowledge and experiences, as well as his or her interest in a particular topic, can affect the difficulty of a text.

PRINCIPLE 4

*M*aintain consistency.

If a child's reading intervention is to be successful, there must be consistency among the many teachers and reading specialists instructing the child. In analyzing a child's total reading instruction, I frequently observe that each instructor is providing a unique and thorough program of instruction. However, the emphasis of methods they're using sometimes conflicts. For example, a student might be receiving explicit phonics instruction with practice reading controlled text in the Resource Room, yet is reading uncontrolled text in the regular classroom with an emphasis on using knowledge of sight words and context clues. The result is confusion that impedes the student's learning. Therefore, to maintain consistency among the methods or techniques being used to teach your students, coordinate with the other teachers who are part of their intervention.

> "The paradox of children with reading problems is that they get more phonics instruction than children reading at expected levels, yet they have continued difficulties decoding words. . . . I recommend a two-pronged solution—first, providing a clear and consistent program of phonics instruction, and second, providing copious amounts of reading of connected text"
>
> (Stahl, 1997).

What About Commercial Intervention Programs?

The number of quality intervention programs is small, but increasing. Several print programs have been available for many years, but there are some relatively new computer programs. Computer programs can assist students during independent reading and skills practice. Today's best offer features that allow students to highlight and hear confusing words read aloud and provide corrective feedback. Computer programs can be highly motivational for struggling readers. Here are exemplary print and computer programs.

- **Read XL** (2000, New York, NY: Scholastic) This program is designed for students in grades 6–8 who are reading one to three years below grade level. Material includes an anthology composed of 60% nonfiction, shared novels for oral reading, audiobooks for fluency models and enjoyment, high-interest independent reading books, practice books for independent skill work, tests to monitor progress, and electronic text for independent reading and motivation.

- **Language!** (J. Greene, 1995, Longmont, CO: Sopris West) This program, designed for the middle grades, contains a comprehensive language curriculum. Each unit includes: phoneme awareness; decoding and encoding isolated words; varieties of word structures; reading sentences, paragraphs, and passages for meaning; understanding and using figurative language; applying principles of composition; pragmatic language use; abstract language interpretation; the grammatical structures of English and their interrelationships; the idioms and collocations of English; punctuation, capitalization, and mechanics in writing; morphology; vocabulary expansion; and expository and narrative writing. A series of readers accompanies the program.

- **The Wilson Reading System** (Wilson, 1996, Millbury, MA: Wilson Language Training) Designed for older students with significant reading problems, this program is based on the Orton-Gillingham instructional principles. It teaches basic reading skills using multisensory, cumulative techniques. The program emphasizes the syllable unit of words and includes decodable text.

- **Lindamoods' Auditory Discrimination in Depth** and **Visualizing and Verbalizing** (Lindamood & Lindamood, 1984, Austin, TX: PRO-ED) *Auditory Discrimination in Depth* teaches the ability to identify speech sounds in words. *Visualizing and Verbalizing* teaches concept imagery to improve reading comprehension.

Teaching Phonics & Word Study in the Intermediate Grades • Scholastic Professional Books

- **Words and Patterns for Reading and Spelling** (Henry and Redding, 1996, Austin, TX: PRO-ED) This tutorial for word study is designed for middle-grade students. It teaches phonograms, syllable types, and Latin and Greek roots. The activities can relate to any texts students are reading.

- **Project Read's Linguistics Kit, Comprehension Kit, Written Expression Kit** (Enfield and Greene, 1996, Bloomington, MN: Language Circle) This program teaches the basic structure of English to students with language learning problems. It uses systematic, direct, multisensory strategies.

- **Read 180** (1999, New York, NY: Scholastic) This state-of-the art computer and print program, directed toward grades 4 through 8, features highly-motivating videos linked to decodable computer passages, computer-assisted learning, books for independent reading, audiobooks, practice books, and teacher support materials. Students receive instruction from the teacher and guided practice from the computer. The program is designed to provide students the level and amount of practice needed to achieve mastery of basic reading and spelling skills.

- **Scholastic Interactive Phonics Readers** (2000, New York, NY: Scholastic) This program contains 72 decodable books on CD-ROM, designed for students who need decoding support at the earliest levels (K–2). As students read each book, they can click on words for decoding support, sound-by-sound. Blending is modeled as often as needed. Three activities—phonological awareness, phonics, and spelling—follow each book along with a timed assessment developed to test decoding accuracy and speed. The hallmark of the program is the corrective feedback students receive throughout the program.

A Final Note

I encourage you to continue your professional development. Consult or join professional organizations, attend local and national conferences, and read professional books and magazines of interest. In addition, continue to take graduate courses and share your expertise with fellow teachers. As I travel around the country, I am struck by the wealth of untapped talent among the teaching staffs in our nation's schools. I constantly remind teachers that their best resources for professional growth are their colleagues.

I wish you all much success!

APPENDIX

Six Quick Word-Identification Assessments

The Nonsense Word Test

Preparing the Test

- Type or print the test and make a copy to record the student's responses.

Administering the Test

- Administer the test to one student at a time.

- Explain to the student that she is to read each word. Point out that the words are nonsense, or made-up, words.

- As the student reads the entire list, put a check mark on the answer sheet beside each word she reads correctly. (The word is correct if the student's pronunciation is correct according to common sound-spelling relationships.)

Scoring the Test

- Total the number of words the student read correctly. Analyze the mispronounced words, looking for patterns that might give you information about the student's decoding strengths and weaknesses.

- Focus future instruction on those sound-spelling relationship categories (short vowels, long vowels, etc.) in which the student made three or more errors.

Teaching Phonics & Word Study in the Intermediate Grades • Scholastic Professional Books

The Nonsense Word Test

A. Short Vowels

1.	lat	6.	fim
2.	ped	7.	hep
3.	sib	8.	yot
4.	mog	9.	rud
5.	vun	10.	cag

B. Digraphs, Blends

1.	sheg	6.	bruck
2.	chab	7.	cliss
3.	stot	8.	smend
4.	whid	9.	thrist
5.	thuzz	10.	phum

C. Long Vowels

1.	sote	6.	shain
2.	mabe	7.	dright
3.	foap	8.	hupe
4.	weam	9.	heest
5.	flay	10.	sny

D. Other Vowels

1.	doit	6.	moof
2.	spoud	7.	lurst
3.	clar	8.	porth
4.	foy	9.	stook
5.	jern	10.	flirch

E. Multisyllabic Words

1.	rigfap	6.	moku
2.	churbit	7.	wolide
3.	napsate	8.	lofam
4.	reatloid	9.	pagbo
5.	foutray	10.	plizzle

Teaching Phonics & Word Study in the Intermediate Grades • Scholastic Professional Books

The Names Test

Preparing the Test

- Type or print the 25 names on a sheet of paper and make a copy to serve as an answer sheet. If you have students who might be overwhelmed by the size of the list, write each name on a note card.

Administering the Test

- Administer the test to one student at a time.

- Explain to the student that he is to pretend to be a teacher and read the list of names as if he's taking attendance.

- Pointing out that you will not help with any names, have the student read the entire list.

- Write a check mark on the answer sheet for each name he reads correctly. Count first and last names separately. (Count a word correct if all the syllables are pronounced correctly. It doesn't matter where the child places the accent.) Write phonetic spellings for the names misread.

Scoring the Test

- Count words where the vowel sound depends on which syllable the consonant is placed with (for example, Ho/mer or Hom/er) correct for either pronunciation.

- Total the number of names read correctly. Analyze the mispronounced names, looking for patterns that might give you information about the student's decoding strengths and weaknesses.

- The average second grader scores 23 correct out of 50.

292

Teaching Phonics & Word Study in the Intermediate Grades • Scholastic Professional Books

The Names Test

(developed by Patricia Cunningham, 1990)

Student: _____ **Date:** _____

Jay Conway	_____	Wendy Swain	_____
Tim Cornell	_____	Glen Spencer	_____
Chuck Hoke	_____	Fred Sherwood	_____
Yolanda Clark	_____	Flo Thornton	_____
Kimberly Blake	_____	Dee Skidmore	_____
Roberta Slade	_____	Grace Brewster	_____
Homer Preston	_____	Ned Westmoreland	_____
Gus Quincy	_____	Ron Smitherman	_____
Cindy Sampson	_____	Troy Whitlock	_____
Chester Wright	_____	Vance Middleton	_____
Ginger Yale	_____	Zane Anderson	_____
Patrick Tweed	_____	Bernard Pendergraph	_____
Stanley Shaw	_____		

The San Diego Quick Assessment

Preparing the Test

- Prepare word-list cards by typing each list on a note card. Write the grade-level on the back of each card for your reference.

- Prepare a typed word list with a space after each word for you to record the student's responses.

Administering the Test

- Start with a card that is at least two years below the student's grade level.

- Have the student read the words in the list aloud. If she misreads any words, go to an easier list until she makes no errors. Now you have identified the student's base reading level.

- Have the student read each subsequent card in sequence, and record all incorrect responses. Encourage the student to read all the words so that you can determine the strategies he or she uses to decode.

- Continue the assessment until the student misses at least three words on one of the lists.

Scoring the Test

- Use the assessment results to identify the student's independent, instructional, and frustration levels. You can provide instructional and independent reading materials for each child based on the results of this assessment.

    Independent level = no more than one error on a list

    Instructional level = two errors on a list

    Frustration level = three or more errors on a list

Teaching Phonics & Word Study in the Intermediate Grades • Scholastic Professional Books

The San Diego Quick Assessment

(La Pray and Ross, 1969)

PRE-PRIMER	PRIMER	GRADE 1	GRADE 2
see	you	road	our
play	come	live	please
me	not	thank	myself
at	with	when	town
run	jump	bigger	early
go	help	how	send
and	is	always	wide
look	work	night	believe
can	are	spring	quietly
here	this	today	carefully

GRADE 3	GRADE 4	GRADE 5	GRADE 6
city	decided	scanty	bridge
middle	served	business	commercial
moment	amazed	develop	abolish
frightened	silent	considered	trucker
exclaimed	wrecked	discussed	apparatus
several	improved	behaved	elementary
lonely	certainly	splendid	comment
drew	entered	acquainted	necessity
since	realized	escaped	gallery
straight	interrupted	grim	relativity

GRADE 7	GRADE 8	GRADE 9	GRADE 10
amber	capacious	conscientious	zany
dominion	limitation	isolation	jerkin
sundry	pretext	molecule	nausea
capillary	intrigue	ritual	gratuitous
impetuous	delusion	momentous	linear
blight	immaculate	vulnerable	inept
wrest	ascent	kinship	legality
enumerate	acrid	conservatism	aspen
daunted	binocular	jaunty	amnesty
condescend	embankment	inventive	barometer

TOWRE *(Test of Word Reading Efficiency)*

Preparing the Tests

- Type or print the two tests on separate sheets of paper and make copies to use as answer sheets to record the student's responses.

Administering the Tests

- Administer the tests to one student at a time.

- For the "Sight Word Efficiency Test," explain to the student that he or she is to read each word. For the "Phonemic Decoding Efficiency Test," point out that the words are nonsense, or made-up, words.

- For each test, have the student read as many words as possible within 45 seconds. Use a stopwatch or other timer to time the student.

- Write a check mark on the answer sheet beside each word the student reads incorrectly or skips. (For the "Sight Word Efficiency Test," count the words read correctly in 45 seconds. For the "Phonemic Decoding Efficiency Test," count a word correct if the pronunciation is correct according to common sound-spelling relationships.)

Scoring the Tests

- For each test, total the number of words read correctly. Analyze the mispronounced words, looking for patterns that might give you information about the student's decoding strengths and weaknesses.

- For information on converting raw test scores to age-based or grade-based scores, see the TOWRE Examiner's Manual (PRO-ED, 1999).

Teaching Phonics & Word Study in the Intermediate Grades • Scholastic Professional Books

TOWRE (Test of Word Reading Efficiency)

(Torgeson, Wagner, and Rashotte, 1969)

Sight Word Efficiency

is	work	crowd	uniform
up	jump	better	necessary
cat	part	inside	problems
red	fast	plane	absentee
me	fine	pretty	advertise
to	milk	famous	pleasant
no	back	children	property
we	lost	without	distress
he	find	finally	information
the	paper	strange	recession
and	open	budget	understand
yes	kind	repress	emphasis
of	able	contain	confident
him	shoes	justice	intuition
as	money	morning	boisterous
book	great	resolve	plausible
was	father	describe	courageous
help	river	garment	alienate
then	space	business	extinguish
time	short	qualify	prairie
wood	left	potent	limousine
let	people	collapse	valentine
men	almost	elements	detective
baby	waves	pioneer	recently
new	child	remember	instruction
stop	strong	dangerous	transient

From *Test of Word Reading Efficiency*, by J. K. Torgesen, R. Wagner, and C. Rashotte, 1999, Austin, TX: PRO-ED. Copyright ©1999 by PRO-ED, Inc. Reprinted with permission.

Phonemic Decoding Efficiency

ip	barp	cratty
ga	stip	trober
ko	plin	depate
ta	frip	glant
om	poth	sploosh
ig	vasp	dreker
ni	meest	ritlun
pim	shlee	hedfert
wum	guddy	bremick
lat	skree	nifpate
baf	felly	brinbert
din	clirt	clabom
nup	sline	drepnort
fet	dreef	shratted
bave	prain	plofent
pate	zint	smuncrit
herm	bloot	pelnador
dess	trisk	fornalask
chur	kelm	fermabalt
knap	strone	crenidmoke
tive	lunaf	emulbatate

From *Test of Word Reading Efficiency*, by J. K. Torgesen, R. Wagner, and C. Rashotte, 1999, Austin, TX: PRO-ED. Copyright ©1999 by PRO-ED, Inc. Reprinted with permission.

Teaching Phonics & Word Study in the Intermediate Grades • Scholastic Professional Books

The Sight-Word Proficiency and Automaticity Assessment

Preparing the Test

- Type or print the test on a sheet of paper and make a copy to record the student's responses.

Administering the Test

- Administer the test to one student at a time.

- Explain to the student that she is to read each word as quickly as possible.

- Have the student read as many words as possible within 90 seconds. Use a stopwatch or other timer to time her.

- Put a check mark on the answer sheet beside each word the student read incorrectly or skipped.

Scoring the Test

- Count the words the student read correctly in 90 seconds.

- Analyze the mispronounced words, looking for patterns that might give you information about the student's decoding strengths and weaknesses.

- Provide additional instruction on words your students read incorrectly or skipped. Retest students every six weeks and monitor progress.

Sight Word Proficiency and Automaticity Asssessment

the	into	also	will	go
of	has	around	each	good
and	more	another	about	new
a	her	came	how	write
to	two	come	up	our
in	like	work	out	used
is	him	three	them	me
you	see	word	then	man
that	time	must	she	too
it	could	because	many	any
he	no	does	some	day
for	make	part	so	same
was	than	even	these	right
on	first	place	would	look
are	been	well	other	think
but	long	as	its	such
what	little	with	who	here
all	very	his	now	take
were	after	they	people	why
when	words	at	my	things
we	called	be	made	help
there	just	this	over	put
can	where	from	did	years
an	most	I	down	different
your	know	have	only	away
which	get	or	way	again
their	through	by	find	off
said	back	one	use	went
if	much	had	may	old
do	before	not	water	number

Teaching Phonics & Word Study in the Intermediate Grades • Scholastic Professional Books

Phonological Awareness Assessment

Preparing the Test

- Type or print the test and make a copy to record the student's responses.

- Make picture cards to use for sections C and D.
  Note that answers are provided in parentheses.

Administering the Test

- Administer the test to one student at a time.

- Follow the guidelines on the test for each section.

- Put a check mark on the answer sheet beside each correct answer

Scoring the Test

- Note areas that the student needs more work on. Students should get a minimum of four correct in each section.

Phonological Awareness Assessment

Rhyme

A. Ask the student if the following word pairs rhyme.

1. cat/hat _____
2. pig/wig _____
3. box/lip _____

4. can/man _____
5. let/pen _____
6. sun/run _____

B. State aloud the following rhyming word pairs. Ask the student to provide another rhyming word.

1. rack, sack _____
2. pop, hop _____
3. wing, king _____

4. goat, coat _____
5. wide, hide _____
6. bake, lake _____

Oddity Tasks

C. Make picture cards for the following word sets. Display each picture-card set. Ask the student to find the two pictures whose names **begin** with the same sound. Circle the student's choices.

1. sun, sock, fish (*sun, sock*)
2. mop, sun, man (*mop, man*)
3. pig, leaf, log (*leaf, log*)

4. pig, pan, dog (*pig, pan*)
5. dog, ten, top (*ten, top*)
6. fan, leaf, fish (*fan, fish*)

D. Make picture cards for the following word sets. Display each picture-card set. Ask the student to find the two pictures whose names **end** with the same sound. Circle the student's choices.

1. bat, rock, nut (*bat, nut*)
2. cup, top, pen (*cup, top*)
3. ten, fan, cup (*ten, fan*)

4. bus, glass, bat (*bus, glass*)
5. sock, cup, rake (*sock, rake*)
6. dog, leg, leaf (*leg, leaf*)

Teaching Phonics & Word Study in the Intermediate Grades • Scholastic Professional Books

Oral Blending

E. Say the first sound of a word and then the rest of the word. Have the student say the word as a whole.

1. /s/ . . . at _____   4. /l/ . . . ock _____
2. /m/ . . . op _____   5. /t/ . . . ape _____
3. /f/ . . . ish _____   6. /b/ . . . ox _____

F. Say each word sound by sound. Ask the student to say the word as a whole.

1. /m/ /ē/ (me) _____   4. /s/ /u/ /n/ (sun) _____
2. /s/ /ā/ (say) _____   5. /m/ /ā/ /k/ (make) _____
3. /f/ /ē/ /t/ (feet) _____   6. /l/ /ā/ /z/ /ē/ (lazy) _____

Oral Segmentation

G. Say each word. Ask the student to clap the number of syllables he or she hears in each word.

1. pencil (2) _____   4. bookmark (2) _____
2. map (1) _____   5. elephant (3) _____
3. tomato (3) _____   6. rock (1) _____

H. Say each word. Have the student say the first sound he or she hears in each word.

1. sun (/s/) _____   4. top (/t/) _____
2. mop (/m/) _____   5. candle (/k/) _____
3. leaf (/l/) _____   6. yellow (/y/) _____

I. Say each word. Have the student say the last sound he or she hears in each word.

1. bat (/t/) _____   4. take (/k/) _____
2. hop (/p/) _____   5. glass (/s/) _____
3. red (/d/) _____   6. leaf (/f/) _____

J. Say each word. Have the student say each word sound by sound.

1. see (/s/ /ē/) _____   4. rain (/r/ /ā/ /n/) _____
2. my (/m/ /ī/) _____   5. tub (/t/ /u/ /b/) _____
3. lake (/l/ /ā/ /k/) _____ 6. rocks (/r/ /o/ /k/ /s/) _____

Phonemic Manipulation

K. Say each word. Have the student say the word without the first sound.

      1. sun (un)   _____   **4.** ship (ip)   _____

      2. mat (at)   _____   **5.** bike (ike)   _____

      3. leaf (eaf)   _____   **6.** stop (top)   _____

L. Say each word. Have the student replace the first sound in the word with /s/.

      1. mad (sad)   _____   **4.** pick (sick)   _____

      2. run (sun)   _____   **5.** hand (sand)   _____

      3. cat (sat)   _____   **6.** chip (sip)   _____

Teaching Phonics & Word Study in the Intermediate Grades • Scholastic Professional Books

Glossary of Phonics Terms

Teaching Phonics & Word Study in the Intermediate Grades • Scholastic Professional Books

affix: a collective term for prefixes and suffixes.

affricative: a subgroup of the fricatives. An affricative is a consonant sound produced by the sequence of a stop immediately followed by a fricative. (For example, /ch/.)

alliteration: the repetition of the same sound at the beginning of a series of words. (For example, Bob busts big balloons.)

allograph: one of the graphic forms of a letter. (*F* and *f*, for example, are allographs.)

allophone: a slightly different version of a phoneme (sound). A sound can have more than one allophone, depending on its position in a word. The difference in sound among allophones is slight and not great enough to affect meaning. (For example, the /l/ sound in *like* and *pill*)

alphabet books: picture books that present, in order, the letters of the alphabet.

alphabetic principle: the assumption underlying any alphabetic writing system that each speech phoneme (sound) is represented by a unique graphic symbol or symbols (spelling).

alveolar: refers to consonant sounds in which the tongue either touches or comes close to the alveolar ridge when the sound is produced. (For example, /t/, /d/, /l/, /n/)

alveolar ridge: the roof of mouth just behind the upper teeth. The alveolar ridge is also called the tooth ridge.

analytic phonics: one of two major instructional approaches used to teach sound-spelling relationships. This approach is also known as implicit phonics or the discovery method. In this approach, readers are expected to learn a spelling-sound relationship by thinking about a sound that is common to a series of words. For example, readers are to deduce from the words *sat, send,* and *sun* that the letter *s* stands for the /s/ sound. The sound is not produced in isolation.

articulation, manner of: the way in which the flow of air is obstructed or altered when a sound is produced.

articulation, place of: the location in which the flow of air is obstructed when a sound is produced.

articulators: the movable parts of the mouth such as the bottom lip, bottom teeth, tongue, and jaw that are used to produce sounds.

aspiration: a burst of air that accompanies a voiceless stop consonant sound such as /p/, /t/, and /k/ when it is produced.

assonance: refers to the repetition of a vowel sound in a series of words. (For example: The green team is mean.)

automaticity: refers to decoding that is rapid, accurate, and effortless. Automaticity develops through extensive practice in decoding words.

basal reader: a book or series of books designed for a specific grade level that are used during reading instruction.

bilabial: refers to consonant sounds in which both lips are used to produce the sound. (For example, /p/, /b/, and /m/)

blending: a procedure used to teach students how to combine the sounds that comprise a word in order to decode and pronounce it. The two most effective blending procedures are successive blending and final blending.

breve: a diacritical mark (˘) used to represent a short-vowel sound.

choral reading: the simultaneous oral reading of a passage by two or more students.

closed syllable: a syllable that ends in a consonant phoneme (sound). (For example, both syllables in the word *pumpkin*—pump/kin.)

cloze passage: a reading passage of approximately 250 words in which, beginning after the twenty-fifth word, every fifth word is omitted. Learners are asked to read the passage and fill in the missing words. A student's independent, instructional, and frustration reading levels can be determined based on the percentage of correct words filled in.

compound word: a word made up of two smaller words. Often the meaning of a compound word can be derived from the meaning of the two smaller words that comprise it. (For example, *pancake.*)

comprehension: the understanding of, or meaning gained from, a written passage when read or an oral passage when heard.

concepts of print: the understanding of the elements of a book (print tells the story, cover, title, author, beginning and ending, left to right and top to bottom sequence), sentences (meaning of a sentence, beginning and ending, role of capital letters and punctuation), words, and letters. Concepts of print is also known as print awareness.

consonant: a phoneme (sound) produced by an obstruction or altering of the air flow through the speech cavities. Consonants can be described as plosives, fricatives, nasals, laterals, and semivowels.

consonant letter: a letter used to represent a consonant phoneme (sound).

consonant blends: the sounds that a consonant cluster stands for.

consonant clusters: two or more consonants that appear together in a word, each consonant retaining its own sound. (For example, the letters *cl* in the word *clown.*)

consonant digraphs: two consonants that appear together in a word and stand for one sound that is different from either sound of each individual consonant. (For example, *sh, ch, wh, th, ph.*)

context clues: clues to the meaning and/or pronunciation of an unfamiliar word derived from the words appearing before and/or following the word.

continuous sounds: sounds that can be prolonged or sustained without distortion. (For example, /f/, /l/, /m/, /n/, /r/, /s/, /v/, /z/.)

controlled text: text that is written with specific constraints. One type of controlled text is decodable text.

cueing systems: the three cues readers use. These include semantic cues (using knowledge of the meaning of the surrounding context to identify a word), syntactic cues (using knowledge of the grammatical structure of sentences to predict what a word might be), and graphophonic cues (using knowledge of sound-spelling relationships).

cursive handwriting: the style of writing in which letters are connected. For example:

cursive

decodable text: text in which all or most of the words are decodable based on the sound-spelling relationships previously taught. This type of text is sometimes used in early reading instruction.

decoding: refers to the process of taking printed words and changing them to spoken words. This generally occurs when the reader maps a sound onto each letter or spelling pat-

306

tern in the words. It can also occur when the reader applies sight-word recognition, structural analysis, and context clues.

descender: the part of a letter that extends below the base line.

diacritical marks: special markings that aid in representing sounds in written form. Some common diacritical marks include the macron (—), breve (˘), dieresis (¨), and circumflex (ˆ). Diacriticals are used in dictionaries to aid in the pronunciation of words.

diagnosis: refers to the careful investigation of a problem, such as a reading difficulty, done to determine the amount and type of remediation needed by a student.

dialect: one form of a given language. In English, different dialects are spoken in certain areas or geographical regions, or by specific racial or social groups. A dialect is characterized by the different pronunciations of words from other dialects. However, a dialect is not sufficiently different from other dialects to be regarded as a distinct language. Any region can have at least two dialects—the standard and nonstandard speech of the region.

digraph: a combination of two letters that stand for a single sound. There are consonant digraphs and vowel digraphs. (For example, the letters *sh* in the word *shop* and the letters *oa* in the word *boat.*)

diphthong: refers to a speech sound in which the position of the mouth changes or "glides" from one place to another as the sound is produced. (For example, /oi/ and /ou/.)

direct instruction: a teaching approach that is focused, sequential, and structured. The teacher presents information to the students and monitors the pacing and learning of the material.

echo reading: a technique used for improving fluency. The teacher reads aloud a passage. The student then tries to duplicate the passage using the same phrasing and intonation.

e-marker: refers to the letter *e* when it occurs at the end of a word such as *rope.* In these words, the letter *e* is a part of the vowel grapheme (spelling) and, although not voiced, signals that the vowel spelling stands for a long-vowel sound.

encode: to spell a word. Encoding is the opposite of decoding.

final blending: a form of blending in which each new spelling in a word is sounded out along with the previous sound-spellings. A word is not completely pronounced until the last sound-spelling is reached. For example, the word *sat* is blended in this sequence: /s/ . . . /sa/ . . . /sat/.

fluency: the ability to recognize words accurately, rapidly, and automatically. Fluency is a term often used synonymously with the term efficiency skills.

fricative: a consonant sound formed by a partial obstruction of the flow of air (for example, /s/ and /f/). Fricatives can be prolonged or sustained.

function words: words other than verbs, adverbs, nouns, or adjectives. Function words are also known as marker words or structure words. In the following sentence the function words are in italics. (For example, *Where* are *the* horses *and* cows *in the* barn?)

geminate: a pair of identical letters appearing together in a word, such as the letters *pp* in the word *happy.*

generalizations: sometimes referred to as rules, generalizations are predictable and fairly reliable sound-spelling relationships.

glide: a sound formed much like a vowel. Glides are sometimes referred to as semivowels. (For example, /w/ and /y/.)

glottal stop: a sound produced by a blockage of the air flow at the glottis.

glottis: an opening between the vocal cords.

grapheme: the written representation of a phoneme (sound). Graphemes can be single letters as in the letter *s* for the /s/ sound, or multiple letters as in the letters *sh* for the /sh/ sound.

hard palate: the part of the roof of the mouth located just behind the tooth ridge.

high-frequency words: the words that appear most often in text and speech. A small number of these words accounts for a relatively large percentage of all the words spoken or read.

homophones: words that sound the same but have different meanings and spellings.

hybrid text: a form of controlled text for the early grades that combines decodable words and high-frequency words, all of which are covered in the instruction prior to the reading of the text.

informal reading inventory: a procedure used to evaluate a student's oral reading. Omissions, mispronunciations, substitutions, additions, and repetitions of words are counted. A reader's inattention to punctuation is also recorded. The scores obtained are used to determine a reader's frustration, instructional, and independent reading levels.

International Phonetic Alphabet: the set of standardized graphic symbols used to represent the sounds for every language in the world.

kinesthetic method: the use of touch, hearing, sight, and muscle movement to teach letters or words.

labiodental: refers to sounds produced by an obstruction of the airflow occurring when the top teeth touch the lower lip. (For example, /f/ and /v/)

Language Experience Approach (LEA): an approach to reading instruction in which the student's own words are written down and used for instruction in reading, writing, spelling, listening, and speaking. Students' oral language is used to develop their reading skills. This approach is regarded as more per-

sonalized and motivating, but less systematic or sequential than other approaches.

lateral phoneme: refers to a sound produced when the airflow passes out of the mouth over the sides of the tongue. (For example, /l/.)

letter knowledge: refers to the ability to discriminate, recognize, and name the letters of the alphabet.

letter-sound correspondence: see sound-spelling relationship.

levels of reading:

Independent or *free reading level:* The level at which a student can read a text without the teacher's assistance. Comprehension should average 90% or better, and word recognition should average 95% or better.

Instructional reading level: The level at which a student should receive reading instruction. The student reads the text with teacher guidance, and is challenged enough to stimulate reading growth. Comprehension should average 75% or better, and word recognition should average 90% or better.

Frustration reading level: The level at which a student cannot read a text adequately. At this level, the student often shows signs of discomfort. Comprehension averages 50% or less, and word recognition averages 90% or less.

linguistics: the formal study of language and how it works.

liquid: a sound produced by only slightly interrupting the airflow. No friction results, and the air passes through the mouth in a relatively fluid manner. (For example, /r/ and /l/.)

long vowels: the phonemes (sounds) /ā/, /ē/, /ī/, /ō/, and /yōō/. The /ī/ and /yōō/ sounds are sometimes referred to as diphthongs. Long-vowel sounds are also referred to as glided sounds.

macron: a diacritical mark (—) used to represent long-vowel sounds.

manuscript handwriting: the style of writing in which letters are not connected. For example

manuscript

metacognition: the knowledge of one's own thought processes while reading. This knowledge enables a reader to select appropriate strategies while reading to help comprehend the text.

minimal pairs: pairs of words that differ in only one sound. In minimal pairs, the differing sound occurs in the same position in each member of the pair, such as *sat/cat*.

miscues: refers to the deviations from a text that a reader makes when reading aloud a passage. Miscues is a term used in place of "reading errors" to indicate that the misreading of a word can be used to glean information about the kinds of cues and strategies the learner is using when reading. This information can be used to modify instructional support.

monosyllabic words: words that have one syllable.

morpheme: the smallest unit of meaning in our language. There are two primary types of morphemes—bound (*un-, -ly, -ing*) and free (*happy, run, cat*).

morphology: the study of morphemes.

nasal: a consonant sound produced when the mouth is closed forcing the air through the nose. (For example, /m/, /n/, and /ng/.)

onset: refers to the part of the syllable that comes before the vowel. An onset can be a single consonant, a consonant cluster, or a consonant digraph. (For example, the letter *c*

in *cat,* the letters *pl* in *plate,* and the letters *ch* in *chair.*)

open syllable: a syllable that ends in a vowel phoneme (sound).

oral blending: the process of combining individual phonemes orally. For example, /s/ + /u/ + /n/ = sun. Oral blending is an important phonemic awareness task. Oral blending is necessary for sounding out words.

oral segmentation: the process of separating a word into its individual phonemes. Oral segmentation is an important phonemic awareness task and is necessary for spelling.

orthography: another name for the spelling system of a language. Orthography is sometimes referred to as the study of spelling.

patterned/predictable text: text written with a predictable plot structure due to the regular repetition of phrases or sentences.

phoneme: the smallest unit of speech sound that distinguishes one word from another in a language.

phonemic awareness: the understanding or insight that a word is made up of a series of discrete sounds. This awareness includes the ability to pick out and manipulate sounds in spoken words.

phonemic manipulation: a phonemic awareness task in which a sound or sounds are deleted or substituted in a word.

phonemics: the study of the phonemes or speech sounds of a particular language.

phonetics: the study of speech sounds.

phonic analysis: the use of phonic information to decode words.

phonic blending: the process of sounding out a word in which a sound is mapped onto each letter or spelling in a word and strung together to pronounce the word. Phonic blending is different from oral blending in which no print is involved.

phonic elements: consonants, consonant digraphs, consonant clusters, vowels, vowel digraphs, and other letter combinations that are the focus of phonics instruction.

phonics: refers to the relationship between sounds and the spelling patterns that are used to represent them in print. The study of these sound-spelling (phoneme-grapheme) relationships is generally included in beginning reading instruction.

phonics generalization: a sound-spelling relationship that occurs as a predictable spelling pattern.

phonogram: a series of letters that stands for a sound, syllable, or series of sounds without reference to meaning. Also known as word families.

phonological awareness: a global term that includes an awareness of words within sentences, rhyming units within words, beginning and ending sounds within words, syllables within words, phonemes within words (phonemic awareness), and features of individual phonemes such as how the mouth, tongue, vocal cords, and teeth are used to produce the sound.

plosive: a sound produced by closing or blocking off the air flow, and then exploding a puff of air. A plosive is also known as a stop sound. (For example, /p/, /b/, /t/, /d/, /k/, /g/.)

polysyllabic words: words that have more than one syllable. Polysyllabic words are also known as multisyllabic words.

prefix: a group of letters that appears at the front of a word. (For example, the letters *un* in the word *unhappy.*)

r-**controlled vowels:** a vowel that comes before the letter *r* in a word. The letter *r* changes and thereby "controls" the sound of the preceding vowel. (For example, *ar, er, ir, or, ur.*)

rime: a vowel and any consonants that follow it in a syllable. (For example, the letters *at* in the word *cat.*)

schwa: a vowel phoneme (sound) that is less accented than other vowels. The schwa is usually heard in polysyllabic words and appears in unstressed syllables. The schwa sound is written as / ə /.

scope and sequence: refers to the skills taught in a reading program and the order in which they are taught.

semantics: the study of the connotations and denotations (meanings) of words.

semivowel: a sound made with a wide opening in the mouth and little disruption of the airflow, such as /w/ and /y/. A semivowel can be either a vowel or a consonant depending of where it is heard in a word.

sequential redundancy: the likelihood that if a certain letter appears in a syllable or word, only certain letters will follow. (For example, the letter *q* is almost always followed by the letter *u.*)

short vowels: the phonemes (sounds) /a/, /e/, /i/, /o/, and /u/.

sight word: any word that a reader is able to recognize instantly. This is often the result of repeated opportunities to decode the word in text. The term "sight word" is sometimes confused with the term "high-frequency word." High-frequency words are the words that appear most often in text. Sight words can be high-frequency words, but can be other words as well.

silent letters: letters that appear in a word but are not vocalized. (For example, the letter *k* in the word *knot.*)

silent speech: the subvocalization, or inner speech, one makes when reading. Skilled, mature readers use less silent speech in reading than do beginning or poor readers.

Teaching Phonics & Word Study in the Intermediate Grades • Scholastic Professional Books

soft palate: the back part of the roof of the mouth. The soft palate is also called the velum.

sound-spelling relationship: the relationship between a phoneme (sound) and the grapheme (letter or spelling) that represents it in writing. Some of these relationships are said to be predictable (reliable/dependable) spellings; others are not. (For example, the letter *s* stands for the /s/ sound.)

stop consonant: a consonant sound produced by the blockage of the airflow. (For example, /p/ and /b/.)

stress: the emphasis on a particular syllable in a word, or a particular word in a sentence. This involves making the vowel sound longer, louder, and higher in pitch.

structural analysis: reading words, specifically polysyllabic words, according to their structural units such as root words, prefixes, suffixes, and possessives.

successive blending: a form of blending in which each letter or spelling in a word is mapped onto a sound and the sounds are strung together as the word is pronounced. For example, the word *sat* is pronounced as *ssssaaaat*.

suffix: a letter or group of letters that is added to the end of a root, or base, word. (For example, the letters *-ly* in the word *quickly.*)

syllabication: refers to strategies used to figure out polysyllabic words.

syllable: a unit of pronunciation. A syllable also refers to the unit into which a word is divided. A syllable usually consists of a vowel and one or more consonant(s) before and/or after it.

synthetic phonics: one of two major instructional approaches used to teach sound-spelling relationships. This approach is also known as explicit phonics. In this approach, learners are taught to say the sounds of individual spellings, which are then combined to form words (part-to-whole). The sounds are produced in isolation.

systematic, explicit instruction: refers to a type of direct instruction. The term systematic means that instruction is sequenced and sounds are introduced at a relatively slow pace but continually reviewed and applied to reading and writing. The term explicit means that relationships are explicitly pointed out and taught rather than implicitly referred to or discovered on one's own.

tactile: having to do with the sense of touch.

trade books: a book published for sale to the general public. The term often refers to commercial books, other than basal readers, that are used for instruction.

unvoiced (voiceless) phoneme: a sound produced with no vibration of the vocal cords. (For example, /t/ and /s/.)

velar: refers to sounds that, when produced, involve the back of the tongue and the soft palate or velum. (For example, /k/, /g/, and /ng/.)

velum: the back part of the roof of the mouth. The velum is also called the soft palate.

virgules: slashes [//] used in the transcription of sounds. (For example, /s/.)

visual perception skills: the ability to see and identify the characteristics of things such as shape, color, size, and distance.

vocal cords: two folds of ligament and elastic membrane found at the top of the windpipe (in the larynx).

voiced phoneme: a sound produced with a vibration of the vocal cords. (For example, /g/ and /z/.)

Teaching Phonics & Word Study in the Intermediate Grades • Scholastic Professional Books

vowel: a phoneme produced with an unobstructed passage of air through the mouth. Vowel phonemes have greater prominence than consonant phonemes.

vowel digraphs: refers to pairs of vowels appearing together in a word. Some vowel digraphs stand for the sound of a long vowel (*ai, ay, ee, ea, igh, oa*); others do not *(oo, oi, oy, ou, ow, au, aw)*.

vowel letters: letters used to represent vowel phonemes.

word-analysis skills: skills a reader must use to determine how to pronounce a word when it is not recognized instantly. These include phonics, structural analysis, and context clues. Word-analysis skills are sometimes referred to as word-attack skills.

word identification: refers to the ability to give the name of a word after seeing it in print. Word identification is sometimes referred to as "word recognition," "word attack," or "decoding." Word identification can involve the use of graphophonic cues (phonics), semantic and syntactic context cues, and structural analysis.

For additional definitions of phonics-related terms see *The Literacy Dictionary: The Vocabulary of Reading and Writing* by T. Harris and R. Hodges (editors), Newark, DE: International Reading Association, 1995.

Bibliography

Adams, M.J. *Beginning to Read: Thinking and Learning About Print.* Cambridge: Massachusetts Institute of Technology. 1990.

Adams, M.J., R. Treiman, and M. Pressley. "Reading, Writing, and Literacy." In I. Sigel and A. Renninger (eds.), *Handbook of Child Psychology, Vol. 4: Child Psychology in Practice.* NY: Wiley. 1996.

Akmajian, A., R.A. Demers, A.K. Farmer, and R.M. Harnish. *Linguistics: An Introduction to Language and Communication* (4th ed.). Cambridge, MA: MIT Press. 1995

Alexander, A., H. Anderson, P.C. Heilman, K.S. Voeller, and J.K. Torgesen. "Phonological Awareness Training and Remediation of Analytic Decoding Deficits in a Group of Severe Dyslexics." *Annals of Dyslexia,* Vol. 41. 1991.

Allington, R.L. "The Reading Instruction Provided Readers of Different Reading Abilities." *Elementary School Journal,* Vol. 83. 1983.

Allington, R.L. "Fluency: The Neglected Reading Goal." *The Reading Teacher, 36,* 556–561. 1983.

Allington, R.L. "Oral Reading." In D.D. Pearson (ed.), *Handbook of Reading Research.* NY: Longman. 1984.

Allington, R.L. "Content Coverage and Contextual Reading in Reading Groups." *Journal of Reading Behavior, 26,* 85–96. 1984.

Allington, R.L., and S.A. Walmsley (eds.). *No Quick Fix: Rethinking Literacy Programs in America's Elementary Schools.* NY: Teachers College Press. 1995.

Anderson, R.C. "The Missing Ingredient: Fluent Oral Reading." *The Elementary School Journal, 81,* 173–177. 1981.

Anderson, R.C., E.H. Hiebert, J.A. Scott, and I.A.G. Wilkinson. *Becoming a Nation of Readers: The Report of the Commission on Reading.* Champaign, IL: The Center for the Study of Reading and The National Academy of Education. 1985.

Anderson, R.C., P. Wilson, and L. Fielding, "Growth in Reading and How Children Spend Their Time Outside of School." *Reading Research Quarterly, 23,* 285–303. 1998.

Avery, P., and S. Ehrlich. *Teaching American English Pronunciation.* Oxford University Press. 1992.

Bailey, M.H. "Utility of Phonic Generalizations in Grades One Through Six." *Reading Teacher,* Vol. 20. 1967.

Baskwill, J., and P. Whitman. *Learner Support Program: A Framework for Classroom-Based Reading Intervention.* NY: Scholastic. 1995.

Bateman, B. "Teaching Reading to Learning Disabled and Other Hard-to-Teach Children." In L.A. Resnick and P.A. Weaver (eds.), *Theory and Practice of Early Reading,* Vol. 1. Hillsdale, NJ: Erlbaum Associates. 1979.

Bear, D.R., S. Templeton, M. Invernizzi, and F. Johnston. *Words Their Way: Word Study for Phonics, Vocabulary, and Spelling Instruction.* Englewood Cliffs, NJ: Merrill/Prentice-Hall. 1996.

Beck, I. "Reading Problems and Instructional Practices." In G.E. MacKinnon and T.G. Waller (eds.), *Reading Research: Advances in Theory and Practice,* Vol. 2. NY: Academic Press. 1981.

Beck, I., and Juel, C. "The Role of Decoding in Learning to Read." *American Educator.* Summer, 1995.

Beck, I., and C. Juel, "The Role of Decoding in Learning to Read." *American Educator.* Summer, 1995.

Beck, I., and E. McCaslin. "An Analysis of Dimensions that Affect the Development of Code-Breaking Ability in Eight Beginning Reading Programs." LRDC Report No. 1978/6. Pittsburgh: University of Pittsburgh Learning Research and Development Center.

Berninger, V.W., S.P. Thalberg, I. De Bruyn, and R. Smith. "Preventing Reading Disabilities by Assessing and Remediating Phonemic Skills." *School Psychology Review,* Vol. 16, No. 4. 1987.

Biemiller, A. "Relationships Between Oral Reading Rates for Letters, Words, and Simple Text in the Development of Reading Achievement." *Reading Research Quarterly,* Vol. 13. 1970.

Biemiller, A. "The Development of the Use of Graphic and Contextual Information as

Children Learn to Read." *Reading Research Quarterly,* Vol. 6. 1970.

Blevins, W. *Phonemic Awareness Activities for Early Reading Success.* NY: Scholastic. 1997.

Blevins, W. *Phonics from A to Z: A Practical Guide.* NY: Scholastic. 1998.

Bond, G.L., M.A. Tinker, B.B. Wasson, and J.B. Wasson. *Reading Difficulties: Their Diagnosis and Correction.* Boston: Allyn and Bacon. 1994.

Bowen, J.D. *TESOL Techniques and Procedures.* Rowley, MA: Newbury House Publishers. 1985.

Bristow, P.S. "Are Poor Readers Passive Readers? Some Evidence, Possible Explanations, and Potential Solutions." *The Reading Teacher.* December. 1985.

Bruck, M., and R. Treiman. "Phonological Awareness and Spelling in Normal Children and Dyslexics: The Case of Initial Consonant Clusters." *Journal of Experimental Psychology,* Vol. 28, No. 5. 1990.

Bruck, M., and R. Treiman. "Phonological Awareness and Spelling in Normal Children and Dyslexics: The Case of Initial Consonant Clusters." *Journal of Experimental Child Psychology,* Vol. 50. 1990.

Bryant, P., and L. Bradley. *Children's Reading Problems: Psychology and Education.* NY: Basil Blackwell, Inc. 1985.

Bryson, B. *The Mother Tongue: English and How It Got That Way.* NY: Avon Books. 1990.

Burmeister, L.E. *Words: From Print to Meaning.* Reading, MA: Addison-Wesley Publishing Co. 1975.

Burmeister, L.E. "Content of a Phonics Program Based on Particularly Useful Generalizations." In N.B. Smith (ed.), *Reading Methods and Teacher Improvement.* Newark, DE: International Reading Association. 1971.

Burmeister, L.E. "The Effect of Syllabic Position and Accent on the Phonemic Behavior of Single Vowel Graphemes." In J.A. Figurel (ed.), *Reading and Realism.* Newark, DE: International Reading Association. 1969.

Burmeister, L.E. "Vowel Pairs." *The Reading Teacher,* Vol. 21. 1968.

Burmeister, L.E. "Usefulness of Phonic Generalizations." *Reading Teacher,* Vol. 21. 1968.

Byrne, B., and R. Fielding-Barnsley. *Sound Foundations.* Artarmon, New South Wales, Australia: Leyden Educational Publishers. 1991.

California Department of Education. *Teaching Reading: A Balanced, Comprehensive Approach to Teaching Reading in Prekindergarten Through Grade Three.* Sacramento, CA. Summer, 1996.

Carnine, L., D. Carnine, and R. Gersten, 1984. "Analysis of Oral Reading Errors Made by Economically Disadvantaged Students Taught with a Synthetic-Phonics Approach." *Reading Research Quarterly* 19.

Caroline, Sister Mary. *Breaking the Sound Barrier: A Phonics Handbook.* NY: The Macmillan Co. 1960.

Carreker, S. "Teaching Reading: Accurate Decoding and Fluency." In *Multisensory Teaching of Basic Language Skills.*

Carroll, J. B. 1990. "Thoughts on Reading and Phonics." Paper presented at the National Conference on Research in English, Atlanta (May).

Carroll, J.B., P. Davies, and B. Richman. *Word Frequency Book.* Boston: Houghton Mifflin. 1971.

Chall, J.S. *Learning to Read: The Great Debate.* NY: McGraw-Hill. 1967.

Chall, J.S. *Stages of Reading Development.* McGraw-Hill. 1983.

Chall, J.S. *Stages of Reading Development.* Harcourt Brace & Company. 1996.

Chall, J.S., and H. Popp. *Teaching and Assessing Phonics: Why, What, When, How.* Cambridge, MA: Educators Publishing Service, Inc. 1996.

Clark, C.H. "Teaching Students About Reading: A Fluency Example." *Reading Horizons, 35* (3), 251–265. 1995.

Clark, D.B., and J.K. Uhry. *Dyslexia: Theory and Practice of Remedial Instruction.* Timonium, MD: York Press. 1995.

Clymer, T. "Utility of Phonics Generalizations in the Primary Grades." *Reading Teacher,* Vol. 16. 1963.

CORE (Consortium On Reading Excellence). 1999. Arena Press. Novato, CA.

Cunningham, A. E., and K. E. Stanovich. 1991. "Tracking the Unique Effects of Print Exposure in Children: Associations with Vocabulary, General Knowledge, and Spelling." *Journal of Educational Psychology* 83.

Cunningham, J. "On Automatic Pilot for Decoding." *The Reading Teacher,* Vol. 32, No. 4. January, 1979.

Cunningham, P.M. "The Names Test: A Quick Assessment of Decoding Ability." *The Reading Teacher,* Vol. 44. 1990.

Cunningham, P.M. "Decoding Polysyllabic Words: An Alternative Strategy." *Journal of Reading.* April, 1978.

Cunningham, P.M. "Investigating a Synthesized Theory of Mediated Word Identification." *Reading Research Quarterly,* Vol. 11. 1975–76.

Cunningham, P.M. *Phonics They Use: Words for Reading and Writing.* NY: HarperCollins College Publishers. 1995.

Cunningham, P.M., and J.W. Cunningham. "Making Words: Enhancing the Invented Spelling-Decoding Connection." *The Reading Teacher,* Vol. 46, No. 2. October, 1992.

Curtis, M.E., and L. McCart. "Fun Ways to Promote Poor Readers' Word Recognition." *Journal of Reading*, Vol. 35, No. 5. February 1992.

Duffelmeyer, F.A., and J.L. Black. "The Names Test: A Domain-Specific Validation Study." *The Reading Teacher,* Vol. 50, No. 2. October, 1996.

Durkin, D. *Phonics, Linguistics, and Reading.* NY: Teachers College Press. 1978.

Durkin, D. *Teaching Them to Read.* Boston: Allyn and Bacon. 1993.

Durr, W.K. (ed.) *Reading Difficulties: Diagnosis, Correction, and Remediation.* Newark, DE: International Reading Association. 1970.

Durrell, D. *Phonograms in Primary Grade Words.* Boston: Boston University. 1963.

Ehri, L.C. "Development of the Ability to Read Words." In R. Barr, M. Kamil, P. Mosenthal, and P.D. Pearsons (eds.), *Handbook of Reading Research,* Volume II. New York: Longman. 1991.

Ehri, L. C. 1987. "Learning to Read and Spell Words." *Journal of Reading Behavior* 19.

Ehri, L.C. "Reconceptualizing the Development of Sight Word Reading and Its Relationship to Recoding." In P. Gough, L. Ehri, and R. Treiman (eds.), *Reading Acquisition.* Hillsdale, NJ: Erlbaum. 1992.

Ehri, L.C. "Development of the Ability to Read Words: Update." In R. Ruddell, M. Ruddell, and H. Singer (eds.), *Theoretical Models and Processes of Reading.* Newark, DE: International Reading Association. 1994.

Ehri, L.C. "Phases of Development in Reading Words." *Journal of Research in Reading,* Vol. 18. 1995.

Ehri, L.C., and C. Robbins. "Beginners Need Some Decoding Skill to Read Words by Analogy." *Reading Research Quarterly,* Vol. 27, No.1. 1992.

Ekwall, E., and J. Shanker. *Diagnosis and Remediation of the Disabled Reader.* Boston: Allyn and Bacon. 1988.

Ekwall, E., and J. Shanker. *Locating and Correcting Reading Difficulties.* NY: Merrill Publishing Co. 1993.

Eldredge, J.L. *Teaching Decoding in Holistic Classrooms.* Englewood Cliffs, NJ: Merrill Publishing Co. 1995.

Evans, M. A., and Carr, T. H. 1985. "Cognitive Abilities, Conditions of Learning, and the Early Development of Reading Skill." *Reading Research Quarterly* 20.

Felton, R.H., and F. B. Wood. "Cognitive Deficits in Reading Disability and Attention Deficit Disorder." *Journal of Learning Disabilities,* Vol. 22. 1989.

Flesch, R. *Why Johnny Can't Read: And What You Can Do About It.* NY: Harper & Row, Publishers. 1955.

Foorman, B. *School Psychology Review.* October, 1995.

Foorman, B., L. Jenkins, and D.J. Francis. "Links Among Segmenting, Spelling, and Reading Words in First and Second Grades." *Reading and Writing: An Interdisciplinary Journal,* Vol. 5. 1993.

Foorman, B., D.M. Novy, D.J. Francis, and D. Liberman. "How Letter-Sound Instruction Mediates Progress in First-Grade Reading and Spelling." *Journal of Educational Psychology,* Vol. 83, No. 4. 1991.

Fox, B., and D. Routh. "Analyzing Spoken Language into Words, Syllables, and Phonemes: A Developmental Study." *Journal of Psycholinguistic Research,* Vol. 4. 1975.

Fox, B.J. *Strategies for Word Identification: Phonics from a New Perspective.* Prentice-Hall. 1996.

Freedman, S. W., and R. C. Calfee. 1984. "Understanding and Comprehending." *Written Communication* 1.

Freyd, T. and J. Baron, "Individual Differences in Acquisition of Derivational Morphology." *Journal of Verbal Learning and Verbal Behavior*, 21, 282–295. 1982.

Fry, E.B., D.L. Fountoukidis, and J.K. Polk. *The New Reading Teacher's Book of Lists*. Englewood Cliffs: NJ: Prentice-Hall. 1985.

Gambrell L. "Reading in the Primary Grades: How Often? How Long?" In M.R. Sampson (ed.). *The Pursuit of Literacy*. Dubuque, IA: Kendall Hunt. 1986.

Gaskins, I. "Word Identification: Research-Based Maxims." Paper Presented at the International Reading Convention, Preconvention Institute. 1997.

Gaskins, I., M. Downer, R.C. Anderson, P.M. Cunningham, R. Gaskins, M. Schommer, and the Teachers of Benchmark School. "A Metacognitive Approach to Phonics: Using What You Know to Decode What You Don't Know." *Remedial and Special Education*, Vol. 9, No. 1. 1988.

Gaskins, I., L. Ehri, C. Cress, C. O'Hara, and K. Donnelly. "Procedures for Word Learning: Making Discoveries About Words." *The Reading Teacher*, Vol. 50, No. 4. December 1996/January 1997.

Gentile, L.M., and M.M. McMillan. "Reading, Writing and Relationships: The Challenge of Teaching At Risk Students." *Reading Research and Instruction*, Vol. 30, No. 4. 1991.

Gillet, J.W., and C. Temple. *Understanding Reading Problems: Assessment and Instruction*. NY: HarperCollins. 1994.

Golinkoff, R.M. "Phonemic Awareness Skills and Reading Achievement." In F.B. Murray and J.H. Pikulski (eds.), *The Acquisition of Reading: Cognitive, Linguistic, and Perceptual Prerequisites*. Baltimore, MD: University Park. 1978.

Gough, P. B., and C. Juel. "The First Stages of Word Recognition." In L. Rieben and C.A. Perfetti (eds.), *Learning to Read: Basic Research and Its Implications*. Hillsdale, NJ: Erlbaum. 1991.

Gough, P. B., C. Juel, and D. Roper-Schneider. 1983. "A Two-Stage Model of Initial Reading Acquisition." In Searches for Meaning in Reading/Language Processing and Instruction, ed. J. A. Niles and L. A. Harris. Rochester, NY: National Reading Conference.

Gough, P. B., J. A. Alford, Jr., and P. Holley-Wilcox. 1981. "Words and Context." *In Perception of Print*, ed. O. J. L. Tzeng and H. Singer, eds. Hillsdale, NJ: Erlbaum.

Gough, P. B., and M.A. Walsh. "Chinese, Phoenicians, and the Orthographic Cipher of English." In S.A. Brady and D.P. Shankweiler (eds.), *Phonological Process in Literacy: A Tribute to Isabelle Y. Liberman*. Hillsdale, NJ: Erlbaum. 1991.

Groff, P. *Phonics: Why and How*. Morristown, NJ: General Learning Press. 1977.

Groff, P. "Blending: Basic Process or Beside the Point?" *Reading World*, Vol. 15. 1976.

Groff, P. "A Phonemic Analysis of Monosyllabic Words." *Reading World*, Vol. 12. 1972.

Groff, P. "Sequences for Teaching Consonant Clusters." *Journal of Reading Behavior*, Vol. 4. 1971–72.

Haddock, M. "Teaching Blending in Beginning Reading Instruction Is Important." *Reading Teacher*, Vol. 31. 1978.

Haddock, M. "Effects of an Auditory and a Visual Method of Blending Instruction on the Ability of Prereaders to Decode Synthetic Words." *Journal of Educational Psychology*, Vol. 68. 1976.

Hall, S. L., and L. C. Moats. 1999. *Straight Talk About Reading*. Contemporary Books, Chicago, IL.

Hanna, P. R., R.E. Hodges, J.L. Hanna, and E.H. Rudolph. *Phoneme-Grapheme Correspondences as Cues to Spelling Improvement*. Washington, D.C.: U.S. Office of Education. 1966.

Hansbrouck, J.E., and G. Tindal. "Curriculum-Based Oral Reading Fluency Norms for Students in Grades 2 Through 5." *Teaching Exceptional Children*, 41-44. 1992.

Harris, A.J., and M.D. Jacobson. *Basic Elementary Reading Vocabularies*. NY: Macmillan. 1972.

Harris, A.J., and E.R. Sipay. *How to Increase Reading Ability: A Guide to Developmental and Remedial Methods*. White Plains, NY: Longman. 1990.

Harris, T., and R. Hodges (eds.). *The Literacy Dictionary: The Vocabulary of Reading and Writing*. Newark, DE: International Reading Association. 1995.

Henderson, E. *Phonics in Learning to Read: A Handbook for Teachers*. NY: Exposition Press. 1967.

Henry, M. 1997. "The Decoding/Spelling Continuum: Integrated Decoding and Spelling Instruction from Pre-School to Early Secondary School." Dyslexia 3.

Henry, M.K. "Beyond Phonics: Integrated Decoding and Spelling Instruction Based on Word Origin and Structure." *Annals of Dyslexia, 38,* 258–275. 1988.

Hiebert, E., and B. Taylor. *Getting Reading Right from the Start.* Boston: Allyn and Bacon. 1994.

Hiebert E. "An Examination of Ability Grouping for Reading Instruction." *Reading Research Quarterly, 14,* 231–255. 1983.

Hoffman, J.V. "Rethinking the Role of Oral Reading in Basal Instruction." *Elementary School Journal, 87,* 367–373. 1987.

Hoffman J.V., and S. Crone, "The Oral Recitation Lesson: A Research Derived Strategy for Reading in Basal Texts." In J.A. Niles and R.A. Lalik (eds.) *Issues in Literacy: A Research Perspective,* Thirty-fourth Yearbook of the National Reading Conference. Rochester, NY: National Reading Conference, 1985.

Honig, B. *How Should We Teach Our Children to Read?* Center for Systemic School Reform, San Francisco State University. 1995.

Honig, B. *Teaching Our Children to Read: The Role of Skills in a Comprehensive Reading Program.* Thousand Oaks, CA: Corwin Press. 1996.

Hull, M.A. *Phonics for the Teacher of Reading* (6th ed.). Upper Saddle River, NJ: Merrill. 1994.

Johns, J.L. 1980. "First Graders' Concepts About Print." *Reading Research Quarterly 15.*

Johns, J.L., and D.W. Ellis. "Reading: Children Tell It Like It Is." *Reading World,* Vol. 16. 1976.

Johnson, D., and J. Bauman. "Word Identification." In P.D. Pearson, R. Barr, M.L. Kamil, and P. Mosenthal (eds.), *Handbook of Reading Research.* NY: Longman. 1984.

Juel, C. "Beginning Reading." In R. Barr, M.L. Kamil, P. Mosenthal, and P.D. Pearson (eds.). *Handbook of Reading Research,* Vol. 2. NY: Longman. 1991.

Juel, C. "Learning to Read and Write: A Longitudinal Study of Fifty-Four Children from First Through Fourth Grades." *Journal of Educational Psychology 80.*

Juel, C., and D. Roper-Schneider. 1985. "The Influence of Basal Readers on First-Grade Reading." *Reading Research Quarterly 20.*

Juel, C., P. Griffith, and P. Gough. "Acquisition of Literacy: A Longitudinal Study of Children in First and Second Grade." *Journal of Educational Psychology,* Vol. 78. 1986.

Just, M.A., and P.A. Carpenter. *The Psychology of Reading and Language Comprehension.* Boston: Allyn and Bacon. 1987.

Koskinen, P. and Blum, I. "Paired Repeated Reading: A Classroom Strategy for Developing Fluent Reading." *The Reading Teacher,* 40, 70–75. 1986

LaBerge, D., and S. J. Samuels. 1974. "Toward a Theory of Automatic Information Processing in Reading." *Cognitive Psychology 6* (2).

LaPray, M., and R. Ross. "The Graded Word List: Quick Gauge of Reading Ability." *Journal of Reading,* Vol. 12, No. 4. 1969.

Lesgold, A. M. and M. E. Curtis. 1981. "Learning to Read Words Efficiently." In Interactive Processes in Reading, ed. A. M. Lesgold and C. A. Perfetti. Hillsdale, NJ: Erlbaum.

Lesgold, A. M., and L. B. Resnick. 1982. "How Reading Disabilities Develop: Perspectives from a Longitudinal Study. In Theory and Research in Learning Disability, ed. J. P. Das. R. Mulcahy, and A. E. Walls. New York: Plenum.

Lindamood, C.H., and P.C. Lindamood. *Auditory Discrimination in Depth.* Hingham, MA: Teaching Resources Corporation. 1979.

Lovett, M.W. "A Developmental Approach to Reading Disability: Accuracy and Speed Criteria of Normal and Deficient Reading Skill." *Child Development,* Vol. 58. 1987.

Lundberg, I. 1984. "Learning to Read." *School Research Newsletter.* Sweden: National Board of Education (August).

Lundberg, I., J. Frost, and O.P. Petersen. "Effects of an Extensive Program for Stimulating Phonological Awareness in Preschool Children." *Reading Research Quarterly,* Vol. 23, No. 3. Summer 1988.

Lyon, G. R. 1995. "Research Initiatives in Learning Disabilities: Contributions from Scientists Supported by the National Institutes of Child Health and Human Development." Journal of Child Neurology 10.

Lyon, G. R. 1996. "Learning Disabilities." *The Future of Children: Special Education for Students with Disabilities 6.*

Manguel, A. *A History of Reading.* NY: Viking. 1996.

Mann, V.A. "Language Problems: A Key to Early Reading Problems." In B.Y.L. Wong (ed.), *Learning about Learning Disabilities.* San Diego, CA: Academic Press. 1991.

Manzo, A., and U. Manzo. *Literacy Disorders: Holistic Diagnosis and Remediation.* NY: Harcourt Brace Jovanovich College Publishers. 1993.

Mathes, P., D. Simmons, and B. Davis. "Assisted Reading Techniques for Developing Reading Fluency." *Reading Research and Instruction,* Vol. 31, No. 4. 1992.

Mazurkiewicz, A. *Teaching About Phonics.* NY: St. Martin's Press. 1976.

McConkie, G. W., and D. Zola. 1987. "Two Examples of Computer-Based Research on Reading: Eye Movement Monitoring and Computer-Aided Reading. In Reading and Computers: Issues for Theory and Practice, ed. D. Reinking. New York: Teachers College Press.

Miller, W. *Complete Reading Disabilities Handbook.* The Center for Applied Research in Education. West Nyack, NY: 1993.

Moats, L.C. 1998. "Teaching Decoding." (Spring/Summer). *American Educator.* In Reading All About It. California State Board of Education. 1999.

Moats, L.C. *Speech to Print.* Baltimore, MD: Paul H. Brookes Publishing Co. 2000.

Moats, L. "Reading, Spelling, and Writing Disabilities in the Middle Grades." In B.Y.L. Wong (ed.), *Learning about Learning Disabilities* (2nd ed.) Academic Press, 1998.

Moats, L.C. *Spelling: Development, Disabilities, and Instruction.* Timonium, MD: York Press, Inc. 1995.

Moats, L.C. "The Missing Foundation in Teacher Education." *American Federation of Teachers.* Summer, 1995.

Morris, D., C. Ervin, and K. Conrad. "A Case Study of Middle School Reading Disability." *The Reading Teacher,* Vol. 49, No. 5. February, 1996.

Murphy, H.A. "The Spontaneous Speaking Vocabulary of Children in Primary Grades." *Journal of Education,* Vol. 140. 1957.

Nagy, W., Anderson, R.C., Schommer, M., Scott, J. and Stallman, A. "Morphological Families in the Internal Lexicon." *Reading Research Quarterly, 24,* 262–282. 1989.

Nagy, W.E. and Anderson, R.C., "How Many Words Are There in Printed School English?" *Reading Research Quarterly, 19,* 304–330. 1984.

Nathan, R.G., and K.E Stanovich. "The Causes and Consequences of Differences in Reading Fluency." *Theory into Practice, 30,* 176–184. 1991.

Nicholson, T. 1992. "Historical and Current Perspectives on Reading." In Elementary Reading: Process and Practice, ed. C. J. Gordon, G. D. Lahercano, and W. R. McEacharn. Needham, MA: Ginn.

Osborn, J., P. Wilson, and R. Anderson. *Reading Education: Foundations for a Literate America.* Lexington, MA: Lexington Books. 1985.

Pavlak, S. *Classroom Activities for Correcting Specific Reading Problems.* West Nyack, NY: Parker Publishing Co. 1985.

Perfetti, C.A., and D. McCutcheon. "Speech Processes in Reading." In N. Lass (ed.), *Speech and Language: Advances in Basic Research and Practice,* Vol. 7. NY: Academic Press. 1982.

Phinney, M.Y. *Reading with the Troubled Reader.* Portsmouth, NH: Heinemann. 1988.

Pinnell, G. S. 1994. "Children's Early Literacy Learning." Scholastic Literacy Research Paper.

Popp, H.M. "Visual Discrimination of Alphabet Letters." *Reading Teacher,* Vol. 17. 1964.

Putnam, L.R. (ed.) *How to Become a Better Reading Teacher: Strategies for Assessment and Intervention.* Englewood, NJ: Merrill. 1996.

Rasinski, T. "Developing Syntactic Sensitivity in Reading Through Phrase-Cued Texts." *Intervention in School and Clinic,* Vol. 29, No. 3. January 1994.

Rasinski, T., and N. Padak. "Effects of Fluency Development on Urban Second-Graders." *Journal of Education Research,* Vol. 87, 1994.

Rasinski, T. V. 1989. "Adult Readers' Sensitivity to Phrase Boundaries in Texts." *Journal of Experimental Education 58.*

Read, C. *Children's Creative Spelling.* London: Routledge and Kegan Paul. 1986.

Resnick, L., and I. Beck. "Designing Instruction in Reading: Initial Reading." In A.J. Harris and E.R. Sipay (eds.), *Readings on Reading Instruction.* NY: Longman. 1976.

Rhodes, L.K., and S. Natehnson-Mejia. "Anecdotal Records: A Powerful Tool for Ongoing Literacy Assessment." *The Reading Teacher,* Vol. 45, No. 7. March, 1992.

Richards, M. "Be a Good Detective: Solve the Case of Oral Reading Fluency." *The Reading Teacher,* Vol. 53, 7, pp. 534–539. 2000.

Rinsland, H.D. *A Basic Vocabulary of Elementary School Children.* NY: Macmillan. 1945.

Rosenshine, B., and R. Stevens. "Classroom Instruction in Reading." In P.D. Pearson, R. Barr, M.L. Kamil, and P. Mosenthal (eds.), *Handbook of Reading Research.* NY: Longman. 1984.

Rosner, J. *Helping Children Overcome Learning Difficulties.* NY: Walker. 1993.

Roswell, F., and G. Natchez. *Reading Disability.* NY: Basic Books. 1971.

Royer, J., and G. Sinatra. "A Cognitive Theoretical Approach to Reading Diagnostics." *Educational Psychology Review,* Vol. 6, No. 2. 1994.

Samuels, J. "The Method of Repeated Readings." *The Reading Teacher, 32,* 403–408. 1979.

Samuels, S.J. "Decoding and Automaticity: Helping Poor Readers Become Automatic at Word Recognition." *The Reading Teacher.* April, 1988.

Samuels, S.J., N. Shermer, and D. Reinking. "Reading Fluency: Techniques for Making Decoding Automatic." In Samuels and Farstrup (eds.), *What Research Has to Say About Reading Instruction.* Newark, DE: International Reading Association. 1992.

Share, D. 1995. "Phonological Recoding and Self-Teaching: Sine Qua Non of Reading Acquisition." Cognition 55.

Share, D. L., and K. E. Stanovich. 1995. "Cognitive Processes in Early Reading Development: A Model of Acquisition and Individual Differences." *Issues in Education: Contributions from Educational Psychology 1.*

Shefelbine, J. "A Syllabic-Unit Approach to Teaching Decoding of Polysyllabic Words to Fourth- and Sixth-Grade Disabled Readers." In J. Zutell, S. McCormick, M. Connolly, and P. O'Keefe (eds.), *Literacy Theory and Research: Analyses from Multiple Paradigms.* Chicago, IL: National Reading Conference. 1990.

Shefelbine, J., L. Lipscomb, and A. Hern. "Variables Associated with Second-, Fourth-, and Sixth-Grade Students' Ability to Identify Polysyllabic Words." In S. McCormick, J. Zutell, P. Scharer, and P. O'Keefe (eds.), *Cognitive and Social Perspectives for Literacy Research and Instruction.* Chicago, IL: National Reading Conference. 1989.

Shinn, M.R. (ed.). *Curriculum-Based Measurement: Assessing Special Children.* New York: Guilford. 1989.

Spafford, C.S., and G.S. Grosser. *Dyslexia: Research and Resource Guide.* Boston: Allyn and Bacon. 1996.

Spear-Swerling, L., and R.J. Sternberg. *Off Track: When Poor Readers Become "Learning Disabled."* Boulder, CO: Westview Press. 1996.

Stahl, S. "Saying the 'P' Word: Nine Guidelines for Exemplary Phonics Instruction." *The Reading Teacher,* Vol. 45, No. 8. April, 1992.

Stahl, S. "Teaching Children with Reading Problems to Recognize Words." In L. Putnam (ed.), *Readings on Language & Literacy: Essays in Honor of Jeanne S. Chall.* Cambridge, MA: Brookline Books. 1997.

Stahl, S., and P. D. Miller. 1989. "Whole Language and Language Experience Approaches for Beginning Reading: A Quantitative Research Synthesis." *Review of Educational Research 59.*

Stahl, S., J. Osborn, and P. D. Pearson. 1992. "The Effects of Beginning Reading Instruction: Six Teachers in Six Classrooms." Unpublished paper. University of Illinois at Urbana-Champaign.

Stanovich, K.E. "Toward an Interactive Compensatory Model of Individual Differences in the Development of Reading Fluency." *Reading Research Quarterly,* Vol. 21. 1980.

Stanovich, K.E. "Has the Learning Disabilities Field Lost Its Intelligence?" *Journal of Learning Disabilities,* Vol. 22. 1989.

Stanovich, K.E. "Speculations on the Causes and Consequences of Individual Differences in Early Reading Acquisition." In P.B. Gough, L.C. Ehri, and R. Treiman (eds.), *Reading Acquisition.* Hillsdale, NJ: Erlbaum. 1992.

Stanovich, K.E. "Matthew Effects in Reading: Some Consequences of Individual Differences in the Acquisition of Literacy." *Reading Research Quarterly,* Vol. 21. 1986.

Stanovich, K.E. "Romance and Reality." *The Reading Teacher,* Vol. 47, No. 4. December 1993/January 1994.

Stanovich, K. E. 1984. "Toward an Interactive-Compensatory Model of Reading: A Confluence of Developmental, Experimental, and Educational Psychology." *Remedial and Special Education 5.*

Stanovich, K. E., and R. F. West. 1989. "Exposure to Print and Orthographic Processing." *Reading Research Quarterly 24.*

Sulzby, E. 1895. "Children's Emergent Reading of Favorite Storybooks: A Developmental Study." *Reading Research Quarterly 20* (4).

Tansley, A.E. *Reading and Remedial Reading.* NY: Humanities Press. 1967.

Taylor, B.M., and L. Nosbush. "Oral Reading for Meaning: A Technique for Improving Word Identification Skills." *The Reading Teacher,* Vol. 37. 1983.

Topping, K.J. "Cued Spelling: A Powerful Technique for Parent and Peer Tutoring." *The Reading Teacher,* Vol. 48, No. 5. February, 1995.

Torgesen, J.K., and S. Hecht. "Preventing and Remediating Reading Disabilities: Instructional Variables That Make a Difference for Special Students." In M. Graves, P. van den Broek, and B. Taylor (eds.), *The First R: Every Child's Right to Read.* NY: Teachers College Press. 1996.

Torgeson, J. K., R. K. Wagner, and C. A. Rashotte. 1994. "Longitudinal Studies of Phonological Processing and Reading." *Journal of Learning Disabilities 27.*

Treiman, R. "The Role of Intrasyllabic Units in Learning to Read and Spell." In P.B. Gough, L.C. Ehri, R. Treiman (eds.), *Reading Acquisition.* Hillsdale, NJ: Erlbaum. 1992.

Treiman, R., and J. Baron. "Segmental Analysis Ability: Development and Relation to Reading Ability. In G.E. MacKinnon and T.G. Waller (eds.), *Reading Research: Advances in Theory and Practice.* Vol. 3. NY: Academic Press. 1981.

Tyler A., and Nagy, W. "The Acquisition of English Derivational Morphology." *Journal of Memory and Language, 28,* 649–667. 1989.

Vacca, J., R. Vacca, and M. Gove. *Reading and Learning to Read.* NY: HarperCollins College Publishers. 1995.

Velluntino, F. R., and D. M. Scanlon. 1987. "Phonological Coding, Phonological Awareness, and Reading Ability: Evidence from a Longitudinal and Experimental Study." *Merrill-Palmer Quarterly 33.*

Wagstaff, J. *Phonics That Works!* NY: Scholastic. 1994.

Whaley, W.J., and M.W. Kirby. "Word Synthesis and Beginning Reading Achievement." *The Journal of Educational Research,* Vol. 73. 1980.

White, T., Power, M., and White, S. "Morphological Analysis: Implications for Teaching and Understanding Vocabulary Growth." *Reading Research Quarterly,* 24, 283–304. 1989.

White, T.G., J. Sowell, and A. Yanagihara. "Teaching Elementary Students to Use Word-Part Clues." *The Reading Teacher.* January, 1989.

Wilde, S. *What's a Schwa Sound Anyway? A Holistic Guide to Phonetics, Phonics, and Spelling.* Portsmouth, NH: Heinemann. 1997.

Wood, K., and B. Algozzine (eds.). *Teaching Reading to High-Risk Learners.* Boston: Allyn and Bacon. 1994.

Wylie, R., and D. Durrell. "Teaching Vowels Through Phonograms." *Elementary Education,* Vol. 47. 1970.

Wysocki, K., and J. Jenkins. "Deriving Word Meanings Through Morphological Generalization." *Reading Research Quarterly,* 22, 66–81. 1987.

Young, S. *The Scholastic Rhyming Dictionary.* Scholastic. 1994.

Zutell, J. "The Directed Spelling Thinking Activity (DSTA): Providing an Effective Balance in Word Study Instruction." *The Reading Teacher,* Vol. 50, No. 2. October, 1996.